# "called to the unpleasing task of a Soldier"

## Writings from the Valley Forge Encampment of the Continental Army

### December 19, 1777–June 19, 1778

### Volume 8

### *Joseph Lee Boyle*

HERITAGE BOOKS
2017

# HERITAGE BOOKS
*AN IMPRINT OF HERITAGE BOOKS, INC.*

**Books, CDs, and more—Worldwide**

For our listing of thousands of titles see our website at
www.HeritageBooks.com

Published 2017 by
HERITAGE BOOKS, INC.
Publishing Division
5810 Ruatan Street
Berwyn Heights, Md. 20740

Copyright © 2017 Joseph Lee Boyle

All rights reserved. No part of this book may be reproduced or transmitted in any form or by any means, electronic or mechanical, including photocopying, recording or by any information storage and retrieval system without written permission from the author, except for the inclusion of brief quotations in a review.

International Standard Book Number
Paperbound: 978-0-7884-5766-1

# CONTENTS

Preface                                                v

Introduction                                           vii

Editorial Procedure                                    xiii

The Documents                                          1

Document Chronology                                    189

Index                                                  197

# PREFACE

While much has been written on the Valley Forge Encampment of the Continental Army, it has only recently been the subject of good scholarly histories. The three volume "Valley Forge Report" (1980-82), by Wayne K. Bodle and Jacqueline Thibaut, written for the National Park Service, is recommended, but only limited copies were printed. It can now be viewed on the "Documents and Publications" segment of Valley Forge National Historical Park's website. John W. Jackson's *Valley Forge: Pinnacle of Courage* (1992), is a readable account. Herman O. Benninghoff III's *Valley Forge: A Genesis for Command and Control* (2001), does not present an overall history of the Encampment. Dr. Wayne K. Bodle produced *The Valley Forge Winter: Civilians and Soldiers in War* (2002). Though well researched, some of his interpretations, such as claiming Washington exaggerated the food crises, are not supported by the preponderance of the primary sources. Thomas Fleming's *Washington's Secret War: The Hidden History of Valley Forge* (2005), is a very good popular history, though I don't concur with some of his conclusions and characterizations.

Several excellent specialized histories include Nancy Loane *Following the Drum: Woman at the Valley Forge Encampment* (2009), and Paul Lockhart *The Drillmaster of Valley Forge: The Baron de Steuben and the Making of the American Army* (2008). Dr. Bruce Chadwick's recent histories deal in large part with events at the Valley Forge Encampment.

Those who are curious how the army happened to be at Valley Forge are directed to John F. Reed *Campaign to Valley Forge* (1965), and John Buchanan *The Road to Valley Forge: How Washington Built the Army that Won the Revolution* (2008). The best work on this period is Thomas McGuire's two volume set *The Philadelphia Campaign* (2006, 2007)

Mark Edward Lender and Garry Wheeler Stone's definitive *Fatal Sunday: George Washington, the Monmouth Campaign, and the Politics of Battle* (2016), underscore the development of the Continental Army into a more effective fighting machine after six months at Valley Forge.

For the development of Valley Forge as a state and national park, the reader is directed to Lorett Treese's *Valley Forge: Making and Remaking a National Symbol* (1995). Thousands of letters and documents written at Valley Forge, have been published in collections such as, *The Papers of George Washington, The Writings of George Washington* and *The Nathanael Greene Papers*. Much is now available on websites such as founders.archives.gov. However these mostly represent the best remembered men of the Revolution. There are many other prominent leaders whose papers are not readily available in print.

There are also thousands of documents by soldiers and staff that have never been published. Others were printed long ago and are not readily available. The intent of this effort is to present a selection of these, as the eighth of a projected nine such volumes. The assistance of staff members at a number of institutions is appreciated. These include the: American Antiquarian Society; Beinecke Library, Yale University; Connecticut Historical Society; Firestone Library, Princeton University; Historical Society of Pennsylvania; Houghton Library, Harvard University; Library of Congress; Maine Historical Society; Massachusetts Historical Society; National Archives; New Hampshire Historical Society; New Jersey State Archives; The Huntington Library; The James Monroe Museum and Memorial Library; The New-York Historical Society; The South Carolina Historical Society; The Watkinson Library, Trinity College; William L. Clements Library, University of Michigan; U.S. Army Military History Institute; University of Georgia Main Library; Valley Forge National Historical Park. A special thank you to Katherine Ludwig and the staff at the David Library of the American Revolution for their assistance and energetic support.

# INTRODUCTION

The year 1777 began well for Washington. The victories of Trenton and Princeton revived the spirits of the Patriots. For the next few months the American army encamped at Morristown, and with the Spring, gradually rebuilt itself from the losses of 1776. In June, British General Sir William Howe attempted to lure Washington into battle in the plains of New Jersey, but Washington declined combat.

In the Summer, with General John Burgoyne advancing from Canada into New York, Howe began an expedition for reasons that have never become clear. Instead of remaining in New York City and then advancing up the Hudson River Valley to support Burgoyne, Howe embarked on an expedition against the American capital of Philadelphia. When Howe sailed from New York Harbor in late July with his army, American spies were well aware of the expedition, but not its destination. Washington suspected that Philadelphia was Howe's object, and moved the bulk of his army into Pennsylvania, leaving Horatio Gates in New York to counter Burgoyne's advance.

Intending to enter the Delaware River, General Howe and his brother Admiral Richard Howe, received information that the banks of the river were heavily fortified, and that it was blocked with submerged obstructions. They then decided to sail south, enter the Chesapeake Bay, land near the head of that bay, and march to Philadelphia.

The destination of the British fleet was not known to Washington until August 22. The next day he marched the army through Philadelphia. The two forces met at the Battle of Brandywine on September 11, which was an American defeat. On October 4, Washington launched an audacious attack on the enemy then encamped at Germantown. Though ultimately defeated, even the defeat cheered the Americans, as they had routed the British in their initial assault.

After Germantown, the focus was on the Delaware River, where Forts Mifflin and Mercer, with a small American fleet, blocked the removal of the obstructions from the river. Opening the river was critical for General Howe, as he needed contact with his fleet for supplies and reinforcements.

On November 2, the Continental Army moved to Whitemarsh, which was to be home for the next six weeks. After clearing the Delaware of American resistance in mid-November, General Howe marched out of Philadelphia on December 4 and faced Washington's position at Whitemarsh for three days. Finding the American position too strong to attack, Howe returned to Philadelphia on December 8.

The oncoming winter weather was becoming unendurable to the poorly clad American soldiers and winter quarters had to be found. The army crossed the Schuylkill on December 12 and arrived at the Gulph, where it remained until December 19, when it marched into Valley Forge and began to build log huts for shelter. Washington never gave a precise reason why the area was chosen, though he had consulted his generals on military alternatives. Captain-Lieutenant James McClure reported "we Have Retired to the barren Hills of Valley forge, & Huted our Hole army, Which Looks Like an Indian City." After a long campaign Andrew Dunlap seemed happy to write that "we have good comfortable hutts."

The six month encampment of the Continental Army at Valley Forge has long since entered the realm of American myths. Though some of the tribulations and triumphs have been exaggerated, and others ignored in popular histories, the enduring patience of the soldiers and the inspirational leadership of George Washington kept the army in being until the supply systems and overall conditions improved in the Spring. Surgeon's Mate Albigence Waldo wrote a poem which included stanzas "to sing the General's praise." Frenchman Maussion de la Bastie recalled "his calmness under a diversity is truly one of the most marvelous sights it has ever been my lot to witness."

An area of contention before and during the early part of the Encampment is what later came to be called the "Conway Cabal." As Washington had lost two major battles, and our capital was in enemy hands, some questions about the effectiveness of his leadership were natural. Horatio Gates, victor at Saratoga, may have been actively intriguing to replace Washington. Some delegates to Congress had misgivings and may have wanted a change. Whatever the extent of this discontent may have been, it has been lost in the fury and zeal of the Washington loyalists as they rallied around their chief. Nathaniel Chipman excused Washington's losses as he "baffled all the stratagems of a wary, politic, and experienced general, and has several times fought him not unsuccessfully" and thought "While *he* lives, be assured, they will never brook the command of another." General Varnum stated "Genl Washington shines with additional Lustre, and is the Adoration of the Army."

Some of the stories that have become legendary are reinforced in this collection. There are many references to the lack of shoes, blankets and clothing. A return on the army on December 23, revealed that 2,898 men were "Unfit for want of Cloaths." James Rix of Massachusetts wrote to his wife Miriam, that he was "badly out of clothes, but we hear there is cloth coming into camp, tho I am better off than the greater part of the men of our state." Washington's Secretary Tench Tilghman lamented "The want of cloathing is a thing which is much to be regretted but not remedied just at this time." The soldiers of the Seventh Virginia "are exceedingly destitute" for clothing according to Major William Davies. While clothing supplies improved markedly in the Spring, there was never an adequate amount to properly supply all the soldiers.

Food was in desperately short supply in December, mid-February and late May. Captain James Bancroft stated "Everything is so dear we are obliged to spend considerable for provision or live very poorly." According to Dr. Samuel Tenny "I—poor I—eat the Scanty Allowance of a common Soldier, drink a little vile Whiskey once in a while." Captain Hugh Maxwell told his wife "my provision is only fresh Beef and flour, and that very Short as well as very poor." If the officers were this bad off, one must pity the common soldiers.

Despite the incredibly severe winter of later fables, references to extremely bad weather in the contemporary documents are few. A review of these letters and numerous other sources leads to the conclusion that the winter weather of 1777-1778 was actually moderate. The Army might have suffered less for food and clothes, had the temperatures been slightly colder. Mud and mire made the unpaved roads nearly impassable at times. No bridges existed over large rivers, and ferries could not bring supplies across with ice floes coming down, though frozen rivers could have allowed supplies to pass over. The winter weather the Continental Army endured at

Morristown in 1779-1780, was considered far worse.

This volume shows the importance of forage for the Army's transport animals. The hundreds of horses in camp needed their own rations of hay and grain, as did the animals that transported supplies to camp. In April Ebenezer Crosby wrote that several months earlier forage was so lacking, that if the British had attacked the army would have had to retreat "leaving all of our artillery and baggage behind, for want of horses, having kill'd hundreds and rendered, I might say thousands, unfit for service during the winter thro' the great scarcity of forage." The new Quartermaster Nathanael Greene jolted the department into action with orders to Commissary General of Forage Clement Biddle to supply 840,000 bushels of grain, with hay in proportion.

Hundreds of officers left the army during the six month Encampment, some being forced out, but many voluntarily resigned. Some complained about their inability to support their families on army pay, the "Difficult Situation of his Family," or health problems, but in the majority of cases little reason appears. Towards the end of the Encampment many North Carolina and Virginia officers in particular left as regiments were combined, as it became obvious that some units would remain woefully understrength in rank and file. Though some excellent officers left the army, many of those departing were marginal, and those who remained were a stronger cadre for the remaining years of war, such at Hugh Maxwell who lamented being "called to the unpleasing task of a Soldier" but served until 1783.

From the distance of more than two hundred years, the bickering and jealousies of some of the officers seems trivial. Major General DeKalb lamented to his wife about "the mutual jealousy of almost all the French officers, particularly against those of higher rank than the rest. The people think of nothing but their incessant intrigues and backbitings. They hate each other like the bitterest enemies, and endeavor to injure each other wherever an opportunity offers." He did mention that Lafayette was a notable exception to the rule."

It may seem unusual but the actions and intentions of the enemy army, occupying Philadelphia barely twenty miles away, are rarely remarked upon, and little real animosity seems to be directed their way. While James McClure could condemn them as "Parricides of

Hell," at the POW exchange meetings Elias Boudinot recalled "We were very sociable" and seemed to be amused that American Colonel Grayson could out drink the British.

This changed in May as rumors began to circulate that the British intended to evacuate. Speculation ran rampant but the arrival of the Carlisle Peace Commission in early June briefly stopped the impending departure of the enemy. Washington held a Council of War on June 17, and requested written opinions from his generals on the practicable options. These were rendered moot as the city was evacuated the same day.

The contribution of Baron Steuben to the discipline of the army has been questioned by some recent historians, but the soldiers in camp highly valued his work. Lieutenant Nathaniel Chipman said "The troops spend their time in discipline, in which they made great proficiency. We have for our inspector general, Baron Steuben, who has been aid-de-camp to the king of Prussia, and lieutenant-general in his service." General Varnum thought "Baron Stupend is very advantageous in disciplining the Troops."

The greatest elation occurred with the news that France and the United States had signed Treaties of Alliance and Commerce. This prompted a huge celebration and a Feu de Joie on May 6. The next day Philip Van Cortlandt to Pierre Van Cortlandt wrote, "I have the pleasure of Informing you that I had the Honour Yesterday of being present at & partaking with the Officers and Soldiers of Our Army the Joys of the greatest Day Ever yet Experienced in our Independent World of Liberty." Another officer wrote: "Doubtless You have heard the Cause, and probably the Particulars of our Rejoicings in Camp on the 6th inst. We were for one Hour employed in returning Thanks to the Supream Governor of the Universe for the signal Display and Manifestations of his approbation, of our just and righteous Exertions in Defence of this infant Empire."

Whatever their position or rank, the men at Valley Forge deserve our utmost admiration and respect, for their steadfast determination and accomplishments in the face of numerous hardships.

Athens, Georgia					Joseph Lee Boyle

## EDITORIAL PROCEDURE

The documents in this collection are arranged chronologically for the six month period of the Valley Forge Encampment. When more than one document of the same date appears, they are arranged alphabetically according to writer.

Letters are introduced by the names of the addresser and addressee. The dateline falls just below the heading, though the original document may have it at the bottom. The complimentary close is usually brought up flush with the last paragraph and the closing signature has been omitted. A descriptive note at the foot of each entry shows the location of the document presented, and identifies the writer and recipient the first time each individual appears.

These documents present a literal translation with spelling, punctuation and grammar remaining as they are found in the original, as are the typographical errors in the printed documents. Each writer's abbreviations and contractions are also preserved as they are found in the manuscripts.

Capital letters follow the text of the originals, although it is sometimes a judgment call whether a letter is a capital or not. Brackets indicate questionable or illegible letters and words. *Sic* is used very sparingly as it would quickly detract from the text, given the numerous variants of spelling and oddities of expression.

Many of the writers of these documents failed to conclude their sentences with periods, and used commas, colons, or semicolons instead, if anything at all. Dashes were frequently used by some, such as Jedediah Huntington, and these have been duplicated.

Crossed out material has been omitted. Margin notes are shown as postscripts, except where obviously keyed to the body of the document.

The index includes the names of all persons and references to key things such as clothing shortages. However place names are selected, depending on relevance and frequency. Casual references to New York, for example, have been omitted.

## James Mitchell Varnum to George Washington

Sir— Camp 22$^d$ Dec$^r$. 1777

    Ensign Bowles of Col°. Greene's Battalion, applies for a Discharge from the Army. Since his ingaging this Campain, his Father died, & left a Widow, whose whole Dependence is upon the Ensign, he being her only Son. The Col°. recommends him to me, And I am persuaded it will be best for him to obtain his Request.
    I am your Excellency's most obd$^t$. Serv$^t$
        J M Varnum
His Excellency Gen$^l$. Washington

Source: RG 93, M 859, Roll 49, f216, National Archives.
Varnum was a Brigadier General from Rhode Island. John Bowles of the First Rhode Island Regiment, was allowed to resign, effective December 27.


## Francis Barber, Certificate Regarding John Conway

+

I certify that John Conway Esq$^r$ Capt in the first Jersey Regiment is the Eldest Captain in the Jersey Brigade
        F. Barber Lt. Col. 3$^d$
Camp Valley Forge    Decem 23$^{rd}$. 1777

To be promoted to the Majority of the 4th. Jersey Regt. vice Major Morrell resigned the 29th: October 1777—

Source: Record Group 93, M 859, Roll 12, Document 3919, National Archives.
The last two lines are in a different hand. Barber was Lieutenant Colonel of the Third New Jersey. Conway was retroactively promoted to Major of the Fourth New Jersey, effective October 29, 1777.


## William Bayley to Jean Bayley

Honored mother    New Providence Penselvana Desembr th 1777.
I take this opertuty to you to let you know that I am well and hope that these few lines will find you the Same I receivd your letter December 2[th] and was very glad to hear that was well I like wise received a pare of mittins and Some needles and thred which obliged very much for I tood in great need of them we arved at genera[l]

Washingtons head Quaters Novembr 20 and are now about 17 miles from Philadelpia I Should have sent you a letter by Lieut Lunt but did not know of his going till it was too late to write we expect to winter whare we are now we are building hutts to live in I dont expect to come home this winter I hope to git nearer home before I git a furlow I would have you wite to me as ofen as you can remember my love to all Brothers and Sisters and all who shall think it worth a while to inquire after me and so I conclude
                    your most obodent Son
                    William Bayley

Source: Andrew Hawes Papers, Coll 64, Box 2, Fl 15, Maine Historical Society. Bayley, a private in the Thirteenth Massachusette Regiment, was writing to his mother Jean Bayley at Falmouth.

## Field Return of the Continental Army

Feild Return of Continental Army, 23d. Decemr 1777

| Brigades | Serjeants | Drums & Fifes | Present fit for duty | Do. Unfit for want of Cloaths | On guard and on detachment |
|---|---|---|---|---|---|
| Muhlenberg's | 78 | | 352 | 199 | 135 |
| Weedon | 66 | 24 | 417 | 372 | 202 |
| Patterson | 70 | 23 | 495 | 150 | |
| Learned | 63 | 42 | 482 | 83 | 118 |
| Glover | 63 | 23 | 607 | 177 | 113 |
| Maxwells | 71 | 35 | 573 | 166 | |
| Late Conway's | 67 | 41 | 355 | 151 | |
| Poors | 44 | 20 | 516 | 299 | |
| 1 pennsylvania Brigade | 32 | 16 | 582 | 205 | |
| 2d. do do | 50 | 31 | 225 | 60 | 111 |
| Woodfords | 44 | 11 | 149 | 257 | 261 |
| Scott | 50 | 30 | 218 | 385 | 171 |
| Varnum | 69 | 38 | 512 | 50 | 192 |
| Huntingdon | 78 | 43 | 700 | 90 | 161 |
| Mc.Intosh | 98 | 66 | 434 | 164 | 119 |
| | 943 | 442 | 6617 | 2898 | 1583 |
| | | | 1583 | | |
| | | | 8200 | | |

Source: Record Group 93, M 246, Roll 137, f 110, National Archives. Note that almost 3,000 men unfit for duty due lack of clothing. A later return on January 19, 1778, showed 3200 men shown in a column as "wanting shoes & Cloathg". There were no entries in the this column for Huntington's, Varnum's, or McIntosh's Brigades.

## Jethro Sumner and Lachlan McIntosh, Certificates for Thomas Granberry/Granberry

Pensylvania Dec$^r$. 24$^{th}$ 1777
These are to Certyfie that Thomas Granberry Esq$^r$. was appointed Cap$^t$. in the third Batt$^n$, of the State of North Carolina, the 16$^{th}$ of April 1776, by Congress of that State, and now desiring leive to resign His Commission, I am to acquaint His Excellency, that He may be suffer'd to make His resignation
   I am &c Jethro Sumner, Colo.

Capt. Granberry is refered to his Excel$^y$. the Commander in Chief for Liberty to resign his Commission—25$^{th}$. Dec$^r$. 1777.
   Lach$^n$. M$^c$.Intosh Br. Gen.

Source: M 859, Roll 45, Document 14433, National Archives.
Granberry/Granbery had been acquitted of charges by a court-martial on December 22, and apparently decided to resign. Sumner was Colonel of the Third North Carolina Regiment. Brigadier General Lachlan McIntosh commanded the North Carolina Brigade. See Henry Dixon on December 27, 1777.

## Anthony Wayne "In Answer to Sundry persons in behalf of the Citizens of Phil$^a$.

Gentlemen           Head Quarters 24$^{th}$ Dec$^r$. 1777
 I mentioned your Proposition to His Excellency—who altho' very desirous to Alleviate the Distress of the Indigent Inhabitants of Phil$^a$, yet he cannot agree to permit the Supplies you require the pass his Guards,—as it is Contrary to a Resolve of Congress which together with Other Considerations prevents him from granting the Indulgence you wish
 I am Gent$^n$. with every Esteem Your most Ob$^t$ Humb Ser$^t$

Source: Anthony Wayne Papers, vol. 4, Historical Society of Pennsylvania.

## Extract of a Letter from an Officer

*Extract of a letter from an officer, dated camp, December 25, 1777.*
    Captain Lee, of whom too much cannot be said, for his activity and gallantry, during this whole campaign, had nearly fallen into the hands of the enemy; that valuable young officer has through the course of this campaign made 132 prisoners without losing a man; his ardor has liked to deprived us of him, on a late occasion, having pushed the enemy so close as to separate himself from all aid of infantry, fell in with 40 of Preston's dragoons, supported by 100 foot, he received the fire of a considerable body of the infantry with no effect on their side, and just as he and his little troop that only consisted of 22, made their charge, which would have put them all in his hands, he found himself the object of the above body of horse, who had till that time concealed themselves, they pursued 3 miles in which distance he several times formed his little squadron, and finally by his bravery got off with the loss of 3 of his troop only, he vowed vengeance, and has already taken it, the enemy being out two days ago on a foraging party near Derby, he equiped himself and with his Lieutenants, Linsey and Peyton, who have also distinguished themselves on every occasion, turned out for satisfaction, and this moment has sent in 13 of Preston's horses and 10 of his dragoons, the other 3 men I supposed he killed by way of retaliation for those he lost. The country between this and Derby is plentifully supplied with provision and forage, and do expect will be the theatre of this winters operations wich will be chiefly by detachments in the foraging way, unless General Howe comes out to fight this army, and that I believe will not be the case.

Source: *The Virginia Gazette*, January 23, 1778.


## Timothy Pickering to Clement Biddle

Dear Sir,                                                                                 Decr. 25. 1777
    Genl. Reed & Major Henry have informed the Genl. of the most atrocious robberies being committed by the soldiers on the other side Schuylkill: The Genl. has therefore directed me to send to-morrow morning a sub. & 10 or 12 men to every ford from Swede's ford to

about three miles up on this side the camp. I have to beg of you an account of the number of fords in that space, and a description of them, that I may know what number of parties are necessary, & be able to direct their routs. If guides in your opinion are necessary to conduct the parties, please to tell me, & how many.

I am, dear sir,     yours sincerely

The Express is to wait for an answer.
Bon Sante Messieurs

Source: Frederic R. Kirkland; ed., *Letters of the American Revolution in the Library at "Karolfred,"* vol. 2 (New York: Coward-McCann Inc., 1952), 42-43.
Pickering was the army's Adjutant General. Biddle was Commissary General of Forage.

## Hugh Maxwell to Hannah Maxwell

My Dear                                December 26, 1777

I with pleasure Imbrace this opportunity of writing to you. So that you may Know I Bear you much on my Mind. Not that I would have you think you alone are more in my thoughts than Lilly, Dorcas or Priscilla Hugh or Chloe or my little Sylvester but I would have you understand that I would be willing to Divide my affections among you all in equall parts  Now my Love towards you and good wishes for you is all I can afford you and this you may be assured of while my life and Reason Lasts.

Now my Dear you must think that it would be the greatest Ingratitude in you to Slight or Set Light by those parents that are Suffering every evill and Distress for you. It is all for my children that I am this exposing my life and Health to danger to which I have hitherto been a Stranger—I have not Lain in a bed Since last June or in a House but twise very offten have I lain in the open air and now in my tent my provision is only fresh Beef and flour, and that very Short as well as very poor.

Now do you consider what Returns you must Make to me for undergoing these things for you to Leave my children in a State of Freedom and liberty—All I ask of you is to follow the paths of virtue—to Honour your parents and love your Brothers and Sisters and if you consider of it that what I ask of you if you perform will turn out to your Infinite advantage you may easily Beleive that what I advise you to is what I think for the best for you therefore I think you will be the easier Induced to preactice it—I dont expect you will write to me very soon for I do not think you can have an opportunity to Send but if you Have I should expect to See you till Spring till that time I commend you to the care of him that preserved your life in Sickness and mine in Battle—he has promised in the Ninety first Psalm he will hear you—Read that Psalm over and over it has promises enough in it to guild the most gloomy providences.

    but I must Draw to a close and Remain you affectionate Father
                  Hugh Maxwell
P. S. Read this Letter to all the Rest of the children

Source: Hugh Maxwell Papers, U.S. Army Military History Institute, Carlisle, Pennsylvania.
A Captain in the Second Massachusetts Regiment, he was writing to his daughter.


## William Alexander, Pass

December 27, 1777.
Permit Mrs. Frazier, Mrs. Harper, and Miss Nancy Frazier to pass to Philadelphia and to return. This pass to continue for eight days after General Howe's Army returns into the City of Philadelphia.
                STIRLING M.G.

Source: *Village Record*, (West Chester, Pa.) November 13, 1860.
William Alexander, usually called Lord Stirling, was a Major General in the Continental Army. Persifor Frazer, Lt. Colonel of the Fifth Pennsylvania, had been captured at the Battle of Brandywine on September 11, 1777, and was being held in Philadelphia. Apparently the ladies were allowed to visit him.


## Henry Dixon, Certificate for Thomas Granberry/Granbery

Camp at the Valley Forge Dec$^r$ 28 1777
    This is to Certifie That I do not Know that Capt Thomas Granbery of the Third North Carolina Regiment is Indebted to the Said Regiment or to the United States
                Henry Dixon Maj$^r$. 3$^d$ N:C. Regim[ent]

Source: Record Group 93, M 859, Roll 45, Document 14421, National Archives.
See Jethro Sumner and Lachlan McIntosh on December 24 and 25.

**Extract of a Letter**

Extract of a letter from an officer at Camp, Valley Forge,
    dated Dec. 27.

There have been brought into camp, within these three days, 60 British foot, 13 dragoons, and 30 waggons; our militia now lies at Germantown: General Howe and his army are lying between Darby and Chester, and Col. Morgan with 700 infantry lies on their lines; the greatest part of our army are detached in parties down the river.

Source: *The Providence Gazette; and Country Journal*, January 24, 1778.


**Nathanael Greene, Furlough for Samuel Waples**

Lt. Samuel Waples of the 9 Virgina Regiment haveing lost all his baggage and there being but few men belonging to the Regement he is permitted to go the Virgina to return and join his corps as soon as order'd or at the first of May without orders.—Given under my Hand at Camp Valey Forge Decem 27 1777
              Nath Greene MG
To all it may concern—

Source: Record Group 15, M806, Pension Applicaton, W6427, National Archives. Waples had been captured, along with most of the Ninth Virginia, at Germatown on October 4, 1777, and later escaped. Major General Nathanael Greene was a division commander. Waples was later allowed to resign on May 22, see below.


**Johann de Kalb to John Adams**

At Valley Forge Camp, December 27, 1777.

    Sir: As you are going to France in a public character from the United States, will you give me leave to present you a letter of introduction for M. le Comte de Broglie, one for M. Moreau, the first secretary to Count de Vergennes, minister of state for foreign affairs, and two for my lady, who will be glad to see you, and to get news from me by your means.

    I wish you a good passage, a safe arrival, health and success in all your enterprises, no one being with more regard and esteem, sir, you most obedient and very humble servant,
              Baron de Kalb

Source: Francis Wharton, ed. *The Revolutionary Diplomatic Correspondence of the United States* (Washington: Government Printing Office, 1889), 2:464.

Kalb, who came from France with Lafayette, had been appointed a Major General in the Continental Army. Adams was a delegate to the Continental Congress, being sent on a mission to France.

## Johann de Kalb to the Comte de Broglie

Enclosure: Johann Kalb to the Comte de Broglie

Mr Count     Camp at Valley Forge 27. of December 1777

You take So great an Interest, in the Success of the American Cause, that I have made so bold, as to recommend to you, Mr John Adams, one of the Members of Congress who goes to France, to treat with the Court upon political Affairs, as Mr Deane will be charged, with the Affairs of Commerce. Mr Adams is a Man of Merit, generally esteemed in this Country, and to whom Mr de Valfort and myself, have Some Obligations relative to our Baggage. Your Credit, will be of great Use to him, if you will condescend to afford it to him.

 I had the Honour to write you a long Letter, two days ago, which I hope will arrive Safe to you. The Poste for Boston presses me, without which, I should also have inclosed a Copy. I am with the most respectfull Devotion, Mr Count,

    your most humble and most obedient Servant,
      The Baron de Kalb

Source: John Adams Papers, Massachusetts Historical Society.

Docketed: "Letter Barron De Kalb to me"; in another hand: "Baron de Kalb Decr 27th 1777." Preceding the date line is the following: "To Monsieur, the Count de Broglio, Knight of the Orders of the King, Lieutenant General of his Army, and Commandant in the Country of Messin, at his House in the Street of St. Dominick, fauxbourg St. Germains, at Paris." Broglie was Kalb's patron.

## Charles West, Certificate for Joseph Baynham

             December 28th. 1777.

 I hereby certify that Lieu[t] Joseph Baynham is not Indebted to the United States as I know of or believe & there is Officers sufficient to do the duty of the Reg[t].—

    Charles West  Maj[r]. 3 Virg[a] Reg[t].

Source: Record Group 93, M 853, Volume 169, Commissions and Resignations, 1776-1780, Roll 13, frame 190, National Archives.
See William Heth to George Washington, in Volume Seven of this series. Baynham's resignation was effective on December 31, 1777.

## List of Stores Near Chester and Other Places

Account of Stores & forrage which may be drawn in from towards Chester.

| | |
|---|---|
| near 100 Tuns of Bar Iron | at John Roberts a Noted Torey |
| sundry other Stores & forrage | Near Merrion Meeting House. |
| 15 Hogshead Rum and sundry other Stores | At Wm. Reese's New town Square |
| a Quantity of Wine, Rum Spirits & other Stores | at John Moulders near Marcus Hook. |
| a Quantity of forrage | at John Adams's near the 6 mile stone Lancaster Road.— |
| a Quantity of Cheese, a large Stock of Hay & other forrage | at Robert Alissons near Uchland Meeting House will take Nothing but Hard Cash |
| a Quantity of Rum pork & flower & other Valuable Stores | at John Smith, John Donally, Edward Corke Andrew Andrew Torten & W$^m$ Goodwin's In the Neighbourhood of Chester Marcus Hook & Potts Landing. |

n the reverse: "List of Stores &c in the neighborhood of Chester &c. 29$^{th}$ Decem 1777—"

Source: Record Group 93, M 859, Roll 79, Document 22880, National Archives. This was a list to be used by the Continental Army's foraging parties.

## Elias Boudinot to Henry Hugh Fergusson

December 31, 1777

While absent I ordered a parcel of Flour to New Castle & Christeen, to go up the Delaware as the most effectual mode & the least liable to objection, but in case the Navigation should be stoped, then to be forwarded by land—I have given Directions that the sloop shall call on the commanding officer of the first sloop of War, that they may meet with & shew him their Orders & take his Directions— The Whole as it gets in, is to be delivered to Mr Tho Franklin agreeable to what passed between us on the lines.

Source: William A. Oldridge Collection, Library of Congress.
Boudinot was the Continental Commissary General of Prisoners. Thomas Franklin was his agent in Philadelphia. Fergusson was the Deputy Commissary of Prisoners with the British Army in Philadelphia.

## Return of Men Needed to Complete the Army

Return of the numbers wanting to compleat the continental troops as taken from the returns of the muster master generl for the month of December 1777.

States and Their Several Quotas        Wanting to Compleat

| | | Serjeants | Corporals | Drums & fifes | Privates | Total |
|---|---|---|---|---|---|---|
| New Hampshire | 2 battalions | 48 | 76 | 16 | 1,509 | 1,649 |
| Massachusets Bay | 15 do. | 73 | 86 | 35 | 4,476 | 4,670 |
| Rhode Island | 2 do. | 8 | 19 | | 731 | 758 |
| Connecticut | 8 do. | | 13 | 12 | 1,584 | 1,609 |
| New York | 4 do. | 12 | 32 | 8 | 1,345 | 1,379 |
| New Jersey | 4 do. | 19 | 47 | 10 | 1,629 | 1,705 |
| Pensylvania | 12 do. | 63 | 165 | 48 | 4,515 | 4,791 |
| Delaware | 1 do. | 9 | 12 | 3 | 407 | 431 |
| Maryland | 8 do. | 72 | 120 | 69 | 3,259 | 3,520 |
| Virginia | 15 do. | 13 | 112 | 71 | 4,736 | 4,932 |
| North Carolina | 9 do. | 224 | 224 | 51 | 4,525 | 5,044 |

30,506

Source: *Public Papers of George Clinton....* (New York: New York State, 1900), 2:618.

## Extract of a Letter from a Captain of Light Horse

HARTFORD, January 20.
*Extract of a letter written by a Captain of Light-Horse in the Southern Department to his friend in Connecticut.*

On the night of the 14th of December by order of his Excellency General WASHINGTON, I took post with a detachment of my troop, consisting of about twenty men, officers included, near Vandeering's mills, on the ridge rode running by the Schuylkill to Philadelphia, with a view of observing the motion of the enemy; the army having crossed the Schuylkill at Sweeds-ford. Notwithstanding we changed quarters every night, at late hours, the enemy got intelligence of our strength and situation, and by the help of some infernal tory, were conducted in a bye road till they had marched near a mile in our rear, by this route avoiding our sentinels and patroles, which were posted on all the main roads leading to Philadelphia; to make my post secure, as guarded on all sides, I ordered a vidette near half a mile in our rear, who at about two o'clock in the morning came in with an account, that a large body of horse, was moving fast down the road directly in our rear. I ordered the men immediately to mount, (the horses being kept constantly sadled, and the men accoutred) and before all could parade in the road they began to fire upon us. We exchanged a few shot, but finding it impossible with about ten men to oppose an hundred, (as I am informed by those who counted them as they passed this is a moderate computation) we moved off as fast as possible. They immediately surrounded the house and barn, pursuing us not far, and took five prisoners, while attempting to escape; whose names for the satisfaction of any concerned, are Quarter Master Samuel Mills, Isaac Brown, John Chauncy, Ephraim Kirby, and Naboth Lewis. After they were brought in, being taken in the field, they were first disarmed, and plundered of their spurs, watches, &c. &c. and then ordered by the officers to be killed; notwithstanding the entreaties and prayers of the unfortunate prisoners for mercy, the soldiers fell upon them, (the officers setting the example,) and after cutting, hacking and stabbing them till they supposed they were dead, they left them (Brown excepted whom after most cruelly mangling they shot) setting fire to the barn to consume any that might be in it. Mr. Mills after being wounded in several places on the head, had his life spared and is now a prisoner. Brown, and Chauncy, are dead.

Kirby and Lewis, have been properly taken care of and I trust will recover.

To add to their barbarity, they fell upon an old man belonging to the house, whom after cutting and wounding badly with their swords, they also shot.

Thus both the army and country have a striking example of what they have to expect from the savage cruelty and barbarity of the British troops.

Source: *The Norwich Packet*, January 26, 1778.
This was probably written by Henry Lee, Jr.

## Albigence Waldo, Certificate for Stephen Caleff

Stephen Caleff, the bearer, in building the Barracks at Valley Forge—by lifting a heavy piece of Timber—brought on a large Rupture at the Groin—for which he has been obliged to wear a Truss ever since—Yet he continued to do his duty as a good Soldier, so far as his situation would possible admit of.—
      Albigence Waldo
      Surgeon of the 1$^{st}$. Con$^t$

Source: Ebay Auction,
http://cgi.liveauctions.ebay.com/183-ALBIGENCE-WALDO-Autograph-Letter-Signed_itemZ320054813874, Dec-10-06 09:00:00 PST
Early American, P.O. Box 3507, Rancho Santa Fe, CA USA 92067.
Waldo was Surgeon of the First Connecticut Regiment. This is undated, and written some time after the army left Valley Forge, as Caleff appears on the Muster Rolls for the rest of the Encampment.

## Isaac Coit, Receipt for Clothing

           Pensylvania valley forge Jany: 1778
I Isaac Coit a Soldier in the Continental army in the first Battallion Raised by the State Connecticut in Capt. Belchers Company have Received of the Selectmen of the Town of Preston, the following Articles of Cloathing. (viz) two new winter shirts—
  Recd: the Same by the hand of Capt. James Morgan—
    Isaac Coit

Source: Photocopy, Valley Forge National Historical Park Library.

## Benjamin Ballard, Receipt for Retained Rations

Camp Valley Forge Jany. 1$^{st}$. 1778—
This is to Certify that there is due to Co$^l$. Bradfords Reg$^t$. of the State of Masachusets Bay; for Retaind Rat$^s$. & Deficiencies from the 12 Aug$^t$. to 31$^{st}$ Dec$^r$. Inclusive 1777, Two Thousand Seven hundred & forty Eight Dollars & fifty four Nintyiths of a Dollar—
$\qquad\qquad\qquad$ Benj$^n$. Ballard DCI
$\qquad\qquad\qquad$ to Gen$^l$. Patterson's Brigade
Dollars 2748 54/90

Source: Record Group 93, M 859, Roll 74, Document 21860, National Archives. Ballard was a Deputy Commissary of Issues, responsible for issuing food to the troops. Retained rations were those that had not been issued due to shortages of supplies.

## Robert, to his Mother

$\qquad\qquad\qquad$ VALLEY FORGE, Pennsylvania, New Year's Day—
Dear Mother:
$\quad$ I thank you heartily for the warm stockings and mittens you sent as a Christmas gift. I am sorry I was not able to send you anything more substantial than a short letter and my best love; but I froze one of my toes last week and so was obliged to buy a pair of shoes. They cost me my month's wages and so I only wear them on extra occasions. I have them and my new stockings on today, and you cannot think how comfortable they feel after having gone without them entirely, or as good as that, for nearly a month. One of the men froze to death a week ago yesterday while trying to get some wood to make a fire with the next day, Christmas. A heavy storm came up and he probably became stupefied with the cold and got lost. We searched for him the next day and found him about a mile from camp.
$\quad$ In honor of the day we each had two potatoes instead of one, and a small piece of dry bread and a little fish. Washington talked with us and encouraged us to stay by him and each other, and wait as

patiently as possible until the time came for us to fight for our liberty or die.

Lady Washington is to be with us the remainder of the week, and she helps us by her patient endurance to bear our sufferings bravely.

It does seem rather hard when we think of the British in Philadelphia, not 25 miles away, living in comfort, nay, even luxury, and we not having even the bare necessities of life. But when we think of Washington, our great commander, enduring suffering so bravely, it gives us courage, too.

Well, mother, I am afraid this is a very dreary letter, but please forgive my despondency, because I have no one to cheer me up, although I ought to be cheerful anyway. Give my love to Jim and Mary, but keep the best for yourself. If any of the neighbors are kind enough to enquire of me, tell them that I am well in body and trusting in God that things will turn out well at least.

Believe me as your ever dutiful son,
ROBERT.

"Through the interest of the Rev. Warren E. Morse, of Atkinson Memorial Church, there has been brought the light a letter written by a soldier boy of the Revolution, one of the heroes of Valley Forge—for they were all heroes—who wrote to his mother describing his fare, which would be pretty poor pickings for a soldier of 1917.

The letter was discovered by Chester N. Hardy, of 873 East Couch street, in Iowa a good many years ago and is a relic of his ancestors."

Source: *The Oregonian*, (Portland), February 22, 1917, page 11.
This letter is included for interest but appears to have been made up long after the Encampment. Christmas gift giving, for example, was not an eighteenth century custom.

## Benjamin Coats, Pay Authorization

Camp Vally forge January $Y^e$. $3^d$. 1778
This is to Authorise Lieut. Derragh to Receive one monts Pay on My Account for Value I $Rec^d$. Wittness my hand
                his Mark
             Benjamin X Coats
Present $Tho^s$. Gourley $Cap^t$

Source: Record Group 93, M 859, Roll 48, Document 15458, National Archives.
Daniel Darragh was a Lieutenant in the Ninth Pennsylvania. Regiment. Thomas Gourley was a Captain in the same regiment. Coats is presumed to have been an enlisted man.

### Griffin Greene, Certificate Regarding Simon Smith

Camp Valley forge Jan$^y$. 3$^{th}$. 1778
These may Certify to all whom it doth or may Concerne that Ens$^n$. Simon Smith of the 1$^{st}$ Rhode Island Battalion Commanded by Col$^o$. Christopher Greene is not Indebted to the Contenent in any way whereby I have Knowledge of the Same
    Griffin Greene P. Mas$^r$.

Source: RG 93, M 859, Roll 49, Document 15610, National Archives.
Smith was discharged from the army on January 5, 1778.

### Griffin Greene, Certificate for Stephen Briggs

Camp Valley Forge Jan$^y$. 3. 1778
    These may Certify to all whom it doth or may Concerne that Ens$^n$. Stepen Briggs of the 1$^{st}$ Rhode Island Battalion Command$^d$ by Col$^o$. Christopher Greene is not Indebted to the Contenent in any way whereby I have knowledge of the Same

Source: Record Group 93, M 859, Roll 49, Document 15607, National Archives.
Greene was Paymaster of the First Rhode Island. Ensign Stephen Briggs was discharged on January 7, 1778.

### Men Reenlisted in the Seventh Virginia

A Return of Men reenlisted of the 7th: Virga. Rt. who have Recd. their Bounty of Paymaster

| Capt. Flemings Company. | Capt. Hills Company |
|---|---|
| 1 Frederick Smith | 1 James Hill |
| 2 Math. Whorley | 2 Edwd. Taylor |
| 3 Claibourn Davenport | 3 Wm. Cardwell |

4 Robert Richeson
5 David Bradley
6. Wm. Mosby
7 Wm. Andrews

Capt. Webb's Compay.
1 Isaac Jeffries
2 Tho. Allen
3 Phill. Patterson
4 John Croxton
5 Williamson Hodges
6 Thos. Marshall
7 Benja. Johnson

Capt. Jouetts Company
1 Wm. Foster

Capt. Poseys Company
1 Saml. Barton
2 Saml. Burks
3 Wm. Bradley
4 Wm. Sutten

Capt. Crockett's Co.
1 Daniel Donaher
2 Jacob Dillering

4 Joshua Crain
5 Henry Cook
6 James Hart
7 Leond. Shackelford
8 Thorow Good Chambers
9 Richd. Boughan
10 Benja. Wain
11 Joseph Newcomb

C: Reubin Lipscomb
1 Ambrose Acre
2 John King
3 John Nicholas
4 John Brightwell
5 George Langston
6 John Samson

Capt. Mosleys Co.
1. Thos. Watkins
2 Smith Kent
3 James Flemister

Capt. Spensers Co.
1 Abm. Cord
2 Edwd. Stivers
3 Abm. Laursee
4 Wm. Willobey
5 Edlen Willobey
6 Thos. Burk

Account of Bounty paid for reeinlisting Men 3d Jan. 1778.

Source: Record Group 93, M 246, Roll 104, f 466, National Archives.
The enlistments of hundreds of the Virginia soldiers expired in early 1778. Those who re-enlisted received cash bounties and furloughs to go home for several months. See Henry Young's report on April 6, 1778, below.

**Enoch Poor to George Washington**

Sir                             Camp at the Valley Forge Jan$^y$ 3$^d$ 1778

I would beg leave to recommend Major Henry Dearborn, who is the Eldest Major in the New Hampshire State, to fill the Vacancy made by Lieu$^t$ Colonel Colburn of Colonel Scammells Regim$^t$ Killed the 19$^{th}$ of Septem$^r$ last.—

His Excellency Gen$^l$ Washington  Enoch Poor, B. Gen$^l$
[Endorsed] Major Dearborn Commission'd

Source: Isaac W. Hammond, ed., *The State of New Hampshire. Part 1, Rolls and Documents Relating to Soldiers in the Revolutionary War* Volume 4 of the War Rolls, (Manchester: John B. Clarke, 1889), 210.
Poor was a Brigadier General from New Hampshire. Dearborn was promoted to Lieutenant Colonel effective September 19, 1777. He was Secretary of War from 1801 to 1809.

## Edward Stevens, Certificate for John Syme

The Bearer Capt. John Syme an Officer in my Regmt. wants leave to resign his Commission and say's that before he can get permission to do so he must get me to Certify that he is nothing indebt to the United States: It is impossible that I can Certify any such thing with Truth. He has settled his Accts. that I am acquainted with—

Edward Stevens Colo 10th Virginia Regiment
January 3rd: 1778

Source: Record Group 93, M 859, Roll 110, Document 31287, National Archives. Syme's resignation was accepted the same day.

## James Bancroft to Joseph Bancroft

Camp Valley Forge, January 5, 1778.
Dear Sir,—While in my tent these cold long evenings, I often think of Reading, and should think myself very happy could I step in and spend a few hours with you and take a pipe and mug of cider, both which are very scarce here, and perhaps it would not be very disagreeable to you to hear something of our fatigues and dangers. Had I had opportunity to write before I came from the northward, I should liked to have written something particular of northward affairs, but it has got too old to write about. I could write nothing new. As we have had some trying times, perhaps you will ask how my courage

held out. If you should, I can't say, as some have done, that they have no fear; but I can say, I had not so much fear but what I could go where I was ordered; and if it had been *much worse* I believe I should have tried to go.

We have a very good corps of officers (one excepted). If the regiments was full of officers and soldiers as good as what we now have, and should be ordered to storm Philadelphia, I am apt to think we should make one bold push for it. The whole campaign has been very hard and fatiguing, but in general healthy. I have not missed one tour of duty since I joined the army.

As to affairs here at the southward, I am at a loss to write. I don't find anything as I expected. I believe the enemy's strength is greater, and ours less, than you imagine. So far as I can judge by the movements, both armies are a little afraid to engage under any disadvantage. There has been, I believe, some misconduct this way among officers, and our army, in most, if not all actions, have retreated, though in that of Germantown, it is said they *retreated from victory*, and that without Gen. Washington's order. I have often heard he has offered a large sum to any that would inform him who gave the orders; but since we arrived, though we have not fought much, we have not run away any. Though the enemy have threatened to drive us off, they have not ventured to make any attack on us; but when we have been about to attack them, they incline to march to Philadelphia. The Battle of Germantown was before we came. I find since that time it has been very sickly here among our officers; more than a hundred have been confined, and some of them broke, one of them a Major-General. The most of the inhabitants here are Friends, or Quakers, who, you know, never bear arms. I believe they are Tories, which is no small damage to us; but being Friends, or Tories, does not save them from being plundered by the King's troops when they have an opportunity. I hope the enemy's having some opportunity to plunder will have the same effect here that it had last year in the Jerseys, and make the Tories become good Whigs.

I hope, sir, if my family should stand in need of your assistance, you will be ready to afford it. It has been out of my power to do anything for them, even so much as to send home any money. The officers, in general, in the regiment, have been obliged to do without or borrow. The army is at present a poor place to get money. Everything is so dear we are obliged to spend considerable for provision or live very poorly. I have been obliged to give half a dollar for one pint of bread and milk; three or four shillings for a fowl; two shillings for one pound of pork. Spirits are three or four dollars a quart, but I seldom use any. Sweetening, butter, or cheese, I have not have for near three months. I expect soon to receive seven or eight months' pay, when I hope to be able to send home some considerable to my wife. I hope the time will come when I shall have the opportunity of seeing you and my friends at Reading; but when that will be God only knows. We have some hard trials to meet yet. If I should tell you what is believed here, that the enemy are more in numbers than we, perhaps you would disbelieve me. The regiments not being full is very great damage to the cause. Had they all been filled up I don't believe Howe would have had any footing in America at this time. They are more deficient this way than with you. Please to give my compliments to Mrs. Bancroft. If you could write to me it will be gladly received by    Your humble servant,

James Bancroft

To Mr. Joseph Bancroft, Reading.

Source: Lilley Eaton, *Genealogical History of the Town of Reading, Mass....* (Boston: Alfred Mudge, 1874), 707-708.
Bancroft was a Captain in the Eighth Massachusetts Regiment.

## Johann de Kalb to Anna Emily van Robais, Madame de Kalb

On the whole, I have annoyances to bear, of which you can hardly form a conception. One of them is the mutual jealousy of almost all the French officers, particularly against those of higher rank than the rest. The people think of nothing but their incessant intrigues and backbitings. They hate each other like the bitterest enemies, and endeavor to injure each other wherever an opportunity offers. I have given up their society, and seldom see them. Lafayette is the sole exception; I always meet him with the same cordiality and the same pleasure. He is an excellent young man, and we are good friends. It were to be wished that all the Frenchmen who serve here were as reasonable as he and I. Lafayette is much liked; he is on the best terms with Washington; both of them have every reason to be satisfied with me also.

Source: Friedrich Kapp, *The Life of John Kalb, Major-General of the Revolutionary Army* (New York: Henry Holt and Company, 1884), 143-44.

## Timothy Pickering, State of the New Jersey Regiments

State of the Non-Commissioned Officers & Soldiers of the four New-Jersey Regiments, according to the weekly return of Jany. 5. 1778.
Regiments

| | | Colo. Ogden's | Colo. Shrieves | Colo. Dayton's | Colo. Martin's | Total |
|---|---|---|---|---|---|---|
| Serjeants | fit for duty | 17 | 19 | 19 | 17 | 72 |
| | Sick present | 2 | 4 | | 1 | 7 |
| | Sick absent | 2 | | | 6 | 8 |
| | On command | 1 | | | | 1 |
| | On Furlough | 2 | | | | 2 |
| | Total | 24 | 23 | 19 | 24 | 90 |
| Drums & Fifes | fit for duty | 8 | 10 | 9 | 7 | 34 |
| | Sick present | 1 | | | 1 | 2 |
| | Sick absent | 1 | | | | 1 |
| | Total | 10 | 10 | 9 | 8 | 37 |
| Rank & File | Fit for duty | 121 | 146 | 172 | 145 | 584 |
| | Sick present | 34 | 7 | 17 | 17 | 75 |
| | Sick absent | 51 | 46 | 35 | 76 | 208 |
| | On command | 9 | 2 | 7 | 13 | 31 |
| | On furlough | 11 | 18 | 1 | 2 | 32 |
| | Total | 226 | 219 | 232 | 253 | 930 |

NB Of the 584 returned fit for duty, about 200 are unfit from the want of cloathing.　　　Tim. Pickering Adjt. Genl.

Source: Record Group: Department of Defense; Subgroup: Revolutionary War; Unbound Mss. 2532, Division of Archives and Records Management, New Jersey State Archives.

The manpower shortage is exemplified by this report as each regiment was supposed to have 692 enlisted men.

## William Davies to William Alexander

My Lord,　　　　　　　　　　　　　　　　　　　　Camp Jany. 7. 1778.

I beg leave to request an order in favor of my regiment for a quantity of cloathing, who are exceedingly destitute, that I return above 120 unfitt for duty on that account alone. Of the proportion allowed at Fredericksburg a considerable number were deficient, which has made the Situation of the regiment still more distressing. I must therefore solicit your Lordship for an order for 211 pair of shoes and 67 blankets for the 14th. Virga. regiment.

I have the honor to be my Lord, with the greatest respect,
Your Lordship's most obedt Servt.
William Davies.
Earl of Stirling.

Source: William Alexander Papers, The New-York Historical Society.
Davies was the Major of the Seventh Virginia Regiment.

**Extract of a Letter**

*Extract of a letter from a gentleman, dated Camp, at the Valley Forge, January 7, 1788. [sic]*

About eight days ago a very large schooner drove on the shore upon the Pea-patch, in the Delaware, with the ice, richly laden; having on board 101 hogsheads of rum and spirits, a large quantity of fine and coarse cloths, India silks, bohea tea, &c. &c. The ice having cut the vessel through, the crew delivered themselves to the militia of Salem county, and the principal part of the cargo has been saved and stored in a place of security.

Source: Francis B. Lee, ed., *Documents Relating to the Revolutionary History of the State of New Jersey*, vol. 2 (Trenton: John L. Murphy, 1903), 9.

**Thirteen Artillerymen's Receipts**

Camp Great Valley Jan$^y$. 7. 1778
Rec$^d$. of Cap$^t$. Will$^m$. Johnston the Sum of Eighteen pound L.M. Eaquel to Sixty Dollars Continental Currancey
    Joseph Driskill Liu[t] Artil$^y$

Camp Great Valley Jan$^y$. 7
Rec$^d$. of Cap$^t$. Leu$^t$. Will$^m$. Johnston the Sum of fourty Eight Shilling LM. Eaquel to Eight Dollars Continental Currancy—

John Gartia

Camp Great Valley Jan<sup>y</sup>. 7
Rec<sup>d</sup>. of Cap<sup>t</sup>. Leu<sup>t</sup>: Will<sup>m</sup>. Johnston of Artillery the Sum of forty Eight Shilling LM. Eaqu[el] to Eight Dollars Continental Currancey— Thomas Sheppard

Camp Great Valley Jan<sup>y</sup>. 7
Rec<sup>d</sup>. of Cap<sup>t</sup>. Leu<sup>t</sup>. W<sup>m</sup>. Johnston of Artil<sup>y</sup> the Sum of forty Shillings L.M. Equael to Eight Dollars Continental Currancey—
John Nick

Camp Great Valley Jan<sup>y</sup>. 7
Rec<sup>d</sup>. of Cap<sup>t</sup>. Lu<sup>t</sup>. Will<sup>m</sup>. Johnston of Artillery the Sum of forty Eight Shillings LM. Eaquel to Eight Dollars
Anthony Kelly

Camp Great Valley Janyy. 7
Rec<sup>d</sup>. of Cap<sup>t</sup>. Lu<sup>t</sup>. Will<sup>m</sup>. Johnston of Artil<sup>y</sup> the Sum of forty Eight Shilling LM. Eaquel to Eight Collars Continental Currancey
his
John X Grangr

Camp Great Valley Jan<sup>y</sup>. 7
Rec<sup>d</sup>. of Cap<sup>t</sup>. Lu<sup>t</sup>. Will<sup>m</sup>. Johnston of Artil<sup>y</sup> the Sum of [for]ty Eight Shilling LM. Samuel Denny

Camp Great Valley Jan<sup>y</sup>. 7. 1778
Rec<sup>d</sup>. of Cap<sup>t</sup>. Lu<sup>t</sup>. W<sup>m</sup>. Johnston of Artil<sup>y</sup> the Sum of forty Eight Shilling LM.— James Russell

Camp Great Valley Jan<sup>y</sup>. 7. 1778
Rec<sup>d</sup>. of Cap<sup>t</sup>: Lu<sup>t</sup>. W<sup>m</sup>. Johnston of Artil<sup>y</sup> the Sum Eight Dollars Continental Currancey Charles Howett

Camp Great Valley Jan<sup>y</sup>. 7.
Rec<sup>d</sup>. of Cap<sup>t</sup>. Lu<sup>t</sup>. W<sup>m</sup>. Johnston of Artil<sup>y</sup> the Sum of forty Eight Shilling LM.— his
Manuel X Lewes
Mark

Camp Great Valley Jan$^y$. 7.
Rec$^d$. of Cap$^t$. Lu$^t$. W$^m$. Johnston of Artil$^y$ the Sum of forty Eight Shillings LM.—
                  his
            John **X** Boughtnow
                Mark

Camp Great Valley Jan$^y$. 7. 1778
Rec$^d$. of Cap$^t$. Lu$^t$. Will$^m$. Johnston of Artil$^y$ the Sum of forty Eight Shilling LM—        William Dockum

Camp Great Valley Jan$^y$. 7.
Rec$^d$. of Cap$^t$. Lu$^t$. W$^m$. Johnston of Artil$^y$ the Sum of forty Eight Shillings LM.—
                his
          Recherd **X** Northover

Source: Record Group 93, M 246, Roll 121, Frames 145-48, National Archives.
All the men were in the Third Artillery Regiment. All the words except the signatures in the same hand. Denny and Kelly deserted on January 8.


**William Alexander to Aaron Burr**

Sir,                                              Camp, January 8th, 1778.
    The receipt of your letter of yesterday's date not a little surprised me, for I can assure you that I have never made use of a word in censure of yourself, or of the court you mention. I some days ago ordered a return to be brought in of the names and rank of the officers of the division, independent of what the two courts were doing, and desired Major Monroe to direct the brigade-majors to make them out as soon as possible: from this, I suppose, some mistake has arose, which I will call upon Major Stagg to explain.
                I am, Your most obedient humble servant,
                      Stirling.
Lieutenant-colonel Burr.

Source: Matthew L. Davis, *Memoirs of Aaron Burr. With Miscellaneous Selections From His Correspondence.* (New York: Harper & Brothers, 1855), 1:123-24.
Burr was Lieutenant Colonel of Malcom's Additonal Continental Regiment. He was the Vice-President under Thomas Jefferson, and killed Alexander Hamilton in a duel.

## William Lee Davidson to Richard Caswell

Sir                                              Valey forge 8 Jany 1778
    Previous to the receipt of this you will have received his excellency Genl. Washingtons Instructions to the Officers of your state respecting the recruiting Service, by the Hand of Col. Lytle: I hope that my long absence from my fammely and the Length of the Jorney will be a sufficient Excuse for my takeing the directest rout home; Especially as I have Ord[ered] Major Hogg to be at Newbern the first Day of March: The Time, & place that I have appointed to [Re]ndezvous unless we receive other Orders sooner, which is very Improbable, as we are likely to be detained through the want of pay. I hope that your Excellency will condesend so far as to acquaint Capt Caswell with your Orders concerning the recruiting service: as I have wrote to him to transmit them to Salisbury by the first oppertunity.
                       I am with the Highist Esteem: your Excellencys
                               most Obedient & Humle Sert
                               William L Davidson Lt Col. 5'B

His Excellency Governor Caswell
Addressed: His Excellency Governor Caswell North Carolina
             favrd by Capt Williams
Docket: Lieut Col. Davidson Valley Forge 8. Jany 1778.

Source: Frederick M. Dearborn Collection, MS AM 1649.6 (33), Houghton Library, Harvard University.
Davidson later left the Continental Army, and was killed in action at Cowan's Ford on February 1, 1781, while serving as a Brigadier General of North Carolina militia, but got a college named after him.

## Elias Boudinot to Thomas Bradford

Instructions for Thos Bradford Esq Deputy Commissary of Prisoners in the American Camp

1st You are to leave notice in writing at the Adjutant General's Office & with Col Harrison at head Quarters, where you are quartered describing the House So as it may be easily found.

2d You are to call at the adjutant General's Office to know if any orders are issued respecting your department or if any Prisoners are in the Provost, which you are to Send to Reading or Lancaster as fast as the number of 8 or 10 are collected—The Guard to be appointed by the Adjutant General on your Application.

3 All Prisoners of War that are Sent off by you, are to be Entered in a Book kept by you for that purpose, Specifying their Names, Corps, Time when & Place where taken & where Sent, in different Columns, a Copy of which is always to be sent with the Prisoners.

4—All Officers are to be admitted to their Paroles, & immediately Sent off under Care of one of our Officers, to Reading or Lancaster, keeping a like Entry of them—

5—When Prisoners are sent off, they are to draw Rations for their Journey, at the Rate of 12 oz Meat & 12 oz Bread pr Day pr Man

6 You are not to Suffer an Officer (Prisoner of War) to have either Horse or Waggon, but at his own Expence, unless wounded or Sick

7 You are to keep exact Entries of all your transactions of every kind—To take up all Letters directed to me, & in case of necessity to forward them on by Express to Baskenridge—

8 Let me hear from you by every opportunity, if it Should be only just to know that all is well: but in Case of any Sudden movement of our Army, or any thing Extraordinary Should happen, Send an Express—Coll: Lutterloh will furnish you with one: otherwise provide one yourself

9 You are to keep exact Vouchers for any disbursements or Expences which may accrue in your Department

10 You are not to allow any officer to be exchanged or go into the Enemy, without Express orders from the Commander in Chief or myself

11 In order that you may know the State of the Prisoners in the City I must inform you, that they are all in close confinement, are Supported

by Rations rec'd from the Enemy @ 8 oz Salt Meat, & 12 oz Bread Pr Man Pr Day— Besides this I have an Agent (Mr Thos Franklin) in the City, who I have ordered to Supply them with every Necessary in his Power as far as the Supplies Sent him by me will enable him—I have already contracted with Robert Haughy of St Georges New Castle County, to Supply him with 1000 Barrels of Flour—500 are already gone in – also have directed him to send in a few Carcases of Beef & about 30 Cords of Wood – also 2000 lb of Indian Meal—Besides this I have Sent them in the last week 68 Barrells of Flour & 24 fat Cattle, & have also engaged Mr Hollingsworth at the Head of Elk to send in 500 Barrels of Flour—So that I think they cannot want anything till 1$^{st}$ of March—If you find they are in want of Beef, Send in a Dozen of good Cattle about the middle or 20$^{th}$ of Feby, which you may get at the Commissy Genl. of Purchases—

12 The Deputy Comissaries you are to Send Prisoners to or Correspond with, in Case of necessity are as follows

| | |
|---|---|
| Massachussets Bay | Joshua Mersereau |
| Connecticut | Ezekiel Williams |
| Albany | Daniel Hale |
| Army at Peeks Kill | John Adam |
| Easton | Robt L. Hooper   Reading |
| Henry Haller | |
| Lancaster | Wm Atlee |
|    York Town | Thos Peters |
| Winchester, Virginia | Joseph Holmes |

13 Whenever you write me, let me have Such letters inclosed as you think may be of any Importance, & do not fail to let me hear from you at least once a week

14 If any Officers (Prisoners) Should be allowed to go into the Enemy, they are not to go thro Camp, & one of our Subaltern Officers is to attend them—The Adjutant General orders one for the purpose

15 Whatever Money or Cloaths are Sent in, for our Prisoners, or are sent out for the Enemy's Prisoners, you will be particularly carefull of & keep Regular Entries for whom they are Sent, the Sum & person by whom & time when you forwarded them —

16 You are to Send every thing, with open letters into the Enemy under Cover to H. Hugh Ferguson Esqr Commissary of Prisoners in Philada—If you write to Mr Thos Franklin, our agent there, the letter must be open & inclosed to Mr Ferguson

17 Whatever is to be Sent to New York, you will forward to me

18 You are carefully to peruse all letters Sent out from the Enemy also those you receive to forward in by flags, to See that nothing improper, is contained in any letter that goes in or comes out

19 Whenever you want to Send any thing into the Enemy, you are to apply to the Adjutant General for a flag & a proper person to go with it—

20t Since giving the above Instructions, I am informed by his Excellency that Genl. Howe will not permit any more Provisions to be sent up Delaware, and that I must fully provide for our Prisoners in the City—You must therefore in Case of necessity give directions for all Provisions to go in by Land – I have already wrote on this Subject to Messrs. Haughy & Hollingsworth—You must immediately inform the Commissary Genl of Purchases, that we must have about 20 Head of fat Cattle on the first of February and about 50 Barrels of Salt Provision or a proportion of Cattle—

    ELIAS BOUDINOT   Commissary General of Prisoners

SOURCE: Thomas Bradford Papers, Series 3, Box 21, vol. 1, p. 124, The Historical Society of Pennsylvania.
Undated. Bradford writes that he was appointed to the position of Deputy Commissary General of Prisoners on January 10, 1778. Boudinot wrote to Hollingsworth on January 11, as referred to in item twenty above, and stated he was just leaving for Jersey, so this document must be dated about January 11, 1778.

## Michael Crous to Thomas Jones, Two Receipts for Cattle.

Camp at Valey Forge Jan$^y$. 14 1778.
    Receiv'd of James Robinson A C. of P$^s$. by Julius Deming Forty Five fat Cattle for which Please to Give him a Reciet for—

Michael Crous
To M$^r$. Jones A. C. G. I.

Camp at Valey Forge Jan$^y$. 1778
Receiv'd of Timothy Bradley A C of P$^s$. by Joseph Smith Thirty Nine fat Cattle for the Use of the Army which please to Reciet to him for Michael Crous
To M$^r$. Jones A. C. G. I.

Source: Peter Force Collection, Mss. 13,778, Series 8D, Container 14, Nos. 2208 and 2209, Library of Congress.
Michael Crous/Crouse was in charge of the cattle brought for the Encampment, which were kept around the French Creek Bridge. Jones was Deputy Commissary General of Issues with the army.

### Richard Kidder Meade, Permission for Hugh Roe to Resign

Hd Qrs Valley Forge Jan 14$^{th}$ 1778
    Lieutenant Hugh Roe of Colo Pattons Regiment at his own request is permitted to resign his Commission in the Continental Army.
    By his Excellys Commd.

Source: William A. Oldridge Collection, from *Delaware Archives*, vol. 2.
Meade was an Aide-de-Camp to Washington. Roe's resignation was effective this date.

### Thomas Jones, Ration Deficiencies of Third New Jersey Regiment

—defeciencies due the officers of the third N. Jersey Regiment—by Col Dayton on Rations drawn for 91 days viz, from Octor 2d to Decemr 31st 1777, both days inclusive.

| Names | Rank | No. defeciencis | L. s. d |
|---|---|---|---|
| Elias Dayton | Colonel | 58 | 17:01 |
| Francis Barber | Lt. Colonel | 182 | 2:15:07 |
| Joseph Bloomfield | Major | | |
| Samuel Shipard | Adjutant | 68 | 1:00:09 |
| Lewis F. Dunham | Surgeon | 68 | 1:00:09 |
| Ephraim Loree | Surg Mate | 54 | 16:06 |

| | | | |
|---|---|---|---|
| Jonathan Dayton | Pay Master | 67 | 1:00:05 |
| Joseph Periam | Qur Master | 78 | 1:03:10 |
| Morgan | Armorer (25 days) | | |
| Peter Dickerson | Captain Resigned Oct 26 | 23 | :07:01 |
| Jeremiah Ballard | 1st Lt Promoted Oct 26 | 56 | :17:01 |
| Edmund D. Thomas | 2d Lt do do | 91 | 1:07:09 |
| Nathan Wilkinson | Ensign | 91 | 1:07:09 |
| Thomas Paterson | Captain | 45 | :13:01 |
| Edward Paterson | 1st Lt | | |
| John Kinney | 2d Lt | 91 | 1:07:09 |
| John Rucastle | Ensign | 91 | 1:07:09 |
| John Ross | Captain | 56 | :17:14 |
| William Clarke | 1st. Lt | 8 | :02:05 |
| William Kersey | Ensign | 91 | 1:07:09 |
| John Mott | Captain | 64 | :19:06 |
| Joseph Anderson | 1st Lieut—Captain Oct 26 | 74 | 1:02:07 |
| William Norcross | 2d Lt Resigned Nov 12 | | |
| Mahlon Ford | Ensign | 91 | 1:07:09 |
| William Gifford | Captain | 45 | :12:09 |
| Cornelius Hennion | 1st Lt—Captain Nov 1, | | |
| Edgar Galaudet | 2d Lt | | |
| Jarvis Bloomfield | Ensign | 8 | :02:05 |
| Samuel Flanagan | Captain resigned Oct 26 | 25 | :07:07 |
| William Bostwick | 1st Lt | 64 | :19:06 |
| Nathaniel Leonard | 2d Lt | 49 | :14:01 |
| James Scobey | Ensign resigned Dec 16 | 33 | :10:01 |
| Robert Hagan | Captain resigned Nov 1, | 30 | :09:02 |
| Marmaduke Curtis | 1st Lieut | 91 | |
| William Catanch | 2d Lt | | |
| George Ewing | Ensign | | |
| Richard Cox | Captain | | |
| John Reading | 1st Lt | | |
| Samuel Hacket | 2d Lt resigned Nov 1, | | |
| Aaron Day | Ensign | | |

Commissaries Office Jany, 18, 1778, as pr Issue Books of Wm. Shute A. C of Issues

Thomas Jones D.C.G. of Issues

Source: Record Group: Department of Defense; Subgroup: Revolutionary War; Roll 6, Mss. 2362, Division of Archives and Records Management, New Jersey State Archives.

## Thomas Antoine, Chevalier de Maudit Duplessis to Henry Laurens

January 20, 1778

I send you my commission. You can see that my appointment is in your Corps of artillery. It is my profession in France. In all the Campaign I have been alwais employ'd by the general Knox in this station and sometimes in the station of engeneer. The desire of general Knox is to conserve me in his corps, and I give you my word that he has promised me to employ me exactly in his corps proper the appointment you will give me. His Excellency and the general Knox have decided together to ask for me the appointment in the artillery. I can say you too that the project is to give me the command of the artillery of the M. de la Fayette's division.

Source: Thomas Birch's Sons Auctioneers, Catalogue 683, (Philadelphia, April 1862), 581. This is the sale abstract from a two page letter.
He was a Captain in the Continental Artillery. On January 19, 1778, the Continental Congress appointed him a brevet Lieutenant Colonel of artillery for his gallant conduct and achievements, the commission to be backdated to November 26, 1777. This was disputed by other officers and Washington convened a board of thirteen generals on June 2. This board confirmed his brevet rank and that "he is annexed especially to the Totality or Aggregate of the Line of Artillery...." Laurens was President of the Continental Congress, then meeting at York, Pennsylvania.

## Alexander Hamilton to Henry Emanuel Lutterloh, Lutterloh to Charles Young

Copy from Coll. Lutterloh, Valley forge, Feb. 20, 1778.
Sir
    I received this morning your favour & acquainted the Hon'ble Committee of Congress with the contents, as your Waggons come in but slow into the Camp, and our distress for Waggons is very great (as you will see by the inclosed note,) I beg you will loose not a

moment's time to get us supplyed, I do not know what to do. In the neighbourhood of the Camp are no Waggons, all are worn out and our own Teams cannot go along being so worked down. I beg for God's sake you will assist us, and let them bring forrage & Commissary stores as I mentioned before. You must send Express again and hurry them on. Tho' the letters mentioned 30, Teams but yet only 20 arrived. Consider the Distress of the army and loose not a moment to assist the Public Service.

  I am, your, &c.  Lutterloh.
 Send the order back.

The Committee ordered me to send this express and request this Exertion of you.

  Copy of the order above mentioned.

Dr Sir,

  You are hereby authorised by order of his Excellency General Washington, to impress any number of Waggons you stand in need of, in the neighbourhood of the Camp. You don't say what number you expect in to-morrow. General Green & Coll. Biddle write, that they meet with the greatest difficulty in foraging for want of Waggons. The General begs you to give them all the assistance you can. For God's sake, my dear Sir, exert yourself upon this occasion, our distress is infinite  Yours,

        A. Hamilton, A. D. C.

To Coll. Lutterloh.

Source: Samuel Hazard, ed. *Pennsylvania Archives*, 1st series (Philadelphia: Joseph Severns, 1853), 6: 283. James Young, Wagon Master General at Reading, was the recipient of this letter. He forwarded it on February 21, to Timothy Matlack, Secretary to the State of Pennsylvania, reporting he received it that day at 3 o'clock P. M. Hamilton was one of Washington's Aides.

**Jedediah Huntington to Mathew Irwin**

Dear Sir,       Camp Valley Forge 20 January 1778.

  I heartily thank you for your kind Offer and wish the Affairs of Camp would allow me to embrace it, one Business crouds so close upon the Heels of another as to forbid Recreation, The Brigadiers are to become Sope boilers, Oilmen Armourers—Tanners—Shoemakers and the Lord knows what. But I hope for better Times when a few more such men as Col. Trumbull & some others lately appointed, have the Direction of our military Arrangements—please to tell him I expect the Pleasure of a Visit from him, by the Time he comes my House will be done which will afford a welcome Reception to him & M$^{rs}$ Irwin—Compliments to Miss Irwin—from d$^r$ Sir

      Your sincere friend & mst obed$^t$
      J Huntington

M$^r$ Irwin Esq:
Endorse Mathew Irwin Esquire  Reading
Gen$^l$ Huntingtons Compliments to Col. Biddle and desires him to forward this.    J. Huntington.

Source: *Pennsylvania Magazine of History and Biography*, 40, no. 1 (1916): 123.
Huntington was a Brigadier General from Connecticut. Irwin was a Captain in Malcolm's Additional Continental Regiment and had just resigned his commission.

## Gaston Marie Léonard Maussion de la Bastie to his Brother

Dear Brother:     Valley Forge Camp 20th January, 1778

 In the midst of all the miseries of our existence here, your recent letter proved most welcome, and I heartily thank you for it. You are kind to say that my descriptions of the things I see and of the battles in which I take part interest you, and since you wish to hear more about this part of my life, I am going to satisfy your curiosity. Having, unfortunately, more spare time on my hands than I should like, I shall take up in detail the story of what happened after the battle of Brandywine.

 The loss of this engagement, a most serious matter to the American army, would have crushed any other man than General Washington. But his calmness under a diversity is truly one of the most marvelous sights it has ever been my lot to witness. We all know how he must feel, and yet never a word is heard to escape his lips that does not express profound trust in Providence and the liberation of his country. Monsieur de La Fayette, who, I believe, knows him better than any other of our officers, has more than once said that he could not conceive how any man could remain so self-controlled under serious disaster. It seems that once our Marquis could not restrain himself and told the Commander-in-Chief how much he admired his attitude in anxiety and misfortune. The only reply was a request never to mention it again. "We are all in God's hands," added General Washington, "and what He permits and ordains we must accept and go on doing our duty regardless of consequences." Now you'll admit that very few, if any, of our brilliant generals would ever have made such a remark!

To come back to my story: when it became evident that we had been beaten at Brandywine, our Commander-in-Chief by a clever retreat brought his army to Chester, and then by a forced march reached Philadelphia where he secured ammunition and provisions for his troops. After this he withdrew to Germantown, having ordered Monsieur de Courdray to complete a series of defensive works along the Delaware River, planned some time before. At the same time he ordered General Armstrong to occupy the line of the Schuylkill River and build redoubts near its fords in case it should become desirable to cross the river.

Our enemy, for their part, were not inactive. General Cornwallis, reaching Chester shortly after our army had evacuated it, took prisoner the governor of the city of Wilmington, while Howe, who occupied a position in our rear, tried to march toward Philadelphia so as to cut General Washington off from the possibility of another retreat. But the General is not a man to be taken unawares; he crossed the Schuylkill himself and so frustrated the British commander's plans.

Nevertheless, General Howe advanced to meet us and was going to attack when one of the most violent thunderstorms ever known in this country prevented him but at the same time ruined all the ammunition we had been able to save, to the great distress of our Commander-in-Chief. Leaving about two thousand men in charge of General Wayne, with instructions to follow and harass the British detachments, General Washington moved with the rest of our army toward a place called Yellow Springs. But as soon as he had left we had another proof that without him everything goes wrong, for General Wayne allowed himself to be surprised at night through treachery and lost more than half his men as prisoners to the British, saving, however, his guns and baggage. General Washington had left a Brigade under an officer named Smallwoud to reinforce Wayne in case of emergency, but although it was encamped only about two miles distant, it failed to get up in time to render aid during the night attack.

This attack saved Howe and allowed him to move on unmolested, because General Washington with his tired troops could not pursue and overtake him. Here again he proved admirable, because, when some one asked him whether he would have Wayne court-martialed for his imprudence, he merely replied that it was he himself who deserved to be censured for having, in such a grave emergency, trusted any one but himself, forgetful of the fact that he could hardly have been in two places at once and that he has performed wonders and kept for himself the most dangerous and responsible task in his brilliant strategy.

But we had lost Philadelphia and had to reconcile ourselves to that fact. It was occupied by Lord Cornwallis, while General Howe established himself at Germantown.

And were we were to witness one of the most extraordinary incidents in this campaign and to see a piece of daring on the part of our Commander-in-Chief such as I am ready to stake my life was never before attempted by a general in the field, no matter in what country.

Our headquarters were at a place called Pennebeque, about eighteen miles from Philadelphia. General Washington conceived the audacious plan of storming the English positions and so reoccupy the city. On the third of October he moved his army, using four roads at the same time, and made straight for the British encampment, intending to attack their whole line at daybreak. He ordered General Sullivane and General Wayne to march on the city and enter it while General Maxwell, General Nash, and another officer whose name I forget were to fall on the British rear and disperse it.

But here again there was regrettable confusion, and this brilliant piece of strategy failed because none of these officers was able to appreciate its importance or the greatness of its conception. General Stefane, who was also there, left General Greene, his superior officer, and hearing sounds of firing, moved in the direction from which it proceeded, and without ascertaining what troops were facing him, ordered his men to fire away before them, which they did, only to discover that they had been attacking one of their own divisions, that of General Wayne, who was in the place assigned him by the Commander-in-Chief. I hasten to add that after this terrible incident General Stefane was dismissed from the service, proof being offered that he had been thoroughly intoxicated at such a critical time and did not know what he was doing nor where he was going.

All this time General Washington had been with General Sulivane whose conduct, in contrast to the others, was quite admirable. From the advance post which they occupied, General Washington had been able to see that, owing to the absence of support, that there was nothing he could do but withdraw his army. He gave the order and with great difficulty regained his headquarters. Again a battle was lost that should have been won.

And here I'll add a detail which probably will interest you. When General Washington saw he could no longer expect assistance from his subordinates, he suddenly passed his hand over his eyes and murmured quite low, but not so low that those who were close to him could not hear, "If only La Fayette had been here, how different it would all have been!" which will prove to you dear Brother, that our Marquis is appreciated as he deserves to be.

Good-by, dear Brother, and keep well till I see you again.

De Maussion

Source: *They Knew the Washingtons: Letters from a French Soldier with Lafayette and from His Family in Virginia* trans. Princess Radziwill (Indianapolis: Bobbs-Merrill Company, 1926), 60-66.

Some experts consider the letters in this book to be of doubtful authenticity. No record of this man's association with the Continental Army could be found. However most of the statements, such as the deluge often called "The Battle of the Clouds" and the attack on Anthony Wayne at Paoli, can be verified.

## James McClure to David McClure

Camp at Valley forge 20 Miles from Philedelphia
up the Schuylkill the 21$^{st}$. January—1778

Dear Brother

I Received your kind Letter by M$^r$. Gookin. Which gave me great pleasure to here of the welfare of your Little family of brothers & sisters. Who I should be glad to see & Spend a little time with But when that will be is uncertain—

you will please to pardon my Neglect in Not writing before now, as I have always been full of Busness & not informed of Conveyances Seasonably, I improve that by Cap$^t$. Rowell of Colo. Hales Regt. who I am informed goes in the morning,—

Instead of Coming Here to do Something Great for the Honor of the nation as Con[fl]an Says. we Have Retired to the barren Hills of Valley forge, & Huted our Hole army, Which Looks Like an Indian City, The Country Supply us with Nothing but what we force from them, at the Most Extrvagant Rates. we are glad to get it any How & at an[y] price, as the Neighbouring states Have Caught the same Distemper, Which Causes us to Live in a miserable Condition for Gentleman soldiers, Not the Least Provision is made Either for Officer or soldier, it is impossible to Discribe the Stupidity & Rascally behaviour of the Inhabitants, who for the sake of the & th[ou] Think it Sacrilidge to look a soldier in the face, but I hope our Roman Gen$^l$. will make them know the Odds before Long—I Could wish D$^r$. Brother I was at my Old Calling again, & Should have been if the Intercession of my Gen$^l$. & Other friends Did not prevail on me to Stay, for I am fairly tired of the army they are So Neglected—I think the States will be inexcusable if they Dont make One Vigorious Exertion. to Enable us to take the field early in the spring. I think it would be the means of bringing it to the much wished for Period [&] of freeing an innocent Country of those plundering murderers. those Parricides of Hell (if I may be allowed the Expression) & that we may once more Enjoy the Happy Days of Liberty & peace—as to News we have none, Only our famous partisan Cap$^t$ Lee of the Light Dragoons, who has Killed & taken 130 of the Enemy since they Landed at the Elk, with his Small Troop, He is posted about Six Miles in our front & keeps out small partys to watch the Enemy, was surrounded in his Quarters, at sunrise with only 7 men, by a party of the Enemy Consisting of 150 who Conceald their march by a Circuitious Rout, on purpose to take him, but he soon bafled their designs. by Judiciously posti[ng] His men at the windows. & after an Hours action he Caused the party Disgracefully to Retire. Leaving 2 Killed & 4 Wounded Not a man Lost on our side, the Enemy Remain Quite Still in their Quarters as we are informed by Diserters who Come out Evry Day.—I hope to set out for Home in about 10 Days from this. Maj$^r$. M$^c$Clintock is hearty & well, Give my kind Regards to Brothers & Sisters, Col$^o$. Long. Deacon Penhallow & familys & Excep$^t$. much Love from y$^r$. Broth$^r$

   James M$^c$Clure

Addressed To the Rever$^d$. David M$^c$Clure        North Hampton

Source: Special Collections, The Watkinson Library, Trinity College, Hartford, Connecticut.

James McClure was a Captain-Lieutenant in the Second Continental Artillery Regiment. David McClure was Pastor of the Congregational Church at North Hampton, New Hampshire. In General Orders on January 20, Washington gave "warmest thanks" to Henry Lee Jr. and his men "for the Victory which be their superior Bravery and Address they gain'd over a party of the Enemys dragoons." Lee, the father of Robert E. Lee, had held a stone house against a vastly superior British raiding force. This action was a major morale boost for the Americans.

## Matthias Ogden to Jonathan Trumbull Jr., John Pierce Jr. to Ogden

Sir,  Camp [Va]lley Forge Jan[y]. 21st. 1778

I wrote you by the post, begging that you would send me a certificate of what Stoppages was retained in your hands at Ticonderoga for the 1st. J: Regiment between the months of June & Sepr[r]. if you have not sent it, or if you have, it is not come to hand, & I beg you will send a duplicate by M[r]. Morris who will hand you this—I am Sir

Yours &c.—

M. Ogden Col 1st J Regt

On publick service   Col, Jon: Trumbull
Paymaster Gen[l] Northern Dep[t]   pr M[r] Morris

Albany Feb[y] 3. 1778

Yours of the 21 Ult. to Mr Trumbull I have recived.—I find that on the 14th Sept. 1776 was stoped eight hundred and fifty two Pounds eighteen Shillings and four Pence NYork Currency from the 1st N Jersey Regiment in favor of Thomas Lowry Esq—there are no other stoppas, [sic] which I can find. I believe M[r] Trumbull has not receiv[d]. any Letter from the post, otherwise I should have known it

I am sir your mot ob[t].

John Pierce Jun[r]

Source: Jonathan Trumbull Jr. Papers, Paymaster General, Vol. 2, 1776-1783, Connecticut Historical Society.

Matthias Ogden was Colonel of the First New Jersey Regiment. Jonathan Trumbull, Jr. was the Paymaster General for the Northern Department.

## Extract of a Letter from an Officer

A Letter from an Officer, at the Southward, dated January 22, 1778, says, "On the 20th Instant, Major Jemason of Foot, Captain Lee, and Lieutenant Lindsay, of Light Dragoons, with four Men of their Corps, were surrounded by near 200 of the Enemy's Cavalry, in their Quarters, at a house in Derby; they made fast the Doors, and fought them through the Windows, made them retreat repeatedly, and at last obliged them to a precipitate Flight, with the loss of two killed and four wounded on the Spot; a slight wound on the Head of Lieutenant Lindsay, is the only Damage on our Side, in this NOBLE Action."

Source: *Independent Chronicle*, (Boston), February 19, 1778.

## Extract of a Letter from an Officer

Extract of a Letter from an Officer dated, Camp, Jan. 22, 1778,

    Nothing new since I wrote you last, save the gallant Defence of a Stone House by 8 Horsemen, against 150 or 200 of the Enemies Horse. This was done by Major Jameson, Captain Lee, Lieutenant Linsey (all of Virginia) and a Corporal and 4 Privates. It was on the Morning of the 20th Instant, just after Day-break. The Enemy fetched a Circuit in Order to surprize Capt. Lee, who commanded the Light Party, Major Jameson being accidentally at his Quarters. Lee had not one Man to a Window, yet baffled the Attempt of the Enemy to force into the House; they then went to the Stable to get the Horses, but they being near, Lee kept up so warm a Fire upon them, that they did not dismount; and just at the Time he ordered his Party to Huzza, (which they did) and cried out, "Now we are safe my Boys, the Light Infantry is come to support us."—The Enemy heard and fled with Precipitation. Captain Lee was about 18 miles from Philadelphia, and 3 Miles from our most advanced Post of 300 Men; from the latter a Party was sent to intercept the Horse, but they fled too fast. Captain Lee is a young Man, but a celebrated Partizan. With his single Troop, he has made 130 of the Enemy Prisoners, since they landed at the Head of Elk. Captain Lee sustained no Loss; Linsey only was slightly Wounded. We have heard 4 or 5 of the Enemy were carried off dead.

Source: *Boston Gazette and Country Journal,* February 16, 1778.

## Andrew Dunlap to Leonard Bronck

Ever Honored Friend     Valley Forge January 24, 1778
    I look on this present as a favourable opportunity to wright to one who I must and am duty bound to say are more a father or relation by behaviour than only a friend, but not doubting that your generous kind nature will be rewarded in a satisfactirous manner.
    Being willing to acquaint you that I am very happly in having my health at this present time and moreso a stedfast resolution to remain a strong libertine as long as my much ronged country may call for soldiers, sword and ball especially, against so cruel, unjust, barbarious and abrupt an enemy, not doubting but we come of victorious.
    We are in the above named place, west from Philadelphia, about 21 miles where we have good comfortable hutts. Nothing strange haith happened only on ye 19th ult. Cap't Lee with 1 Sub. 1 Corpl. and 4 privates was attacked by a detachment of 200 of the dragons they being harisd, maraccilously drove the enemy leaving 2 dead and 4 wounded
                    Your Humble Servt
                      Andrew Dunlap

    Desiring that you would be so kind as to favour me in remembering my kind respects to Rachiel Dotherick and Thany Irvin and their respective families and all enquiring friends. I have hopes of comeing home soon.

Source: *The Spirit of '76* (January 1900), 6, no. 5, 83-84.
This was addressed to Bronck at Coxsackie, N.Y. Dunlap was a Sergeant in the Second New York Regiment.

## Charles Porterfield, Certificate for Daniel Reagan

                                  Camp January 24th. 1778
    I do certify That Lieutenant Ragan of Capt. Rices Company is not Indebted to the United States, To the best of my knowledge, or from any Information I can get
           Chas. Porterfield Capt Comdt. of the 11th. V. R.

being unacquainted with Lt. Ragan, his Capt absent, & he being but Short Time with the Regt. I know not further, than as above Certifyd.

Chas. Porterfield Capt. 11th. V. R.

On reverse: "Resignat. Lieut. Reagen of 11th. Virga. 25th. Jany 1778"

Source: Record Group 93, M 858, Roll 110, Document 31279, National Archives.

**Tench Tilghman to William Alexander**

My Lord                    Head Quarters 24th. Jany 1778

As His Excellency is very busy in preparing matters to lay before the Committee of Congress and Board of War, he commands me to acknowledge your Lordships favour of this day, inclosing a very melancholy letter from Colo. Spencer.

The want of cloathing is a thing which is much to be regretted but not remedied just at this time. A considerable quantity upon public account ought to have been here by this time, but thro' the negligence of the officer who had it in charge it was left at Fishkill. The General has sent an Express to bring that forward. The State of Pennsylvania have collected a large parcel of Cloathing for their Troops, for which Genl. Wayne went to Lancaster a fortnight ago, and as the whole of Colo. Spencers Brigade except his own Regiment are Pennsylvanians, they will come in for part of that cloathing when it arrives from Lancaster. The Waggons were called in from the Brigades that an exact arrangement of them might be made, that a more effectual mode of forraging might be fallen upon, (by appropriating a particular number of Waggons to that use) than had hitherto been practised. I should. I should think, my Lord, if the Commissaries of Forage were ordered to bring in a load or two of Straw with each Brigade of Waggons, that the men might constantly have enough for Beds. I hope you will evade the attack of Gout that has threatned you.

                 And am my Lord yr. most obt. Servt.
                         T. Tighman

Source: *Letters on the American Revolution in the Library at "Karolfred."* ed. Frederic R. Kirkland, vol. 2 (New York City: Coward-McCann, Inc., 1952), 46.

Tench Tilghman, from Maryland, was Assistant Secretary on Washington's staff, and was responding to a letter of Stirling's of the same date.

## Jonathan Allen to Unidentified

Sir,                    Camp Near Valley Forge, 25th Jan., 1778.

I take this opportunity to inform you of my good state of helth, hoping these will find you and your father and mother in as good a state of helth as I could wish them.

I have nothing extraordanery to inform you with only that we are in close hall with the enemy watching their motion, but we do not engage except now and then our scouts and light horse has a small scratch but not to much purpose, we live here in houses of our own making, and they barrack in Philadelphia.

But we secure in our all conquering charmes
Laugh at their vain efforts of false alarm
We magnifye their conquest who complains
For none would struggle were they not in chains.

Sir, I wrote you one dated the 15th Dec., 1777, but not receiving an answer I flatter myself that it did not arrive to your hand, acquaint your unkel that I spoke to Colo. Bailey in regard to the salt he mentioned to me, but got no answer.

My best compliments to Miss Hannah Knine and Catty, and hope to be maid so happy as to here of their wellfare, my compliments to the family, my compliments to Fanny and all the ladies of my acquaintance, my respects to you all while I have the honour to remain.

               Your humble servt.
               JONTH. ALLEN

On reverse: Sir,

I have the honour to inform my Colo. that by my interest I have procured him a Brigadeers commission and my Major to be first Colo. and the Capt. of Graniders to be Major.

I congratulate them with their promotions. My only dependant the brigadier to a major gen'l.

Source: *The Spirit of '76* (January 1900), 6, no. 5, 84.
In the General Orders for June 9, 1778, it was stated that: "At a Division Court Martial on June 7th. 1778, Adjutant Allen of Colo. Michael Jackson's Regiment, tried first, for repeated disobedience of Orders; 2nd. for abusive language to Major Hull and refusing to leave his hutt when ordered; unanimously found guilty of the Charges exhibited against him and sentenced to be discharged the service."

## Timothy Bigelow to Nancy Bigelow

Camp Great Valley Jany: 25th 1778

Dear Nancy

I received your obliging favor of the 15 of Decemr. I am sorry for Andrew's Misfortune, I could willingly lick the rogue that should serve my honest Veteran in such a manner—I am exceeding glad you learn Rufus to read, I think it would not be amiss for you to hear Andrew read too, especially when there is no School.

Your letter is very well wrote & better spelt than letter [*sic*] are in general, but I take notice there is two words not spelt proper viz. the word scaring, you should have left out the e final of the word scare, for in most verbs, when they become participles, or when the ing is added, the final e is left out, as in making, taking &. c. the next is School werein you omitted the h, I should have thought it had been a mistake had not you spelt it twice in the same way.

I shall now take notice of your french which your wrote as follows
je lisez Francois chaque oppertunité
you should have wrote
je lisle francois a chaque occasion—
you misused the person of the verb <u>lire</u>, if you look into the conjugation in your Grammer you will find that it is <u>je lis</u>, and <u>vous lesez</u>. Oppertunité is a french word but if you look in the Dictionary you will there find it marked as word out of use, on the whole I think you made out exceeding well I am glad to know that you read french every oppertunity, Miss no oppertunity in writing to me, I hope in your next to see more than one line of french. The receipt of your letters will always give me please pleasure

Give my love to Timmy Andrew Rufus & Lucy tell Timmy he must write me every oppertunity he has

I hope he has received his bl[ue] coat I sent him some time since. I ha[ve] no news to write nothing extraordinary has happened here since my last

From my dear child your affectionate Father
Timo: Bigelow

P.S. Give my compliments to Mr Baldwin an tell him I have received his letter have not time now to write but will send him an answer to his question the first oppertunity

Miss Nancy Bigelow

Addressed: Miss Nancy Bigelow
Worcester N. England

Source: Timothy Bigelow Papers, American Antiquarian Society.

## John Fitzgerald to Hammond Beaumont

Sir                                                          Head Quarters 26th. Jany. 1778.

I have received your Favor of yesterday and was a little surprised at your meeting any Detention on the Way—The circumstances have been represented to His Excellency Genl. Washington, and it is found that the whole have been grounded upon a misrepresentation of Facts—as soon as the Letters which will be carried by Lieut. Patterson, are delivered to Lieut. Colo. Smith, you and the other Gentlemen will be set at Liberty to pursue to business on which you came out.
                            I have the honor to Be &c &c.
                                    John Fitzgerald
To Dr. Beaumont

Source: Copy, Henry Laurens Papers, Roll 11, South Carolina Historical Society.
Fitzgerald was an Aid-de-Camp to Washington. Hammond Beaumont had been surgeon of the British 26th Regiment of Foot since March 1761. General William Howe, by agreement with Washington, had sent a number of wagons from Philadelphia in January, with clothing for Hessian and British prisoners in American hands. There were problems with the authorities in Lancaster and the envoys were detained for a time.

## A Lieutenant Colonel

THOUGHTS on the present state of the ARMY ;
addressed to the MILITARY.
Quod verum aique desens, curo et rogo et omnis in hoc sum.

BESIDES the love of our native country, which ought to actuate every honest man, ambition and glory are the secondary principles that encourage us to endure every hardship necessarily attending the profession of a soldier, and to sacrifice even life for the attainment of those desirable ends. Doubtless the service of our country, considered abstractly and independent of subsequent contingencies, is a *most honourable service*; and with regret it may be remembered that at the beginning of this war, our army consisted of men of property and popular influence, who entered into it from the most laudable and disinterested motives, who sacrificed every private view to the public good.—But tempora mutantur—we see men without education, without experience and without influence, advanced to the most important offices; looking upon the army as a resort for pensioners and placemen, whose regard for the prosperity of our cause is in exact proportion, and runs parallel with their *rank* and *pay*.

The very nature of this contest deprecates such depravity of soul, and with justice it may be said, while we are Forced to make use of such engines,—Flectere fi nequeo superos, *Acheronta* movebo.

Let us first take a view of the *military* line, and we shall find that some officers are in the field promoting the good of their country, and suffering every fatigue and danger, others are in *safe quarters*, dancing attendance on their respective legislatures for promotions, in which they seldom fail of success. Every country village, in the vicinity of the camp, you will find crowded with pot valiant heroes and fire side soldiers ; yet of so little importance are they to every thing but the *funds*, that the service flourishes best without them.

These are some, among a number of other causes of the dissatisfaction that prevails in the *military* line, among such I mean as do their duty like men, and never turn their backs upon the enemy.

We now see boys, of yesterday's growth, raised to the command of veterans, who have distinguished themselves in war before these striplings were born : And what is the efficient cause ?—They have friends in C—s & A—y.—These veterans have nothing to recommend them but the *stale, ineffectual* plea of their own *personal* merit, evidenced by their long and faithful services.

Every officer in the army ought to be considered as a man of *sense* and *courage*: Actual service is the only test to prove this hypothesis ; and by that alone are we to determine of his merit. It is a touchstone that will make useful discriminations, by separating the *fool* and the *coward*, from the man of *sense* and the *soldier* ; and until such an alternative is proved, every officer has an indubitable right to rise according to his seniority.

Discipline is the life of an army, and until subordination is fully established, the former will never take place. Ignorance of military affairs, and a clownish diffidence of their own importance, are some of the causes of this defection. The primary cause may be traced to that *stupid* contempt, with which our inferior officers are treated by many of their haughty superiors: Such improper conduct will ever discourage the efforts of a young soldier, and damp the genius of every man of spirit.—And where does this *pitiful* despotism takes its rise ? In *Ignorance* and *vanity*—they are void of politeness, and (unused to command) they are foppishly vain of their power. I have seen a subaltern arrested, struck, and charged with *stealing* and *pillaging* fruit from an orchard; I have known him tried and acquitted with honor: Yet such was the greatness of this non-entity in letters! this demi god of power! that it was mutiny, if not treason, to ask reparation. This, I aver, is a tyranny, that so far from existing in the British, is not tolerated in the armies of the most despotic princes on earth. I have read an anecdote that happened at the surrender of Fort St. David, in the East Indies, to the French in 1758.—A subaltern being charged by Monsieur Lally, conscious of his error, made full reparation in the face of his army. To a conduct the antipodes of this, we may palliate, that the goddess of politeness, (if there be such a deity in ancient mythology) has never shed upon us the light of her reconciled countenance, but has suffered us, like the Goths and Vandals of old, to work out our own salvation in boorish darkness ; holding all refinements to be inconsistent with the principles of primitive freedom.

 Let me now make some observations on the Staff of the army, which our rulers have thought expedient to divide and subdivide into so many departments; of the utility of which, I refer the curious to an inspection of the Pay-Master General's accounts.

 In mechanics, simplicity and efficacy are certain and concomitant Redundancy ought to be ever avoided: Too great a combination of powers impedes the motion, and eventually destroys the use of the machine or structure. The same rule applies to military, as well as civil government; by multiplying such offices, the business of the army is much perplexed, greatly retarded, and sometime totally neglected. For, like true statesmen, none of these officers will deign to discharge the duty of their respective appointments, till it passes thro' an infinite series and concatenation of clerks, assistants, subs and deputies, and finally arrives at the *grand* fountain head; where, like a Nabob in his durbar, he vouchsafes to settle an account with as much pomposity, as a capitulation or a definitive treaty of peace ceding and guaranteing to a poor countryman the just equivalent only of his merchandise, taken for the use of the army.

The Quarter-Master General's department includes the Commissaries General of ordinance [sic] and hides; the Clothier, Forage, and Waggon-Masters General, with all their deputies and assistants; subtract these *latter*, and the business of the *former* is a vox et praeteria nihil, a mere pensioned sine-cure, a nullity and an incumbrance on the public. To increase the chagrin and lessen the importance of the military, (for as we are under a Commonwealth, the levelling principle should extend even to the army, where nothing can be done without proper subordination) every one of these staff gentlemen have a military title either *given* or *assumed*; and so great is their contempt for the army, and of so little importance are commissions, that few will except of *any* rank under that of a Field Officer. Not a fellow will shoe a horse or skin a beef, unless you flatter him with a *Captaincy* at least; and *he* who retails whisky, and chops up provisions for the soldiers, must be dubb'd a *Colonel*. These are mortifying considerations to an officer who commands a regiments [sic] or a company, to be rank'd and parallel'd with those greasy moneymaking fellows. Take a view of our bitter enemies, the British army, and contrast their military police with our own ; we all accede to this maxim, fas est et ab hoste doceri. Every staff office in *that* service is generally filled by officers holding military command ; there is no rank whatever affixed to those several posts independant of the military line, and consequently they cannot pretend to take precedency by virtue of such staff appointments, only as their battalion commissions specify.

Adjutants General, Aids de Camp, and Majors of Brigade, may be properly called *military staff*, because their duty is such; and should be officers taken out of the military line, who notwithstanding, ought to hold no new rank, having nothing to do but deliver and execute the orders of others, there is not the least necessity for such indulgence.

Rank implies pre-heminence, [sic] and commissions specify command: Therefore, when neither is the case, in consequence of such appointments, rank and titles are abstract ideas. Nevertheless we find in our army a number of unexperienced boys delegated to those important duties, taking rank accordingly, and rising in battalion equally with those in the regular line. Officers of sound judgment and great experience, are the only men proper to fill those active departments—the most fatal errors prove the truth of this observation.

The *civil staff* includes all the rest, and are never invested with rank only under the circumstances aforesaid. The Quarter Master General, in his line of duty, is so connected with the army, that none but a military man can discharge that trust with propriety, and therefore in most armies we find it occupied by some experienced Field Officer.

The Commissaries General of Provisions and Musters, not being fighting men, are entitled to military rank. [*sic*] The Clothier, Forage and Waggon Masters General, being appendages of the Quarter Master General, are involved and necessarily lost therein, and having no command only over their clerks, waggoners and horses, it would be absurd to dub them with rank.

Suppose, in case of capture (which seldom happens) a *Colonel* or *Brigade Major* of waggons is taken, would either be included in a cartel with the *Commander* of a British regiment or *Major* of battalion? Certainly not.

Therefore it is not only my wish, but that of many officers in the army, to see those degeneracies done away. If then our Governors would be less generous in lavishing honours so indiscriminately on such, as by their situation, are neither intitled or necessitated to receive them—the service would be more respectable, the army better officered, and the troops more effective. Commissions not being so cheap, would be of importance;—and the grand business of the whole would go on with facility.

By what has been said, I do not mean to censure any *Gentleman* now serving in those several stations, but would wish, by attempting to remove so *ridiculous* a precedent, to make us more respectable not only among ourselves, but with the enemy and all other nations. These few remarks are humbly submitted to the Gentlemen of the army, by

A LIEUTENANT COLONEL.

Source: *Continental Journal and Weekly Advertiser*, (Boston), January 29, 1778.
The modern reader wonders who the officer was, and what his future was with the army. Some of his complaints were exaggerated such as a farrier requiring the rank of Captain to shoe a horse, but other officers complained about rank being given to those in non-combat positions. And by 1778, the *rage militaire* had long since passed.

**Elias Boudinot**

VISITS THE CONTINENTAL PRISONERS IN NEW
YORK TO EXAMINE INTO THEIR GRIEVANCES.

 In the spring of 1777 General Washington wrote me a letter requesting me to accept of a Commission as Commissary General of Prisoners in the Army of America—I waited on him and politely declined the task urging the wants of the Prisoners & having nothing to supply them—He very kindly objected to the conduct of Gentlemen of the Country refusing to join him in his Arduous struggle,—That he had nothing in View but the Salvation of his Country, but it was impossible for him to accomplish it alone, That if Men of Character & Influence would not come forward & join him in his Exertions all would be lost—Affected by this address, and supposing that I could be of some service to the Prisoners, and at the same time have an Eye on the Military Power & prevent its Incroachment, on the Civil Authority, I consented to accept the Commission on the Generals assurance that I would be supplied by the secret Committee of Congress with hard Money for the relief of Prisoners, and that I should only subject to his order in the Conduct of my department—

 Soon after I had entered on my department, the applications of the Prisoners were so numerous and their distress so urgent, that I exerted every nerve to obtain Supplies but invain—Excepting £600—I had rec'd from the Secret Committee in Bills of Exchange, at my first entrance into the Office—I could not by any means get a farthing more, except in Continental Money, which was of no avail in New York.—I applied to the General describing my delicate Situation and the continual application of the Officers, painting their extreme distress, and urging the assurance they had rec'd that on my appointment, I was to be furnished with adequate means for their full relief—The General appeared greatly distressed & assured me that it was out of his power to afford me any supplies—I proposed drawing Clothing from the public Stores, but to this he objected as not having any thing like a sufficient supply for the Army. He urged my considering & adopting the best means in my power to satisfy the necessities of the Prisoners, & he would confirm them—I told him I knew of no means in my Power but to take what Monies I had of my own, & to borrow from my friends in New York, to accomplish the desirable purpose—He greatly encouraged me to the attempt, promising me that if I finally met with any loss, he would divide it with me—On this I began to afford them some supplies of Provisions over and above what the Enemy afforded them, which was very small & very indifferent.

The Complaints of the very cruel treatment our Prisoners met with, in the Enemy's lines rose to such a Heighth that in the Fall of this Year, 1777, the General wrote to General Howe or Clinton respecting there complaints & proposing to send an Officer into New York to examine into the truth of them—This was agreed to, and a regular Passport returned accordingly—The General ordered me on this Service—I accordingly went over on the third of Feb 1778 in my own Sloop—supposing that my treatment would be very harsh, I prepared to meet with it in a proper manner. at Staten Island, the Commanding General, put on Board of us a Sergeant & file of Men we arrived at the wharf at New York, a little before Sun down, when I sent the Sergeant to the Commandant of the City (who was General Robertson, who I had formerly known) to inform him of my arrival & request to land. In a very short time, the Sergeant returned, with an answer that I must send to the General my rank & Business before I could be permitted to land—knowing that the General knew both, I was chagrined at this Answer, and immediately turning to the Captain of my Sloop in the presence of the Sergeant, asked him if the Wind would suit to return over the Bay, to which he answered in the affirmative—I then took out my Watch & addressing the Sergeant, told him to return to his General & inform him that I would neither send him my rank or business, as he well knew both, and that if I was not suffered to land in Ten minutes, I should return from whence I came—The Sergeant surprised at such a message to the Commanding General, ran with great haste to deliver this answer, and much sooner than I could have expected, Major Courtland returned with the Sergeant & very politely desired me to land, as he was ordered to conduct me to the Commissary of Prisoners—When I came to Mr. Commissary Lorings, he behaved very civilly, and after taking Tea with him, desired me to attend him to the General.

I found no ceremony of blinding me or any other restraint which I had expected I wore a uniform & sword by my side. The General rec'd me with great politeness and appeared as friendly & sociable as he had used to do before the War—He conversed very freely with me for near two hours, without mentioning anything relative to the manner of my conducting myself while in the Garrison—At length he informed me that lodgings were prepared for me, and the Commissary would wait upon me to them—I answered that my being in a garrisoned Town, was an entire new thing to me, and therefor if I asked anything improper, I hoped it would be imputed to my want of knowledge of military caution—That I had a Brother in Law in the City who was my agent, and therefor should be glad, if consistent with order, to lodge with him—The General, with great politeness assured me that the lodgings were prepared, yet I might go where I pleased, on Condition of my breakfasting with him in the Morning—This I promised to do, & retired—Taking it for granted that I was to be put under the expected restriction in the Morning, I waited on the General at Breakfast, he behaved as before with the greatest civility & good humor—After breakfast he asked a great many questions about the News in our lines, and conversed on common Topicks, but said nothing about my Conduct while in the City, on which I at last introduced the business on which I had eorne.—That I was a stranger to military rule—I knew that I was in a garrisoned Town, and therefor wished to know what line of Conduct it was expected that I should pursue—The General answered me that he knew we had heard strange stories within our lines of their Conduct to our Prisoners, that he rejoiced that General Washington had taken the measure of sending me in to examine for ourselves, for that he was sure that we should find them a parcel of damned lies—that he had ordered every Place I should choose to visit to be freely opened to me, and that as I was a gentleman, all that he expected was that I should behave as such, and that I might use my own pleasure & go where I pleased—I confess I was surprised at this generous conduct, and immediately replied, that I could not accept the Gentlemanly offer—That I had come on a fair and open Business That I had no secrets to communicate & would not receive any from any person whatever,—That I could not put myself so far in their power, as after my departure to render it possible for them to Charge me with improper behaviour unworthy my Character, by communicating or recieving secret intelligence to or from our Officers—That my intentions were not only to be convinced myself of the truth of the treatment the Prisoners had received, but if it had been cruel, that the General also should be convinced of the fact also, as necessary towards their relief; That therefor I should not see a Prisoner or have any communication with one but in the presence of a british Officer, who I hoped he would oblige me by appointing to attend me—The General expressed himself well pleased with the proposal, and appointed one accordingly, observing again, that he was sure I should find the reports we had heard totally false—Accordingly I went to the Provost, with the Officer, where we found near 30 Officers from Colonels downwards, in close confinement in the Gaol in New York. After some conversation with late Ethan Allen, I told him my errand, on which he was very free in his abuse of the British on account of the cruel Treatment he had rec'd during Months close confinement. We then proceeded up stairs to the Room of their Confinement. I had the Officers drawn up in a Ring, and informed them of my mission,—that I was determined to hear nothing in secret, That I therefore hoped they would each of them in their turn report to me faithfully & candidly the Treatment they severeally had recieved—that my design was to obtain them the proper redress, but if they Kept back anything from an improper fear of their keepers, they would have themselves only to blame for their want of immediate redress—That for the purpose of their deliverance the British Officer attended that the British General, should be also well informed of Facts.—On this after some little hesitation from a dread of their keeper, the Provost Martial, One of them began & informed us that they had been confined on the most frivolous pretenses, some for having been oppressors of the friends of Government,—for taking refugees' Property, while officers under command & in obedience to orders—for being out of their bounds of Parole, the week after their return—some confined in the Dungeon for a Night to wait the Censure of General to examine them, & forgot for months—for being Committee Men, &c., &c.—That they had rec'd the most cruel Treatment from the Provost Martial, being locked up in the Dungeon on the most trifling pretenses, such as asking for more water for drink on a hot day than usual—for sitting up a little longer in the Evening than orders allowed—for writing a letter to the General making their Complaints of ill usage & throwing out of the Windows.—That some of them were kept 10, 12 & 14 weeks in the Dungeon on these trifling Pretenses — a Captain Vandyke had been confined 18 months for being concerned in setting fire to the City When, on my calling for the Provost Books, it appeared that he had been made Prisoner, & closely confined, in the Provost 4 days before the fire happened—A Major Paine had been confined 11 months for killing a Capt. Campbell in the Engagement when he was taken Prisoner, when, on Examination it appeared that the Captain had been killed in another part of the Action—The charge was that Major Paine when taken had no Commission tho' acknowledged by us as a Major—Capt.———was confined for breaking a soldiers thigh with the but of his Gun after he was shot down, when the British Surgeon on examination acknowledged that the thigh was broken by a Ball, &c., &c., &c. Most of the cases examined into turned out wholly false or too trifling to be regarded—It also appeared by the Declaration of some of the Gent' that their water would be sometimes, as the Caprice of the Provost Martial led him, brought up to them in the Tubs they used in their Rooms, & when the weather was so hot that they must drink or perish—On hearing a number of these instances of Cruelty—I asked who was the Author of them, they answered the provost keeper—I desired the Officer to call him up that we might have him face to face—He accordingly came in, and on being informed of what had passed, he was asked if the Complaints were true. He, with great Insolence answered, that every word was true—on which the British Officer, abusing him very much, asked him how he dared to treat Gent' in that cruel Manner, he, insolently putting his hands to his side swore that he was as absolute there as Gen'l Howe was at the head of his Army—I observed to the Officer that now there could be no dispute about Facts as the fellow had acknowledged every word to be true—I stated all the facts in substance & waited again on Gen'l Robertson, who hoped I was quite satisfied of the falsity of the reports I had heard—I then stated to him the facts, and assured him that they turned out worse than any thing we had heard. On his hesitating as to the truth of this assertion, I observed to him the propriety of having an Officer with me, to whom I now appealed for the truth of the facts. He being present confirmed them,—on which the Gen'l expressed great disatisfaction, & promised that the Author of them should be punished. I insisted that the Officers should be discharged from his Power on Parole on long Island as other Officers were—To this after recieving from me a copy of the facts I had taken down, he assented and all were discharged except Seven, who were detained some time before I could obtain their reliese—I forgot to mention that one Officer, Lieut———was taken Prisoner and brought in with a wound thro' his leg. He was sent to the Provost to be examined the next morning—He was put into the Dungeon & remained there 10 weeks totally forgotten by the General, and never had his wound dressed except as he washed it with a little Rum and Water, given to him by the Centinels thro' the hole out of their own rations. Cap———& a Cap Chatham were confined with them and their allowance was 4 lb hard spoiled Biscuit & 2 lb Pork per week; which they were obliged to Eat raw—while they were thus confined, for the slightest Complaints, the Provost Martial would come down and beat them unmercifully with a Rattan & Knock them down with his fist—After this I visited two Hospitals of our Sick Prisoners and the Sugar House; in the two first were 211 Prisoners & in the last about 190—They acknowledge that for about two months past they fared pretty well. being allowed 2 lb of good Beef and a proportion of flour or Bread per week by Mr Lewis my Agent over and above the Allowance rec' from the British which was professed to be 2/3r Allowance—but before they had suffered much from the small allowance they had rec' & that their Bread was very bad being musty biscuit, but that the British Soldiers made the same Complaint as to the bread.—From every account I recieved, I found that their treatment had been greatly changed for the better., within a few months past., except at the Provost. They all agreed that previous to the capture of Genl Burgoyne, and for some time after, Their treatment had been cruel beyond measure, That the prisoners in the French Church, amounting on an average to 3 & 400, could not all lay down at once, that from the 15th Oct. to the 1stt Jany. they never recd a single stick of wood, and that for the most part they eat their Pork Raw, when the Pews & Door & Wood on Facings failed them for fuel.

But as to my own personal knowledge, I found Genl Robertson very ready to agree to every measure for alleviating the miseries of War: and very candidly acknowledged many faults committed by the inferior Officers, and even the mistakes of the General himself, by hearkening to the representations of those around him, He showed me a letter from Genl Howe who was in Philadelphia. giving orders that we should not be at liberty to purchase Blankets within their lines,— and containing a copy of an Order, I had issued, that they should not purchase provisions within ours, by way of retaliation but he represented it as if my order was first—I stated the facts to Genl Robertson who assured me that Genl Howe had been imposed upon & requested me to state the facts by way of letter which he immediately wrote to Genl Howe. urging the propriety of reversing his orders, which afterwards he did in a very hypocritical manner as will appear hereafter.

One Day Calling on Genl Robertson he asked me if I had any objection against a free private political Conversation. I answered that I could not have any.—He asked me up into his Bed Room, and began by asking me, why so much blood was shed, among those who were once brethren, when it was apparent that no valuable end could be answered by it. Why no one had yet stepped forth to stop so unnatural a breach & prevent the cutting each other's throats—I replied, that no good reason could in my opinion be as signed—That the fault lay with them—They had invaded our Land—we had not troubled them—that all we had asked was to be heard—That this was refused and War and desolation was brought by them into our Country.

It was therefor with them to make propositions, that we might know which it was they would be at. That we were not only strangers to & ignorant in the Art of War and almost wholly unprepared for it, but were lovers of Peace & only wished to enjoy our Habitations in quietness, without quarrelling with any one.—He expressed himself very strongly agt the war, as an unnatural destruction of each other by which nothing valuable was to be obtained,—That he was authorized to assure me that if any one would step forward & heal the unhappy difference, that he should be rewarded in any manner he shou'd ask, even to a Pension of Ten Thousand Pounds Sterling—I observed to him that there could be no necessity for this, that the Americans were desirous of Peace, and would eagerly seize every opportunity of embracing it, but the proposition from the nature of the thing must come from them.

He observed that Lord Howe & Genl Howe had been authorized to make peace with us on almost any Terms. I assured him that I had been conversant with the proceedings of Congress & the knowledge of Genl Washington and I did not believe that any such thing was known. After a little reflection, he insisted that the fact was so, and that Lord Howe had actually written an account of it to Genl Washington before his landing, while off the Hook at Sea.—On my repeating my disbelief of it, he told me that this was one of the evils of the present dispute.—That a parcel of Demagogues had professed themselves of the Govt and kept the people in entire Ignorance of the true principles of the differences between us, That he was sure if the people of America were left to themselves, They had too much good sense to continue the Breach, after such offers of Peace on our own Terms—at last starting as from a reverie, he said we must know it, as he had seen lord Howe's letter in our News Papers, I asked him if he did not know that Lord Howe's Authority went no farther than merely to grant Pardons, &c. He seemed confused and said that any Agreement he made would be ratified by the Parliament of Great Brittain—I then reminded him that the war had been brought on by the British Ministry having refused to suffer Parliament only to hear us, that being the sum of our last Petition and whether (as he had said, he knew many very sensible and Worthy men in America) he thought those sensible men would ever submit to make a Treaty with any British Commissioners (and thereby loose the Friendship of France), and Trust to a British Ministry (whose treatment had hitherto been so unworthy Men of Probity or Political understanding) to have ratified by Parliament. He now seemed a little chagrined, and said with some seeming petulance, that he did not know what the American Gentn. had done with their Oaths of Allegiance—Indeed Sir, I know not how you have got over, your Oath of Allegiance for I know you have taken one. I answered that it had been matter of some difficulty to me till I was legally discharged by an Act of the British Parliament. He said he had never heard of any such Act. I told him (much in the language he had used in the beginning to me) that I had long known the misfortune of the British Officers. That they were kept hoodwinked and in total ignorance of the Causes and Reasons of the War in which they were engaged—That they were obliged to obey & fight in every cause whether right or wrong.—That I supposed that this Act was kept from getting to their knowledge, but I knew the fact, and had seen it in St Jame's Chronicle published by Authority. He assured me that it must be a congressional false hood and that no such Act, had ever been passed. I then asked him if he was acquainted with the British Constitution—He answered in the affirmative. I asked him what he thought of Allegiance & Protection. He said they always went together, and that without Protection no Allegiance was due. I replied Have you never seen Sir, an act of Parliament putting all the Colonies (friends & foes) out of the King's protection—The Old Gentn. seemed alarmed at his Confession, and with warmth said.—A damned act.—a damned Act—I told the Ministry so at the time—They were distracted.— A damned Act—let us go down Stairs—and our Conversation Ended—

Source: Elias Boudinot, *Journal of Historical Recollections of American Events During the Revolutionary War*, (Philadelphia: Frederick Bourquin, 1894), 9-23.

## Jonathan Todd, Jr., Receipt for Pay

Received of Henry Daggett Qr Mast'r to Colo Swifts Regt One Months Extraordinary pay as allowed by Congress and all other Wages due to me for service in the above sd. Regt. since the first day of Jany. 1778 'till discharged, also all Money due for Rations in the Year 1777—

      Jonth. Todd jur.

Source: General Collection Manuscript Miscellany, Group 1518, Item F-1, Henry Daggett Papers, Beinecke Library, Yale University.
Daggett was Quartermaster of the Seventh Connecticut Regiment. Todd, Surgeon's Mate of the Seventh Connecticut Regiment, left camp on furlough of February 4, and resigned March 28, 1778.

## George Weedon to Richard Henry Lee

           Valley Forge, Feb. 1st., 1778.
—Nothing extraordinary between the two armies since my last, except a *coup de main* attempted by two hundred British Light horse on your relation Capt. Harry Lee. That little Hero is quartered about 6 miles below this Post; the Enemy formed a scheme of taking him by surprise, on the 20th Jan'y at night set out upon this Expedition, by a circuitous route of 20 miles eluded the vigilance of his Videttes, and arrived at his Quarters just at day light. By his activity he first secured the doors, which they made many fruitless attempts to force; he then mustered up his garrison which he found to consist of a corporal and 4 men, Mayor [*sic*] Jamieson, who happened there by chance, his Lieut., Lindsay, and himself, amounting to eight in the whole, and by his judiciously posting his men, tho' he had not a sufficient number to man each window, he obliged them disgracefully to retire after an action of near half an hour. Lieut. Lindsay rec'd a slight wounded in his hand, four or five of his men who were out of the house got taken; five of the Enemy were killed, and several others are licking their sores. When they found forcing the doors was rather hazardous, their next attempt was to take off his horses that were in a stable some small distance from the House, which were enfiladed by the end windows, to which he immediately drew his troops. Here he found it necessary to perform a manoeuvre, and cheering up his men, called out aloud, "Fire away my dear Fellows, here comes our Infantry, we will have them all by G—." This produced

a precipitate scamper, he sallied, mustered his troops together, which were stationed in different parts of the neighbourhood for the conveniency of Forage, and pursued, but to no purpose. This is allowed to be as brave a thing as has happened this war, and is confessed by all a piece of distinguished merit. Indeed his hidden impulses for military achievements are daily transpiring.

Source:   Excerpt of a Letter, "Selections and Excerpts from the Lee Papers," *The Southern Literary Messenger*,(December 1858), 453-454.
Weedon was a Brigadier General from Virginia. Lee was a member of the Continental Congress and a signer of the Declaration of Independence.

### Ephraim Blaine to Alexander Blaine

Sir                                                                            Camp $3^{rd}$. Feb$^y$. 1778
Please pay M$^r$ William Brown or his Order Five Hundred Dollars which charge to Acc$^t$. of Sir—
                        Your Hbl Serv$^t$
                        Eph Blaine
M$^r$. Alex$^r$ Blaine    Carlisle

Source: Peter Force Collection, Ephraim Blaine Papers, Mss. 13,778, Series 8D, Roll 1, Frame 232, Library of Congress.
Blaine was Deputy Commissary General of Purchases, his brother Alexander purchased for the army.

### The Marquis de Lafayette to Henry Laurens

Dear Sir                                         the [ ]th a five in the morning
I am not yet out of camp tho' I did not loos a minute, but the roads and My business detained me longer than I thought—however I'l push very quick and you wil hear very soon from me—the bearers of these letters are two gentlemen while the first is I believe intended by his excellency to be an ingeneer, the second wants too some employement—they were, say they, Strongly recommanded to me by one who was taken—if you see only one of those officers it will be a merit that the first schall be reccommanded by his excellency himself—There will be an also officer Jehue already emploied in our army to whom il beg you to say that I have mentionned hime for going in the northern army—I can not be so hot for Men unknown to

me, but as french men I'l recommand allwais them and make the best wishes for theyr succes —I am glad they could know that I have mentionned them—don't forget if you please the [litle] Martiniena who brought letters for me.

You have seen Mr de fleury—I fancy <u>entre vous</u> that he [ perllion which could hurt the commander in chiefs nights

I have showed to Colonel Fleury the first lines of my letter, in order to let him know my giving willingly the reccomendation he asks for You—you know that gentleman's merit and that duplessis and himself were made lieutenant colonels as reward of fine actions.

With the most tenderest affection and highest reward I am
    dear Sir Your most obedient servant

Addressed: To the honorable the president of Congress at York Town
Docketed: Recd. 6th Feby 1778 by Colo. Fleury

Source: Henry Laurens Papers, Roll 14, South Carolina Historical Society.
Lafayette was leaving Valley Forge for Albany, New York, where he was to command a force to invade Canada. When he got to Albany he discovered everything in disarray and returned to Valley Forge.

## James Rix to Miriam Rix

Dear Wife:                      Camp Valley Forge, Feb. 5, 1778.

With pleasure I embrace this opportunity of writing to let you know that I am in extraordinary good health at present and have been so for two months past, thank Good for it. I hope you are well but I have not heard from you since I saw Dudley Dustin at Stillwater, tho I have sent to you several times. I have a great mind to come home, but the time I was promised a furlough, orders came the day before not to give any more until further orders, and being disapointed of our money by the paymaster's fault and the expence of so long a journey, I will content myself to stay till spring. By what is learned and by every thing we see, the wars will not be continued very much longer here in America at present. I am badly out of clothes, but we hear there is cloth coming into camp, tho I am better off than the greater part of the men of our state. I have sent here an Indian Broach to each of my sons and a ribbon to my eldest daughter Anna. I have nothing else to send but my love and that I have for all.

I remain your loving husband
James Rix.
Directed to Miriam Rix, In Haverhill, West Parish, With care deliver.

Source: Guy S. Rix, *History and Genealogy of the Rix Family of America Containing Biographical Sketches and Genealogies of Both Males and Females* (New York: The Grafton Press, 1906), 18.
Rix was a Sergeant in the Ninth Massachusetts Regiment.

## William Russell, Discharge for William Wroe

William Wroe a Continantal Soldier in the fifth Virginia Ridgment having Serv'd as a Good and faithfull Soldier two years and is hereby discharged from Service, given under my hand this
    William Russell Colo.
    Commdr. Genl. Mulinburg Brigd.

A Return of Clothing that I have Drawn during my service for two years
1 Coat, 1 waistcoat, 1 pr. Cloth Breeches, 1 Hatt
2 pr. Stockings, 2 pr. Shoes, 1 Hunting Shirt 1 pr. Overalls, 3 Shirts
Sworn before me 6 Feby 1778,      William Wroe
    W. Russell Colo. Commdt. of
    Genl. Muhlenberg's Brigade

Source: Record Group 15, M 804, Pension Application S39918, National Archives.

## Johann de Kalb to Henry Laurens

Sir                        at Camp 7th. February 1778
    By the return of Marquis de la Fayette and the orders I am to receive from the Commander in Chief in consequence of a Resolve of Congress to Serve in the Northern department I prepare to set out in a Few days as soon at chevr. Dubuysson will be back from York and Lancaster where he repairs this morning to get several Necessarys for this my change.
    May I recommend to your Excellency and to the consideration of Congress said chevr. Dubuysson my Aid de Camp for the Commission of Lieutenant Colonel as was promised me by a Resolve

of Congress October 4th. 1777. The only objection made at that time for granting him the same was that his promotion to that rank would create uneasiness and discontent among the aids of other Major Generals, there having been no precedent of the like, without some extraordinary occasion. This rule being broke for the Aids de Camp of the Marquis and of General Conway I hope the same Favour will be granted to one of mine, who has the same right, being an Officer of ten years in the French Service beside the promise of the above mentioned Resolve. Though I think it will be but doing him justice I shall consider it as a new Favour conferred upon myself and an increase of obligations towards you. I have the honour to be with the greatest respect
    Your Excellency's Most obedient and most
      humble Servant
      Baron de Kalb

Source: Henry Laurens Papers, Roll 9, South Carolina Historical Society.
Le Chevalier Charles-Francois Du Buysson des Hays was promoted to Lt. Colonel on February 11, 1778. He served until the Battle of Camden in which the Baron was killed and he was wounded.

## An Officer to His Friend

We therefore presume that the public will be glad to see the following Letter from an officer of no small importance in Gen. Washington's army. We can assure our readers that it is a *genuine* Letter, the original of which is in the possession of gentleman in this city, of strict veracity and honour, and who has been formerly well acquainted both with the writer and the person to whom the Letter is addressed.

*Dear Sir,*         *Lancaster*, *7th Feb.* 1778.
  The length of time which has elapsed since I have wrote you, and being indebted to you for the favour of two letters while I was in Morristown last summer, makes me almost ashamed to put pen to paper to you now—but I rely on your friendship to excuse an omission which, I assure you, did not proceed, by any means, from disrespect or ingratitude—let this, I pray, apologize for the neglect, and believe me at the same time, that among the number of your friends, there is not one that holds you in higher respect than I do. I have also to beg your pardon for not returning your —— —— but

really I was so bare of —— after my return from —— that I found myself under an absolute necessity to trespass on your goodness by keeping them, till I could have an opportunity of replacing them with others, not imagining at that time that any thing would have happened to cut off our intercourse—I thought to have mentioned this matter to you when I was on my march with the army to Chester county, but I was so circumstanced that I could not spare time to spend one hour with my friend, and the fatal consequences that attended us afterwards in our encounter with the British troops, has rendered it impossible for me to see you since.

I came to this place about ten days ago from our camp at the Valley, in a poor state of health, owing, I suppose, to the wretched situation we are in for want of some necessaries of life, such as clothes, salt, vegetables, &c. &c. of fresh meats we have as yet plenty—but there is no variety in our food—and as for any of the comforts of life, that is intirely out of the question with us—we have no liquors of any sort except now and then a little whisky, the very smell of which is enough to knock a man down. I have not drank a glass for two months past, till I came here, so that may easily judge what hardships I must have experienced in the field at this inclement season. Yet my dear friend, my sufferings, or those of other officers, are very trifling to what the common men undergo—what they must feel is not to be described, let it be sufficient to say, that the different scenes of distress that daily present themselves to my view, is shocking to humanity—and the country round about with hospitals full of those miserable creatures, and by what I can learn they have neither medicines nor blankets to cover them, at least, one of the young doctors here says so. What the consequences of the next campaign will be, God only knows—much will depend upon circumstances—at present things bear a very gloomy aspect on this side, but we are extremely industrious in devising methods to keep up our drooping spirits.—Our men in power tell us that we shall have a larger army than ever in the field next spring—where it is to come from, am sure I don't know, unless the New-England folks, elated with their success against Burgoyne, may once more *feel bold*,—but as to the southern states, for my own part, judging from what some of their first officers tell me, and what I know myself of their situation, I have little expectations from them—though the legislators in Virginia have determined to compel the people to turn out by classes—a measure which I think will rather tend to hurt the cause than otherwise; but at the best those men will be only militia, and I would not give a dollar a hundred for them, for they will not fight, nor indeed I don't know how it can be expected of them—and besides we never can keep them under any degree of subordination, for every fellow of them thinks himself on a footing with his officers, and in fact there is very little distinction can be made between the one and the other—for I believe the world never before produced such a set of shabby officers as we have among us from time to time, insomuch that I think it a curse to be obliged to mix with them;—and it's true there are some exceptions, for we have a few genteel men with us, who are very agreeable, and men of resolution—but they are few compared to the number of the others. As to this state, I don't believe it will turn out many people—and if they do turn out numerous, still what are they? a parcel of lazy fellows, that in the hour of danger cry out for their wives and children, and in the first onset run home as fast as they can.—I can say nothing of our standing army in point of it's numbers, but it did not exceed 13000 men at any time last summer:— since then our losses by deaths, sickness, and desertions have been very great, not to mention what have been killed in battle, and taken prisoner—so that you must of course think we can't muster very thick in camp, and many of them are almost useless to us.—We have some militia, which serves to hunt the people going to market, and they will always do very well for that service, when the weather is not cold nor wet,—however they are true Dutchmen, they must have their bellies full, their fling every morning, or else away they go, and that happens frequently.—In regard to the recruiting, that is at an end, for I believe that all the men that would inlist in the different states, have already inlisted long ago, besides our common men now look upon the money to be of no value, for they can get nothing for it.

    Thus, my friend, have I given you a history, instead of a letter, because I know you will be curious to know how matters are with us:—I could say more, but I can't at this time,—except only that I most sincerely wish I had never engaged in the damned dispute, according to what you so strenuously recommended to me;—but I may thank my friends at ———— for it; they persuaded me into the matter,—and then I thought they would themselves engage in it also;—but instead of that, they staid at home by the fire-side, influencing every one they could to turn out,—and if they took any part, it was by getting into some office, from which they derived an advantage, and some have made great fortunes in that way, while we, poor devils, are suffering every species of hardship and danger; and yet how to get myself clear I know not, for I have some friends in camp, who will not hear of my resignation: My friend —— has resigned, as well as some others;—they gave some reasons, which proved sufficient,—but the true reasons were, they got tired of it:— Our great Conway talked of leaving us;—he did not like a great many of the officers being neither gentlemen nor soldiers; however he has got a place of greater profit, if he can but convert his paper into a more solid stuff.

My best respects wait on Mrs. ——, and be assured I am, with unalterable esteem and regard, my dear Sir, Your affectionate friend, &c.

Source: *The Pennsylvania Ledger; or the Philadelphia Market-Day Advertiser*, February 28, 1778.
This was published in British-held Philadelphia. It could have been a piece of British propaganda, but the information within sounds accurate. The places with missing words are that way in in the published version.

## Thomas Jones to Unidentified

Sir,                        Camp, near Valey Forge, Feby 8th, 1778.

Underneath you have an acct of what constitutes a Ration, as agreed on by a Board of General officers, on 28th December last, to be delivered out to the Troops, viz:

1 ¼ lb Beef, 1 lb Pork, or 1 ¼ lb Salt Fish pr Man a Day; 1 ¼ lb Soft Bread, of Flower, 1 lb Hard Bread, ½ Gill Wisky, or Rum, pr Man pr Day, in Lieu of Beer; 3 lb Candles pr 100 Men pr Week for Guards, 24 lb Soft Soap, or 8 lb of hard Soap, pr 100 Men pr Week.

N. B. The Liquer to be Issued only on General or Special orders.

Your are therefore Requested, on any account whatsoever, not to Deliver any more but agreeable to the above orders, untill further Direction from me.

I am sir, your humble serv't

Source: Samuel Hazard, ed. *Pennsylvania Archives*, 1st series (Philadelphia: Joseph Severns, 1853), 6:247.
At this time of the Encampment, the troops would have been very happy to get the above listed daily rations.

## Ephraim Blaine to John Lacey Jr.

Dear General          Camp Valley Forge Febry 10th 1778
     The army is like to suffer for want of Provisions and without a speedy supply it cannot be avoided The nearest Magazine is at Coryells ferry Where there is a quantity of Salt Provisions but cannot be brot forward for want of teams The necessity is so great That His Excellency has desired me to apply to you for parties to impress teams in the Neighbourhood of Buck sufficient to bring forward all the Stores at Coryells Your Compliance will particularly oblige
          Your most Obdt Servt
          Eph:Blaine D.C.G.

Addressed Genl. Lacey
     Brigadier General Lacey near Cross Roads
Docket: Letter from Eph Blaine D.C.G. Feby 10 1778

Source: Frederick M. Dearborn Collection, MS AM 1649.6 (18), Houghton Library, Harvard University.
Lacey was a General in the Pennsylvania Militia.


## George Weedon, Discharge for James Hungerford

This may certify that James Hungerfoot Soldier in the sixth Virginia Regiment has faithfully served his time of Enlistment and is hereby discharged. Given under my hand at Valley Forge this 11th day of February 1778          Weedon B. Genl

Source: Record Group 15, M 804, Pension Application S38856, National Archives.
Hungerford is the way the name is spelled in the pension application.


## Charles Scott, Discharge for David Grate/Great

David Grate A Soldier of the 8th Virginia Regiment, having served his time for which he enlisted, is hereby discharg'd
Given udner my hand at the Valley Forge 12th Febru'y 1778
     Chs. Scott B. G.

Source: Record Group 15, M 804, Pension Application S38747, National Archives. Scott was a Brigadier General from Virginia.

## Thomas Jones, Return of Food Delivered at the Bakehouse

Return of Bread, Flour & Pork delivered at the Bakehouse

| Date 1778 Feby. | For what Division Brigade & ca. | Barrels Flour. | Wt. by Estimate | Barrels of Bread | lbs. Ditto | Barrels Pork | lbs. Do: | Amount of Bread & Flour in pounds |
|---|---|---|---|---|---|---|---|---|
| 12 | Gen. Weedons B | 20 | 4.400 | | | | | |
| 13 | Ditto | | | 10 | 1.000 | | | 5.400 |
| 9 | Muhlenbergs | | | | 2.800 | | | |
| 12 | Ditto | | | 5 | .600 | 3 | | |
| 13 | Ditto | 16 | 3.500 | | | | 630 | 6.900 |
| 9 | Maxwells | | | | 2.400 | | | |
| 12 | Ditto | 12 | 2.640 | | | | | |
| 13 | Ditto | | | 12 | 1.200 | 3 | 630 | 6.240 |
| 12 | Conway's | | | | 3.500 | | | |
| 13 | Ditto | 20 | 4.400 | | | | | 7.900 |
| " | Brodheads | 30 | 6.600 | | | | | 6.600 |
| " | Chambers's | 11 | 2.420 | | | | | 2.420 |
| " | Varnums | 16 | 3.500 | | 1.600 | | | 5.100 |
| " | Huntingtons | 6 | 1.320 | | | 3 | 630 | 1.320 |
| 9 | Pattersons | 20 | 4.400 | | | | | |
| 13 | Do | | | 16 | 1.600 | | | 6.000 |
| 9 | Learneds | 8 | 1.760 | | 2.000 | | | |
| 13 | Do | | | | 2.600 | | | 6.360 |
| 13 | Poors | 12 | 2.640 | | 2.600 | | | |
| 9 | Do | 15 | 3.300 | | | | | 8.540 |
| 11 | Glovers | | 2.640 | | | | | |
| 13 | Do | | | | 1.500 | | | 4.140 |
| 9 | Knoxes Arty | 10 | 2.200 | | 2.000 | | | |
| 11 | Do | | | | 2.000 | | | |
| 12 | D | | | 10 | 1.000 | 2 | 420 | |
| 13 | Do | 26 | 5720 | | | | | 12.920 |
| 9 | Mc.Intoshes | | | | 3.300 | | | |
| 12&13 | Do | 40 | 8.800 | 7 | 700 | | | 12.800 |
| | Staff Dept. | | | 2.070 | | | | 2.070 |
| | Capt Lees Troops | 3 | 660 | | | | | 660 |
| | Detachments | | | | 11.770 | | 210 | 11.770 |
| | | | 60.900 | | 46.240 60.900 | | | 107.140 |
| | | | | | 107.140 | | | |

Errors Excepted Camp near Valley Forge  Februy. 13th. 1778
Thomas Jones D.C.G of Issues

Source: Papers of the Continental Congress, RG 360, M 247, Roll 199, p405, National Archives.
The traditional Bakehouse at Valley Forge is close to Washington's Headquarters.

### Joseph Vose and William Shepard to George Washington

May it please your Excellency—  Valley Forge 13$^{th}$ Feb$^y$. 1778
 Upon the Application of Ensign Hill of my Reg$^t$. for a discharge from the Service he having settled off all his Accounts with the Army, I would thereby Recommend him to your Excellency for the Same—
 Joseph Vose Colo
 W. Shepard Col. Commdr.

Source: Record Group 93, M 859, Roll 8, Document 2347, National Archives.
Vose was Colonel of the First Massachusetts Regiment, Shepard was Colonel of the Fourth Massachusetts. Ensign Daniel Hill of the First Massachusetts was allowed to resign on February 14, 1778.

### George Weedon, Discharge for John Turnley

I do hereby certify that John Turnley, a soldier in the sixth Virginia regiment has faithfully served his time of inlistment and is hereby discharg'd, given under my hand at Valley Forge camp
 Feby 13th 1778—
 Geo. Weedon Bridgr General
John Turnley Pension Application, W6327.
Source: Record Group 15, M 804, Pension Application W6327, National Archives.

### Hugh Maxwell to Bethiah Maxwell

My Dear  February 14th, 1778
 the day before yesterday I have the good Fortune to Receive a letter from you Dated the 11th of January which gave me the Very agreable New that you and our Dear little ones were all well—I Hope I Sincerely Join with you in Thanks—My Dear Health is a principall Blessing. But at the Same time your complaints are great and I fear have to much foundation. I am almost Discouraged. Our Foreign Enemy I am Satisfied cannot conquer the land under Heavens Smiles

I think we Have not much to fear from them but O the oppression the Extortion and Hard Heartedness to one another thro the land. you say I must come Home well I think So too. I believe I Shall at Spring I am Resolved to if I can get clear with Reputation and I am Sure you dont want to See me in Disgrace pray my Dear dont be Discouraged hope on—dont let little loses or croses trouble you. I Know you have many of them but I also hope you Have a Spirit within you that Dispises them.

I would Send Some money but I am afraid to Venture it now. I have not Drawed Seargent Howards yet nor Shal till I can have a good opportunity to Send it to him give my Service to him tell him I thank him for his care and am glad to hear he is growing better—Let him Stay with you till he is able to Join the Army again—make your Self as Easy and as comfortable as you can.

  my Love to you all and Remain yours only,
    Hugh Maxwell.

P. S. My love to Ben Thompson their wives and children and all your good Neighbors. I Have Sent you three letters lately—I want some Shirts I Should be glad you would get me Half a Dozen and 2 or 3 pair such Stockings as you made me last Sumer. if I am forced to stay I Shall want them and if I dont they will bring a good price. I am surprised that Seth Temple has not finished the barn yet tell him I think I have good Reason to be affronted with his Neglect it is what I did not Expect of him and I See no Reason why Should not pay the Damages—Likewise Josiah warfield has not used you well in not doing the same—tell him I Expect it done this Spring by all means.

To Bethiah, at Charlemont

Source: Hugh Maxwell Papers, U.S. Army Military History Institute, Carlisle, Pennsylvania.

## William Russell, Discharge for David Street

Camp Valley forge february th14 1778
  David Street a Soldier in the 5th Virginia Rigment and detached with Col. Morgan haveing served two years from the Date of his inlistment as A good & faithful Soldier is hereby Discharged from the servis with a blanket being his own property

W. Russell Colo. Comm'dt.
Gen'l Muhlenberg's Brigade

Source: Record Group 15, M 804, Pension Application W6164, National Archives.

## William Davies, Certificate for Le Roy Edwards

I do hereby certify to the Colonel Commandant of the Brigade, that Mr. Le Roy Edwards of the 5th. Virginia regiment was entitled to a First Lieutenancy in the regiment, So long since as the 21st. day of February 1777, in consequence of the promotion of Capt. Colston.
Feby 15. 1778.            William Davies Lt. Col. Comt. 5th. Vir. Regt.
                 W Russell Col. Commdt. of Genl.
                 Muhlenberg's Brigade

Russell's signature is an endorsement. On the reverse: "Certificate of a 1st Lieutenancy to Mr Le Roy Edwards 21st feby. 1777"
Source: Record Group 93, M 859, Roll 110, National Archives.
Edwards was promoted to First Lieutenant effective February 21, 1777.

## Receipts by Robert Blair and John Chaloner

Feby. 16, 1778—
Received of Mr. Alexander Steel one Hundred & forty pounds of Beef, which taken from persons Carrying it towards the Enemy.—
    & by me apply'd to the Use of Gen Greenes Detatchment at the lines.—
        received also one Hide, which I deliver'd Col Ewing—Wt. 32 lb
            Robt Blair ACI.
140 Pounds.

£0..5.. Pay the amount of the above to James Darah AC of I—
            Alexr. Steel
John Chaloner, Esqr.
    A C of Purchases.—

Source: Peter Force Collection, Ephraim Blaine Papers, Roll 77, f2217, Library of Congress.

## William Davies to William Russell

Sir  Camp Feby. 16 1778.
Lt. Thomas M'Reynolds of the 5th. regiment is desirous to resign and settle his accounts, and I find he have received lately from the State of Virginia 1 1/2 yds green broad cloth, 7 yds linen & 2 pair worsted hose, the price not known as yet. He has drawn nothing from the Continent, and thinks the money due to him for rations agreeable to his sworn account, and one month's pay left it the Paymaster's hands will be sufficient. I believe they will too, and have no objection against your recommending him to Head Quarters for leave to resign.
        I am, Sir
           Your most obedt. Servt.
             William Davies Lt. Col. Comt 5. V. Rt.
To Col. Russel Comt. of the Brig:

Source: Record Group 93, M 859, Roll 110, Document 31259, National Archives. First Lieutenant McReynolds was allowed to resign.


## George Washington to Richard Howell

Major Howell,  Head-Quarters, Valley Forge, Feby. 17, 1778.
    Please have the Moreland stable put in shape to be used as a temporary Barracks for one hundred men. You may take as many men as you need to do the work. The Quartermaster will furnish the necessary material.
           G: Washington

Source: Sol Feinstone Collection, David Library of the American Revolution. In Washington's hand. Richard Howell was Major of the Second New Jersey Regiment.


## James Chambers, Plantation for Sale

TO BE SOLD, A VALUABLE Plantation in Cumberland County, State of Pennsylvania, lying at the mouth of Green Spring, on Canadaguinet Creek, fourteen miles above Carlisle, containing about 150 acres, 63 of which is patented and excellent for bearing hemp or corn, and 50 more can be watered: There are on said place a gristmill

and sawmill, on a never failing limestone spring, about a mile and a half from the head. An indisputable title will be given. Any person inclining to purchase may know the terms by applying to Mrs. CATHARINE CHAMBERS, in Chambersburgh, or the subscriber now in Camp.
JAMES CHAMBERS, Col. 1st P. Reg.

Source: *The Pennsylvania Packet*, February 18, 1778.

## Samuel Tenny to Peter Turner

Brother Peter, Camp, Feby 18, 1778.

Let these hasty, unconnected Lines, convince you that I am still alive and not altogether unmindful of absent Friends. The latter is not so extraordinary, for so long as I breathe, my Friends will share my Affections & Thoughts: but when you are inform'd that we have been five Days without Provisions, the former will appear a little strange. I believe there are a Set of Men about the Army endeavouring to ruin it, with the D. Commy Genl. of Issues at their Head. He is detected in his Villanies; & we all hope he will suffer, with Thieves Spies, & money makers, in this World & with Hypocrites & unbelievers in the next.

It continues very sickly in our Regt. 76. in my last Return 51 of them in Col. Greene's Regt. We loose bout one per Week of late, & the Rest will never get well. They relapse, & rerelapse & relapse two or three Times more. The Officers are all well and hearty. But indeed, Sir, we are very Dull. The Clever Fellows are chiefly absent, a few however remain.

We have been pleas'd with the Notion of being sent to Rhode Island, for some Time past, of late however little has been said. I know not how it will turn. A Committee of Congress have been sometime sitting from which very great Things are expected. An Establishment & half Pay for the Officers during Life is one. I rather wish than expect it. Parturient Montes, nascetur ridiculus Mus, may be a proper Motto for their Proceedings. If it should, the Army will be ruind. Disappointment will stimulate many to resign their Commissions, who never before tho't of it, & God knows we can spare but few more except only the Slimslacks will apply; & they are commonly the last to seek a Discharge.

I ardently with to hear from you, Doctor, & be inform'd what the people at home are about: whether the Black Regiment does on, or whether there is any recruiting at all. I needn't inform you I expect the Favour of a Letter by the First Opportunity.—With my sincerest Regards to your agreable Eliza & her beloved Peter, I am, Sir
  Your Friend & Servant
   S. Tenny
Addressed: Dr. Peter Turner Rhode Island Favored by Lt. Hicks.

Source: Peter Turner Papers, Box 1, William L. Clements Library.
Tenny was the Surgeon of the Second Rhode Island. Peter Turner was Surgeon of the First Rhode Island Regiment. He appears on the muster rolls as On Command at Rhode Island from January through April 1778.
slimslack – someone who is mentally or physically disabled.
Latin phrase: Mountains will be in labour, and an ridiculous mouse will be born.

**Charles Scott to Samuel Gill et al.**

Sir,—You are to proceed to Virginia with a party of Discharged Soldiers. You will draw provisions for them at the different Stages as you may think Convenient. Attention must be paid that the Soldiers march with some Regularity, & particularly that they are prevented from straggling and Injuring the Inhabitants
  Chas. Scott, B. G.
To Lieut. Sam'l Gill, 4th Virg'a Reg't.

  Issue provisions for a party of Discharged Soldiers under the care of Lieut. Gill upon his order.
feb'r 21st, 78.   Ch's Scott, B. G.
To the Commissarys between Camp and Leesburg, Virga.

Permit Lieut. Gill to pass over all Ferries between Camp & Leesburg in Virg'a free without cost.
Feb'y 21'st.  Ch's G. Scott, B. G.
To the Keeper of all Ferries.

Source: *Virginia Military Records From The Virginia Magazine of History and Biography, the William and Mary Quarterly, and Tyler's Quarterly* (Baltimore: Genealogical Publishing Co., 1983), 681-82,

## John Wilson and Lachlan McIntosh, Certificate for Joshua Curtis

Feby 21st. 1778

I hereby certify that Ensign Curtis has acted in my Company ever since his appointment untill the first January, and that he has settled for all the public Money in his hands, and as he wishes to leave the service, I think he might be admitted to resign, without doing the servis [*sic*] much injury—

J Wilson Capt. Comt 4th. N Carolina Regt.
The Honourable Brigr. Genl. Mc.Intosh

I have no objection to Ensign Curtis's Resignation
Lachn. Mc.Intosh B.G.
On the reverse: "Resigned 21st Feb 1778"

Source: Record Group 93, M 859, Roll 45, no. 14428, National Archives.

## Jedediah Huntington to Jabez Huntington

Hon$^d$ Sir, Camp Valley Forge 22$^d$ Feb$^y$ 1778.

I wrote You Yesterday by M$^r$. Fanning—since which the Officers of Col Prentices Reg$^t$. have been with me to desire my Influence in the Appointment of a Commanding Officer—they were afraid that Colonel Prentice would make Interest to get himself appointed by the Governor & Council. I told them it was not to be supposed the Governor & Council would fill up Vacancies at the very Time when General Washington was doing the same, as it must create Confusion—besides it was in Contemplation to reduce the Number of Regiments, in which Case there might not be Occasion for any more Officers—the Officers of that Reg$^t$. understand they have not had an Allotment of Clothing in Proportion to their Numbers on account of the Surplus of Prize Clothing remaining of what they had last Year—the Officers themselves are as needy as those of any other Regiment—and it is to be wished they might receive an equal Share of the new Clothing for the Soldiers for the sake of Uniformity—it was the Generals Wish that all the Troops might be dressed alike and a snug Uniform has been recommended accordingly—Colonel Swift has a Lieut gone Home to superintend the making up his Clothing who knows what the Patterns are—the clothing left in your Store ought to be coloured some other Colour as many Inconveniences arise from our Troops being clad in the usual Habits of our Enemies—

The Comm[ee] of Congress are still on Business and when they will finish I cannot say—I am very desirous to wait the Result of their Session and to see to any new Arrangements and Appointments that may take Place in my Brigade—I have no Letter from Norwich since the 12th. of January. I remain with the warmest Affection for my Friends there—

your dutiful son

I have been expecting M[r] Ellis these some Days with my Gray Horse and a blue Waistcoat

Source: Huntington Papers, The Connecticut Historical Society.
Jabez was Jedediah's father.

**James Monroe, Pass for John Wallace, Jr.**

Lieut. Wallace of the sixth Pensyla. Regt. has Lord Stirling's permisson to be absent from the army 7 weeks

Jas. Monroe
Feby. 23.        Aid De Camp

Source: The James Monroe Museum and Memorial Library in Fredericksburg, Virginia. This is the earliest known signature of the future president.
Major Monroe was serving as an Aide-de-Camp to William Alexander. Wallace was a Second Lieutenant in the Sixth Pennsylvania Regiment,

**Rations Certifications by Jesse Baldwin, William Shute, and John Conway**

I Certify that Capn. John Conway's full Rations as a Capn. was retained in the 1st. Jersey Reg[t]. from the 30th. Day of October 1777 to the Time he joined the 4th. Reg[t]. as Major; both Days inclusive,

Jesse Baldwin Q.Mr. P. T.
Camp 28th. Feby. 1778.

I Certify that no Rations was drawn or Retained for a Major in the fourth Jersey Reg$^t$. from the 30th. Day of October to the 26$^{th}$. of Dec$^r$: both Days inclusive and that John Conway Esq$^r$: was appointed Major to said Reg$^t$. the 29$^{th}$. of October

W$^m$. Shute A. C. Issues<br>Gen$^l$ Maxwells Brigade

I Certify on Honor that I Retained my full Ration[s] and am justly intitled to pay for them from the 30th$^h$. Day of October to the 31$^{st}$. of December last, both Days inclusive, and that I am Commissioned as Major in the fourth Regt. of Jersey the 29th. of October, 1777. the Time of Major Morrel's Resignation,

John Conway, Major<br>4$^{th}$. Reg$^t$. of Jersey

Source: Record Group 93, M 859, Roll 74, Document 21865, National Archives.

## Return of the North Carolina Brigade

Monthly Return of the Troops under the more immediate Command of his Excellency George Washington, Esqr., General and Commander in chief of the armies of the independent States of America.

Camp, Valley Forge, Feb'y 29th 1778.

McIntosh's Brigade (N. C.)

**OFFICERS PRESENT-Field**
Colonels 2   Lieut. Colonels 3   Majors   2

**OFFICERS PRESENT-Commisioned**
Captains 19   Lieutenants 24   Ensigns   2

**OFFICERS PRESENT-Staff**
Chaplains 2   Adjutants 3   Pay Masters 3
Qr. Masters 3   Surgeons 1   Mate 1

**NON-COMMISSIONED**
Sergeants   115 Drums & Fifes   77

**RANK AND FILE**
Present Fit for Duty    490
Sick Present        178        Sick Absent        210
Unfit for duty for want of Clothes.    30
On Command        100
On Furlough        16
Total            1024
Dead            24
**Discharged**        3

**Joined**
Sergeants    3    D. & Fifers    4    R. & File    62

Source: *State Records of North Carolina*, 13:377.
The nine North Carolina regiments were so short of men that the entire Brigade had less less than one regiment's total of men present fit for duty. They were later consolidated into three regiments.

### Robert Hanson Harrison to Clement Biddle

Dr Sir                                          March 3, 1778
    His Excellency requests that you will transport the inclosed immediately thro the channel of the Stationary Expresses.—He would have sent it to Col. Lutterloh but apprehended he might not be acquainted with them.
        I am Dr Sir Yours Rob: H: Harrison

Source:    http://www.hcauctions.com/valley-forge-letter-by-washington-aide-de-camp=lot33816.aspx, Raynors' Historical Collectible Auctions, Lot 7, Sold for $829.50, on January 30, 2014. The enclosure is not known.
Harrison was Military Secretary to George Washington.

### Lachlan McIntosh to Robert Hanson Harrison

Sir                              Camp Valley Forge 3$^d$. March 1778.
    The bearer Lieut. James Luten, of the Second No. Carolina Regiment inclines to Resign his Commission which his Colonel (Patten) rather approves of than otherwise; & assures me he is not

Indebted either to his Company or the Regiment.—therefore I can have no objection to it—

     Lachn. M$^c$.Intosh B. G.
To Colo. Harrison

Source: Record Group 93. M 859, Roll 45, Document 14500, National Archives. James Luten's resignation was accepted March 3, 1778.

## Samuel Bartlett to George Washington, with an Endorsement by James Mellen

        Camp Valley Forge March 4 1778
To His Excelency Gen$^l$. Washington
Commander in Chief of the Army of the United
States of America

  I would beg leave to acquaint your Excelency that by reason of the Fateigues of the Past Campaign I am Reducd. to so low a State of Health that I am intirely unfit to do Duty in the Camp, and as it is very improbable that I shall recover so long as I continue in the Camp, must beg your Excelency to grant me a Discharge from the Service

  Your Excelencys Granting my Request
    will much Oblige your most Obed$^t$. Hum$^{bl}$. Ser$^{vt}$
    Sam$^l$ Bartlett Cap$^t$ in Co$^l$ Wessons Reg$^t$

This may Certify that the Above Cap$^t$. Bartlit of Col Wessons Reg$^t$ is not Indebted to the Continent for Publick moneys and likewise has settled all Accompts in said Regiment as to Debts due from him

  I would Recommend him to His Excellency for a Discharge Knowing him to be Unable to Endure the Fateague of the Camp.
    James Mellen Lt Col

Source: National Archives, Record Group 93, M859, Roll 8, Document 2390. Bartlett was a Captain in the Ninth Massachusetts Regiment His resignation was accepted on 6 March 1778. Mellen was Lieutenant Colonel of the same regiment.

## John Chaloner to Jacob Anderson

Sir        Commissaries Office March 4th, 1778

I expect eer this Col Biddle has wrote to the Forrage Mr. at Pottsgrove, to grind Forage on the Terms that Col. Blaine wrote to you about, if he still neglects or refuses to comply with them terms, must trouble you, to inform me or Col Blaine, pr first Oppy.

The purport of this is to request of you to call on <u>Mr. Mc.Caskey, Forrage Mr. at the White Horse</u> deliver the inclosd inquire how many barrels of Flour he has, and urge him to forward them to Camp as speedily as possible—Mr. Aston has been with you lately, he doubtless has set the Mills to Work and must expect of you to forward the flour as speedily as possible to Camp, where it is much wanted. Your compliance with oblige   Sir Yours &c.

      John Chaloner
To Mr. Anderson  A C of Ps

Addressed: On Publick Service
 Jacob Anderson Esqr  Commissary of Issues at Pottsgrove

Another hand wrote "dated March 4th. 1778—" and "No. 5"
Source: New Jersey State Archives, RG Dept. of Defense, Subgroup: Adjutant General's Office (Revolutionary War), Numbered Manuscripts, Roll 11, Mss. No. 4338.

## Henry Daggett, Receipt

                March 5th. 1778
Receiv'd of Captn. Watson by the hand of Sergt. Hunt one Gun, Bayonet likewise a Catuch Box unfit for use.
     Henry Daggett Qr Mr.

Source: General Collection Manuscript Miscellany, Group 1518, Item F-1, Henry Daggett Papers, Beinecke Library, Yale University.
Daggett was Quartermaster of the Seventh Connecticut Regiment. Titus Watson was a Captain in the same regiment.

## Thomas Hughes, Certificate for James Hord

March 6$^{th}$. 1778
 This may certifie that Ensign James Hord of the 7 V. R$^t$. has Settled till the last of Feb$^y$ And that I have no charge against him—

He has not Rec$^d$. the Months extra pay—Agreeable to resolve of Congress which he is Enteteled to by Certificate from the Gen$^l$ and may receive at York Town.
    Thomas Hughes, Paymaster 7$^{th}$ VA.

Source: Record Group 93, M 859, Roll 110, Document 31220, National Archives.
James Hord of the Seventh Virginia Regiment was allowed to resign on March 7, 1778.

## John Paterson and Tench Tilghman, Discharge for Joseph Morse

Dear Sir                        Head Quarters 7th March 1778
    The Case of Mr Morse is very particular and His Excellency therefore desires that you may do what you think proper in this If he leaves the Service as a private Soldier, which is a station below his merit, he will come in, in some other way
                I am Dear Sir Your obed$^t$ Serv$^t$
                Tench Tilghman.
    (on the reverse)
Joseph Morse a Soldier in Colo Marshalls Regiment being under peculiar Circumstances is by leave of his Excellency Gen$^l$ Washington discharged the Service of the United States and from doing any Duty in said Regiment has leave to pass from Camp to Boston
    Given under my hand in Camp this 7$^{th}$ Day of March 1778
                Jn$^o$ Paterson B Gen$^l$

Source: Thomas Egleston, *The Life of John Patterson, Major-General in the Revolutionary Army* (New York: G. P. Putnam's Sons, 1894), 91.
Morse was a soldier in the Tenth Massachusetts Regiment. Paterson was a Brigadier General from Massachusetts.

## George Washington to Caleb Gibbs

Caleb Gibbs Esqr.
    Capt. Comg.
Sir,                     Head Quarters Valley Forge March 9th 1778

Send Leiut. Livingston and fifty men to Norristown as an escort to Messrs. Potts [Tr]ower and Clymer as far as West Chester, and with the enclosed order for the transfer to his command of the recruits, horses and Waggons awaiting there, an [sic] escort to Head Quarters.
Go: Washington   Comr. in chf

Source: Antiques Roadshow, March 24, 2015.
http://www.theindychannel.com/newsy/antiques-roadshow-george-washington-note-worth-thousands. Document valued at 30-40,000 dollars
The document was written and signed by Washington. Gibbs commanded the Commander-in-Chief's Guard.

## Samuel Jones, Pay Certificate for Horatio Turpin

This may Certify that Ensign Horatio Turpin enter'd in the Jany & February Pay Rolls for the Sum of One hundred & Twenty two & two third Dollars. & is not indepted to me.
Saml. Jones. PM 15 VR

Source: Record Group 93, M 859, Roll 111, Document 31683
Turpin's resignation was effective this day. Heitman shows his first name as Thomas, and sometimes known at Horatio. On June 6, 1778, Jones was convicted of conduct unbecoming an officer, possessing mittens that were not his, and gaming. He was convicted and dismissed from service. But on June 11, "The commander in Chief having received ample testimony of the general good character and behavior of Lieutt. Jones who was sentenced to be dismissed the service by a General Court-Martial, which sentence was approved by HIM on the 6th instant, and being further satisfied by Generals Woodford, Scott and other Officers that that Gentleman is not addicted to the Vice of Gaming restores him to his Rank and Command in the Regt. he belong'd to and in the line of the Army."

## Walter Stewart, Discharge for Thomas Fleeman

This may certify that Thomas Fleeman Soldier in the 2nd. Regiment has faithfully served his term of Enlistment and is hereby discharged Given under my hand at Valley Forge the 12th day of March 1778.
   W. Stewart Commanding
            Gen. Weedon's Brigade

Source: Record Group 15, M 804, Pension Application S39525, National Archives.

Walter Stewart, Colonel of the Thirteenth Pennsylvania Regiment, was then commanding George Weedon's Brigade.

## Joseph Ward to Richard Varick

Dear Sir                                    Head Quarters March 13th, 1778

Your Favour of Jany 28th, came to hand Febry 27$^{th}$. And yours of Febry. 20th. I received this day, inclosing your Abstracts &c.

I am much obliged to you for the particular account of matters relating to the late intended Expedition. I conceive, with you, that it was more wisely laid aside, than undertaken. However, it is possible some advantage may accrue from the Design, as the British Court will doubtless hear of it long before they can know the consequence, and may thereby be the more puzzled to plan their operations.

Your Letter directed to Major Fish, I left with Col. Cortland, with whom he quarters, he being out of Camp. As soon as he returns, I shall favour him with the reading of your account of the Secret Expedition.

The difficulties you mention, respecting Furloughs, men left in Hospitals, &c., are too much experienced here, as well as with you. I consulted his Excellency General Washington on these matters, and his direction was, that Soldiers who did not join their Corps at the expiration of their Furloughs, (unless their Officers, or others, could make it appear that they were necessarily detained) should be returned Deserters. If upon joining their Corps, they should then make it appear they had been necessarily detained, they will notwithstanding their having been returned Deserters, draw their whole pay. Officers, are not to be returned Deserters, unless they have been long absent after the expiration of their Furloughs, but are to be answerable to the Commander in chief of the Department, for absence beyond the limited time. But when their is good reason to apprehend an absent Officer will never join his Corps, or that he has any fraudulent design to keep out of Camp & at the same time draw pay, you may strike him off the Roll, until he joins and does duty. This I think may be a more eligible method than to return them Deserters, and more consistent with that delicacy which Officers ought to deserve.

With respect to men in Hospitals, their Officers ought to know from the Surgeons what their state is, whether dead or alive, and whether they are likely ever to join the Corps; but when men have been left sick at a great distance and their Officers cannot obtain proper information respecting them, immediately, they must be notified to obtain such information against the next muster; and if the Officers neglect a proper attention to this duty, they must answer for the neglect before a Court-martial. When you are satisfied any absent men who were left in Hospitals or elsewhere, who by reason of incapacity, desertion, or other cause, will never join their corps, you may strike them out of the Rolls. You are not obliged to wait for proof of their death or desertion. If any such should after being struck out of the Rolls, join their Corps, and give reasons for their absence sufficient to justify them, they may be inserted in the next Roll for the whole time of their absence; by which means no honest man will suffer by being struck off the Roll—

One piece of News only have we in this Quarter, Capt. Barre with some armed Boats a few days since took on armed Vessel of 8 Carriage Guns, & two other Transports, as they were coming up the Delaware about 30 miles below Philadelphia; as some men of war were apprised of this event & were making towards Capt Barre, he was obliged to take out the most valuable articles & burn the Transports.

In great haste I am Sir Your Obedient Hum Servt
Joseph Ward C.G.M.

P.S. The Instance you mentioned of an Artillery Officer refusing to swear to his Muster Roll, & yet was found worthy to be reprimanded only, is to me unaccountable. However, I don't conceive that a Mustering Officer is obliged to accept any Roll until it is sworn to. If he thinks it proper under certain circumstances, to receive a Roll that is not sworn to, he may; but it is at his option whether he will accept it or not.

Col. Richd Varick DMMG
[docket:] Head Qurs March 13. 1778 / from Colo Ward

Source: Inventory Number 22299, Priced at $10,000 by Seth Kaller Inc., 914-289-1776. On sethkaller.com website May 19, 2013.
Ward was Muster Master General of the Continental Army. Varick was Deputy Muster Master General in the Northern Department. The Muster Rolls were critical for tracking the location of the men in the army, and were used to determine pay.

## Dan Leet to William Russell, Peter Muhlenberg to Robert Hanson Harrison

Sir,                                                                   March 15$^{th}$. 1778

    I have Examined Capt$^n$. John Lemons Accounts with the United States & find him Indebted for 7 Yards Linen 2 Yards Holland & 1 ½ Yards of Check Linen—& there is one Month & a Half of pay Due him together with Seventy five Days Rations—Exclusive of his Accounts with Col Crawford—
    pr Me Dan Leet
    P M$^r$ 13 VR

To Colonel William Russell

Source: Record Group 93 M 859, Roll 110, Document 31293, National Archives.

Sir                                                                    March the 16$^{th}$. 1778
Capt$^n$ Lemon of the 13th. Virginia Reg$^t$. has applied for leave to Resign his Commission, on Account of his Family, who are on the Frontiers, exposed to the Indians; If Capt$^n$. Lemon be indulged The Regt. would not suffer by it, as it is fully officer'd.—
    Peter Muhlenberg B Genl.

Source: Record Group 93, M 859, Roll 110, Document 21292, National Archives. Muhlenberg was a Brigadier General from Virginia. Lemon's resignation was accepted on March 16, 1778.

## Joseph Jay, Deserter Notice

    SIXTEEN DOLLARS REWARD.
DESERTED from the first New-Jersey regiment, a certain JOHN BARLOW, about five feet eight or nine inches high, well set, and about twenty-seven years of age. Also a certain HUGH WELSH, about five feet seven or eight inches high, of a dark complexion, and has a down look. Whoever takes up the said deserters, and delivers them to the subscribers, or to any officer of the regiment, shall have the above reward and reasonable charges, or Eight Dollars for either, paid by                   JOS. JAY, Lieut.

Source: *The New Jersey Gazette*, March 18, 1778.

The bearer hereof Elisha Arnold a Solder in the 6th Virginia Regt. having served his term of enlistment is hereby dischared from the service.

Chas. Lewis Colo. Comm of the 2d Virg'a Brigade

Source: Record Group 15, M 804, Pension Application, S6523, National Archives
Stokes was a First Lieutenant in the Sixth Virginia. Charles Lewis was Colonel of the Fourteenth Virginia Regiment. That Stokes, a lieutenant, was commanding the regiment, indicates how weak some of the units were.

**Bounty Paid to Massachusetts Soldiers**

Valley Forge March 23d, 1778.
I acknowledge to have received Timothy Bigelow Esqr. [*sic*] twenty Dollars as a Bounty from the Continent.

John Morein<br>Joseph Jones<br>Josiah Dodge<br>Nathal Young<br>David Parker

Source: RG 2, M 859, Roll 7, Document 2185, National Archives.
Bounties were paid to soldiers who reenlisted.

**Samuel Goff, Payment from John Nixon**

| Coll. Moylan | Dr. To James Vaux | | |
|---|---|---|---|
| 1777 | | | |
| Decemr. | £ | S | D |
| 19th. To four Dozen of Sheaf Oats | 1 | 10 | 0 |
| 20th To Three Do Do | 1 | 2 | 0 |
| To One Dozen of Do | 0 | 7 | 6 |
| 21st. To Two Dozen of Do | 0 | 15 | 0 |
| 22th To One Dozen of Do | 0 | 7 | 6 |
| To One Do of Do | 0 | 7 | 6 |
| 23d. To Two Dozen of Do | 0 | 15 | 0 |
| 24th To One Dozen of Do | 0 | 7 | 6 |
| 25th To One Dozen of Do | 0 | 7 | 6 |
| 26th To One Dozen of Do | 0 | 7 | 6 |

|  |  | £ | s | d |
|---|---|---:|---:|---:|
| | To Two Bushels of Oats | 0 | 15 | 0 |
| | To Two Dozen Sheaf Oats | 0 | 15 | 0 |
| 27th | To Two Dozen of Do | 0 | 15 | 0 |
| 28th | To Two Dozen of Do | 0 | 15 | 0 |
| 29th. | To Two Dozen of Do | 0 | 15 | 0 |
| 30th | To One Dozen of Do | 0 | 7 | 6 |
| 31st | To Two Dozens of Do | 0 | 15 | 0 |

Jany 1778.

|  |  | £ | s | d |
|---|---|---:|---:|---:|
| 1st | To Two Dozen & ½ of Do | 0 | 18 | 6 |
| 2th | To Three Dozen of Do | 1 | 2 | 6 |
| | To Three Bushels of Oats | 1 | 2 | 6 |
| 3d | To One Dozen of Sheaf Oats | 0 | 7 | 6 |
| 4th | To Keeping one Horse to the 12th at 6 Sheafs pr day | 1 | 10 | 0 |
| 15th | To One Dozen of Sheaf Oats | 0 | 7 | 6 |
| 16th | To One Dozen of Do | 0 | 7 | 6 |
| 17th | To One Dozen of Do | 0 | 7 | 6 |
| 18th | To One Dozen of Do | 0 | 7 | 6 |
| 19th | To One Dozen of Do | 0 | 7 | 6 |
| 20th | To One Dozen of Do | 0 | 7 | 6 |
| 21st | To One Dozen of Do | 0 | 7 | 6 |
| 22th | To Three Dozen of Do | 1 | 2 | 6 |
| 23d. | To One Dozen & a half Do | 0 | 10 | 9 |
| 24th | To Two Dozen of Do | 0 | 15 | 0 |
| 25th | To Two Dozen of Do | 0 | 15 | 0 |
| 26th | To Two Dozen & a half of Do | 0 | 18 | 9 |
| 27th | To Two Dozen of Do | 0 | 15 | 0 |
| 28th | To One Dozen of Do | 0 | 7 | 0 |
| 29th | To Four Dozen of Do | 1 | 10 | 0 |
| 30th. | To Four Dozen of Do | 1 | 10 | 0 |
| 31st | To Four Dozen of Do | 1 | 10 | 0 |
| | | 28 | 13 | 3 |

|  |  | £ | S | D |
|---|---|---:|---:|---:|
| Feby. | | | | |
| 1st | To Three Dozen Sheaf Oats | 1 | 2 | 6 |
| 2th | To Three Dozen of Do | 1 | 2 | 6 |
| 3d. | To Three Dozen & a half of Do | 1 | 6 | 3 |
| 4th | To Two Dozen & a half of Do | 0 | 18 | 9 |
| 5th | To Three Dozen of oat Sheafs | 1 | 2 | 6 |

| | | | | |
|---|---|---|---|---|
| 6th | To Two Dozen of Do | 0 | 15 | 0 |
| | To four Bushels & a half of Oats | 1 | 13 | 9 |
| 7th | To One & a half Dozen of Do | 0 | 11 | 3 |
| 8th | To One Dozen of Do | 0 | 7 | 6 |
| 9th | To One Dozen & a half of Do | 0 | 11 | 3 |
| 10th | To One Dozen of Do | 0 | 7 | 6 |
| 11th | To Do Do | 0 | 7 | 6 |
| 12th | To Do Do | 0 | 7 | 6 |
| 13th | To Do Do | 0 | 7 | 6 |
| 14th | To Three Dozens of oat Sheafs | 1 | 2 | 6 |
| | To five Bushels of Oats the last Week Coll Moylan & Bayler's Horses were at J V | 1 | 17 | 6 |
| | To One Tun of Hay given the Horses at Sundry times from Decr 19th 1777 To Feby 1778 | 10 | 0 | 0 |

$$£ \quad \underline{24 \quad 1 \quad 3}$$
$$\underline{28 \quad 13 \quad 3}$$
$$\text{Tol. } £ \quad 52 \quad 14 \quad 6$$

Providence Town March 26 1778
    Reced of John Nixon on Acct. of Col. Moylan the above Amts. In full for James Vaux—
        Saml Goff

RG 93, M 859, Roll 55, frames 285-86, National Archives.
James Vaux owned Fatland Farm, across the Schuylkill from Valley Forge. Colonel Stephen Moylan commanded the Fourth Continental Light Dragoons, and in March, 1778, succeeded to the command of all the American cavalry. Baylor was Colonel of the Third Continental Light Dragoons.

## William Woodford to Oliver Towles

Dear Majr.                  Camp Valley Forge 27th March 1778
    I have not been favour'd with an Answer to my Letter about a Fortnight past respecting Colo. Taliaferros Affairs—since that yours of the 21st Feby. directed to Genl. Scott (who is gone to Virginia) fell into my Hands, with several of yours to Mrs Towles & other Friends in Virginia, all which I Seal'd & forwarded the next Day pr post—you inform Genl. Scott that Taliaferros Effects would be sold & amount to

sufficient to pay his Debts in the City, if you recd. my Letter, you'll observe that I desired they might be sent out to be sold here, this was from a certainty of them selling to more advantage. I have this Day a Line from his Brother who desires his Sword & Ring, Shoe & Stock Buckles with a small Pocket Book may be sent to Virginia, if you have any of these things on Hand, you'll please to secure them—

I have it in [ ] from Colo. Pendleton to make particular enquiry after John Curd, a youth that listed from Goochland County & whose Friends have heard he was a prisoner in Philadelphia—if he is there & alive you'll very particularly oblige my by rendering him any service in your power—if you can spare him a small supply of Cash I will be answerable to you for it—my respectfull compliments to Capt. Spotswood & all the Virga. Officers

    I am Dr Sir Your Obedt. humble Servt.
    Wm Woodford

Majr. Towles

Source: Frederick M. Dearborn Collection, MS AM 1649.6 (224), Houghton Library, Harvard University.
Woodford was a Brigadier General from Virginia. Towles was Major of the Sixth Virginia Regiment, and had been captured at the Battle of Germantown. William Taliaferro, Lieutenant Colonel of the Fourth Virginia, had been taken prisoner at the Battle of Brandywine, and had died a prisoner in Philadelphia, on February 1, 1778. Captain John Spotswood had also been captured at the Battle of Germantown.

## Robert Hanson Harrison to John Lacey, Jr.

On Tuesday next Commissioners between the two Armies are to meet at German Town on the subject of prisoners. That place is to be neutral during their negotiations, and his Excellency desires that while the Commissioners are there that none of your parties be suffered to enter the Town.

    I am sir, Your Most Obed. Servt.,
    Robert Harrison, Secy.

Head Qrs. Valley Forge, March 28, 1778

Source: Simon Gratz Collection, Historical Society of Pennsylvania.

## Henry Bicker, Certificate for Philip Clumburg

This is to Certify That Lieutenant Philip Clumburg, of the Second Pennsylvania Regiment has my Permission to Resign his Commission, having settled his Accounts to the Satisfaction of the Regiment—

      Henry Bicker Coll
      the $2^d$ Rieg$^t$ Penna

Source: Record Group 93, M 859, Roll 110, Document 31409, National Archives. Clumburg had written to Washington on March 30, asking for permission to resign which gives an approximate date of the same day for this document. A notation on the document show his resignation as effection on April 1, 1778.

## Rowland Evans to Edmund Physick

Friend Physick:—            March 30, 1778.

  Having consulted my Friends and more maturely considered of the Propriety of taking this place for another year. I have at length come to the Determination to take it if it may be had on such terms as are tolerable, and as I knew of no other way of consulting thee have dispatched the Bearer for that purpose.... The meadow fences are very much gone with the Fresh (freshets) as I told thee in my last letter and likewise great part of the Division Fence between, the Meadow and Fields. The season is now grown late and unfavorable for cutting timber for lasting....Work men are very hard to be got and their wages extravagantly high, so that repairing of Fences will be very difficult and expensive....When we likewise consider the uncertainty of their standing, as many Fences have been and probably will be burnt by the armies. I should think the Governor (John Penn, Esq.,) would incline rather to let them remain in their present condition than to go to the great expense where there is such risque of losing them....Thee may remember in my last I informed thee ye Mill produced scarce anymore than paid the Man who attended it as there is nothing to grind but the Grist for Farmer's home consumption....If you chuse to let the place as it is, without repairing the Fences, I am willing to take it, and take all care I can of it during the next coming year, provided you agree that the Rent shall be fixed upon by three Judicious Men whom we may chuse for that Purpose at the end of the year.

As I have another place in view which I may have when ever I apply for it, in case we do not agree about this, and it would not suit me with any delay, I shall expect an answer by the Bearer as will determine me on his return.
      Truly Thine,
       Rowland Evans.
To Edmund Physick.

Source: Dr. W. H. Reed, "Reminiscences of Audubon," *Historical Sketches, A Collection of Papers Prepared for the Historical Society of Montgomery County, Pennsylvania* (Norristown, Pa.: The Society, 1910), 188.

Evans was a Philadelphia merchant and Justice of the Peace, and rented the property near Valley Forge. See Evans' letter of March 2, in volume five of this series, and his later letter in this volume. Physick had been the Agent for the Penn family, whose property, now known as Mill Grove, was on the north side of the Schuylkill River. As happened commonly to civilians in the area, he had lost property to both armies.

## Nathanael Greene to Clement Biddle

Sir         Camp Valley Forge March 31, 1778
  You are immediately to carry into Execution the within plan by forming Magazines of Forage agreable thereto & erecting the Screw presses, puting up the hay in bundles
    Nathanael Greene
     Q M General
To Col Clement Biddle
  Com Genl Forage

200,00 Bushels of Grain and as much Hay as can be drawn in from both sides of Delaware to be lodged on the banks of Delaware from Trenton upwards.
200,000 Bushels of Grain & as much Hay as can be procured at different points of Schuylkil
200,000 Bushels of Grain & as much Hay as can be procured within forty miles of the Camp to be fixed at different points from the head of Elk to Camp—
100,000 bushels of Grain & a proportionable Quantity of Hay on the line from Reading to Wrights Ferry on Susquehana at different posts.

100,000 Bushels of Grain & a proportionable Quty of Hay on the line of Communication between Delaware & Hudsons River—
All the Hay to be screwed in Bundles—
40,000 Bushels of Grain & Hay in proportion, at Trenton, Allentown, & other lower parts of Jersey.

Sir I approve of the above places for magazines with this proviso, that the one at Trenton shall not (in its full extent) be immediately formed, and that the others upon that river shall be tolerably high up for security—The quantity is I presume the result of Estimation—For obvious reasons I should prefer a number of small magazines to a few large ones and think if they were laid in quarterly or for a term not exceeding four or six months it would be advisable & proper and the Theatre of War may change—and taxation must reduce the price of every commodity.
             Signed Geo Washington
Valley Forge March 31. 1778
To the Qur Mr General

Source: Nathanael Greene Papers, Huntington Library.
This gives some idea of the magnitude and complexity of providing forage for the thousands of draft and food animals needed by the Continental Army, particularly when it was not known how the 1778 campaign would unfold.

## William Henry, Roll of Recruits

A Roll of Recruits in Capt. Mathew Scotts Company, 13th Pennsa. Regiment, commanded by Walter Stewart, March 31, 1778.—

| Names | Enlisted | Country | Place of Abode | Age | Complexion | Hair | Size. |
|---|---|---|---|---|---|---|---|
| Patrick Dougan | Feb. 16 | Ireland | Cumberland Co. | 21 | Fair | Sandy | 5 ft. 6 in. |
| Mathew Horner | Feb. 13 | do. | Shippensburgh | 26 | do. | Black | 5 ft 8 in. |
| John Otney | Feb. 15 | France | Cumberland Co. | 20 | Yellow | do. | 5 ft 6 in. |
| Henry Miller | March 23 | Germany | do. | 24 | Dark | do. | 5 ft 5 in. |
| Richard Star | " 14 | Ireland | Shippensburgh | 20 | Brown | do. | 5 ft 2 in. |

| John Fiday | " 2 | do. | do. | 35 | Fair | Brown | 5 ft 6½ in. |
| Peter Miller | Feb. 6 | Germany | Westmorland Co. | 30 | Black | Black | 5 ft 5½ in. |

This is to Certify that the above named Men were solemnly Sworn before me to Serve the United States of America for during the War, and that they were enlisted by Capt. Mathew Scott of the 13th Pennsa Regt. Given under my Hand the 31st day of March 1778.

William Henry

Source: *Pennsylvania Magazine of History and Biography*, 25, (1901), 582.


**Ebenezer Smith, Certificate for Nathan Thayer**

This May Certify that the Continent has Not any Demands on Ensn. Nathan Thayer of Colo. Edward Wigglesworths Regiment—
        Eben. Smith
        Pay Master said regt
March 31st. 1778

Source: RG 93, M 859, Roll 6, Document 1857, National Archives.
Ensign Thayer of the Thirteenth Massachusetts Regiment was allowed to resign the same day.


COLONEL ELIAS BOUDINOT'S NOTES OF TWO CONFERENCES HELD BY THE AMERICAN AND BRITISH COMMISSIONERS TO SETTLE A GENERAL CARTEL FOR THE EXCHANGE OF PRISONERS OF WAR, 1778.

[The exchange of civil and military prisoners of war was a matter which continued in a very unsatisfactory state until the appointment by Congress in June of 1777 of Elias Boudinot, Esq., as Commissary General of Prisoners. The Historical Society of Pennsylvania in its manuscript collection has much of the correspondence and many notes of conferences of Colonel Boudinot on the subject, and we have selected one of the latter, for the interesting account it gives of the attempt to settle on a general cartel for the exchange of prisoners of war. The American Commissioners were Colonel William Grayson, Lieutenant-Colonels Alexander Hamilton and Robert Hanson Harrison, of Washington's staff, and Colonel Elias Boudinot, and the British, Colonel Charles O'Hara, of the Coldstream Regiment of Foot Guards, Colonel Humphry Stephens, of the Third Regiment of Foot Guards, and Captain the Hon. Richard Fitzpatrick, of the First Regiment of Foot Guards. Their meetings took place in the Benezet mansion, on Main street near the Square, Germantown, and in the inn of Amos Strickland, at Newtown, in Bucks County.]

On Tuesday the 31$^{st}$ March 1778 Col. W$^m$ Grayson, Lieut Col. Rob$^t$ H. Harrison & Alexr Hamilton and Elias Boudinot Commissioners appointed by his Excy Gen. Washington, (for meeting Commissioners of like Rank from Genl Howe to sett & agree upon a general Cartel for the Exchange of Prisoners &c.) set out from the Camp at the Valley Forge, and proceeded to German Town, and arrived at 11 o'clock in the forenoon, where they met Col. Charles O'Hara, Col. Humphrey Stephens & Capt. Rich$^d$ Fitzpatrick, Commissioners from Sir William Howe. The Commissioners on each side were attended by an Escort of 12 light Dragoons under the command of a Cap. of light Dragoons—Americans by Capt. [Robert] Smith of Baylor's reg$^t$.

After the usual Introduction, Col. O'Hara mentioned their coming with the most upright Intentions of acting with Candour & Openess. That they doubted not of our coming with the same resolutions, and that therefore, they hoped for a favourable Issue. Col. O'Hara presented their Commission from Sir William Howe dated the 5th Inst. for meeting on the 10th, whereupon Col. Grayson produced the Commission from Genl Washington and Com$^s$ were examined & exchanged. Col. O'Hara previously observed, that he understood the two Generals meant the negotiations to proceed between the military Gent$^n$ and if necessity required to call in Mess$^s$ Boudinot & Loring for Information occasionally, but on seeing that Mr. Boudinot was mentioned in the Commission, waived the Matter and proceeded to introduce rough Notes of their Ideas of the principal Parts of a general Cartel, leaving them and desiring they might be considered by tomorrow. Then proposed their going to Town this Evening, & returning by Ten o'Clock tomorrow Morning.[1] Col. Harrison mentioned the necessary attendants passing & repassing to the respective Camps under Passes from each other. Col. O'Hara agreed for this Day & promised to Obtain proper Authority for the purpose

for this Day & promised to Obtain proper Authority for the purpose by tomorrow. It was mentioned that German Town should be a place of neutrality & no Troops besides the mutual Escorts to enter. Col. O'Hara also proposed at the Introduction, that we should take up the matter of our Business in the first Place by settling a general Cartel, to answer the Purposes of our Commissions and afterwards to settle all other disputes as secondary Matters, to which we assented, provided nothing was considered as binding on either Party until the whole was settled.

In another communication Colonel Boudinot states: "The British Commissioners after dinner told us, that they had engaged to attend a grand Ball that was to be given that evening in the City, and earnestly solicited that we should gratify them by consenting to their going into the City, when they would mention our Objections to their powers and they would be out early in the morning. They accordingly went and I suppose reported to Gen. Howe. The next morning, they came out in good time. In granting this request, we were guilty of a great Blunder."

Dined altogether at Benezet's; spent the Evening in considering the rough Minutes left with us & preparing our Objections for the morning.

Wednesday, April 1.—After settling our Minds on the rough Notes of a general Cartel, & making the proper Notes, we attended at the Place of Meeting, where after waiting an Hour, we were joined by the Commissioners on the Part of Gen$^l$ Howe.

After making our Objections to Gen$^l$ Howe's Commission to the Gentn viz. That it did not contain an Averment of Gen$^l$ Howe's Power and that it was restricted to the 10th March, which was past, we proceeded, (through Col. Grayson) to examine the rough Notes Paragraph by Paragraph, and after discussing the several propositions separately, we agreed in our general Ideas on the most material of them making Notes thereof. The Gentlemen then proposed amplifying the rough Notes & reducing them to the form of a Cartel before the next meeting, but as this must be the work of Time they agreed to adjourn till Friday morning.

Having finished Business, they informed us that they had rec'd orders to acquaint us that it was Gen$^l$ Howe's intention that as German Town was within 4½ miles of their Posts, the Truce should be considered to be in force no longer than we were actually sitting excepting that when his Commissioners went off towards

Philadelphia every Evening we should immediately set off towards our Posts, and that we should be mutually protected in going & coming. On this we immediately demanded to know if these were their positive orders from Genl Howe, they answered, that how ever they might consider this matter themselves, that these were the orders they had rec'd from Sr Wm Howe, to which we ans$^d$ that we should depart to our Camp as soon as possible, and that they could not expect our attendance again until a farther Agreement between our Genls respecting this matter.

It is to be remembered, that in the Notes we made of our agreement of Ideas on the rough Proposition, we went no farther than the general Principle of each, which we agreed was to be mutually modified & enlarged with such restrictions & Conditions & applied to such purposes as per measure to be adopted on our part, as we conceived it to be an extraordinary step on their side to start such doubt on so clear a point and which had been so fully settled by the two commanders in chief: & at the same time looking upon it as derogatory to the dignity of the States, & a reflection on our own personal honor. We informed them we should set out in the morning to give an account to Gen$^l$ Washington of the reasons which suspended the negotiation.

April 4.—Genl Washington having informed us that he had rec'd a Letter from Gen$^l$ Howe on the Subject of our negotiation & leaving German Town, in Consequence of which he had appointed another Meeting of the Commissioners at New Town in Bucks County on Monday next, which was to be the Place of our residence till the negotiation was finished, unless an adjournment should take Place to any other Place, by mutual Consent, we agreed to set oft early on Monday Morning.

Monday, April 6.—We arrived at New Town about 6 o'Clock in the afternoon Escorted as before, where we met Genl Howe's Commissioners just arrived, with the addition of a Commissary & Subaltern officer. Lodgings were provided for the English Commissioners, & their Escort. It appearing that they were unprovided with either Provisions or Forage, we agreed to make the necessary Provision for their Escort, & to keep one Table for the Commissioners, they having provided Liquors. It was agreed to adjourn all Business till to-morrow morning.

April 7.—The Commissioners met at the house of Mr. Strickland, and previous to opening the Business, Col. O'Hara informed us, that Sir Wm Howe had been made acquainted with the objection taken to their Commission, when at German Town. That his wish & desire was to treat in the present Business with Gen$^l$ Washington in the personal characters of the two Generals. That however, he thought himself justifiable in exceeding his express Powers, in negotiating an Exchange from the necessity & mutual convenience of the measure and would take the risque upon himself; yet he could not think or consent to setting forth any Assertion in the Powers or Commission that would convey the Idea of a national compact or Agreement, and therefore the English Commissioners desired our Consideration of the question, whether we thought ourselves authorized to treat with them under the Commission as it now stands as otherwise they could not proceed in the Business. That if we could not think ourselves thus authorized as to the Cartel at large, because of such want of Powers, that there could be no just Objection to our going into an Exchange of the Prisoners now actually in Possession, as this would be merely a personal Business to be executed immediately.

After some altercation on the subject, they proposed to adjourn till tomorrow morning, when they would expect our final answer.

April 8.—On meeting this morning we desired the Gentn would give us an answer to a previous Question, viz. Whether they considered their Proposition as a positive Term on the Compliance to which, we could only proceed to Business, or whether they considered it as a point of discussion, and therefore that they were ready to hear our Arguments on the subject. On a little disputation we informed them that we considered ourselves as unauthorized either to treat under the Idea of representing our General in his personal character, or of negotiating partially for the exchange of the present Prisoners only. They replied, that they considered it at present as a positive preliminary, and that none but Sir Wm Howe could fully answer the Question and authorize them to proceed, and that to settle this Dispute, two of them Col. O'Hara & Capt. Fitzpatrick would immediately go to Philadelphia & take his further Instructions on the subject, and return tomorrow morning. To this we agreed and adjourned till tomorrow morning.

As they chose to take their Waggon to the City to return with some necessaries, a Passport was signed by Col. Grayson & Col. Hamilton for the purpose.

April 9.—The Gentn returning from Philadelphia so late, that no Business could be done.

April 10.—On meeting this morning Genl Howe's Commissioners informed us, that they were ready to treat with us on the Commission as it stood, but it could not be altered. Having had a great deal of private confidential conversation on the subject, we proposed, that our objections should be put into writing, and that they should give us an official answer in writing, to prevent mistakes, to which after some dispute they consented. We retired, and drew up our objections to their Powers (for state of objections see appendix) and delivered it to them, which they refused to read, and returned back, alledging that having considered the matter, they did not think themselves authorized to give any other than a verbal answer. This altercation put off the Business for this day.

April 11.—Having corrected & amended our State of Objections, we insisted on Genl Howe's Commissioners receiving them, which they did with great difficulty, and in the afternoon returned us a written Paper (see appendix) declaring that it was no answer to our Objections but only a declaration of their readiness to treat. To this we immediately prepared a reply, and delivered it to Col. O'Hara, who refused to read it, alledging that if we could not meet them on that Commission the negotiation was at an end, and after keeping it some time, he returned it to us, on which Col. Grayson read the Paper aloud to them. They insisted that we had gone out of the present Business with our Objections, which ought to have been confined to their Commission, in which there was nothing contained relative to any thing civil but was altogether military. That the Exchange of Citizens was a ground they never could meet us on, as the inhabitants were all their Citizens, and the Terms were unequal—and that with regard to the publick Faith, if we held up Language of that kind it must forever prevent any negotiation, as it could not be pledged with People in our situation. On this we replied, that Citizens were an express object of our negotiation—that they were mentioned in the most positive Terms in the Correspondence between Genl Washington & Genl Howe, and that if they considered them excluded from their Commission, it was a new Objection to the sufficiency of their Powers, which we could never give up. That with regard to the publick Faith, we relied on our reasoning upon that subject being conclusive, and desired to know officially from them, whether they considered their Powers as enabling them to hold the Conference as a personal Treaty between the two Generals only, or whether the publick were also to be concerned in it. They answered that they could agree only on a personal Treaty as between the two Generals only, and that the publick faith could not be pledged or concerned in the matter, and that the Cartel if settled would be binding but during Sir Wm Howe's administration and on him alone.

In the course of the conversation it was added, that Citizens were expressly mentioned in our Powers, which being interchanged, pointed them out as one object of our negotiation, that we conceived them to be comprehended in theirs, under the general description of Prisoners of War, since we know no other light in which Citizens could be made the subjects of Captivity, that Sir Wm Howe in his correspondence with Genl Washington expressly refers the affairs of Citizens to a personal description between the Commissioners, and that their own proposition to us, contained a clause respecting Persons in Civil Employment, which we looked upon as only the words for Citizens in office. Genl Howe's Commissioners answered that they considered the negotiation as at an end, and therefore to dispute further on the subject was vain. On this we broke off Business and agreed to return tomorrow.[2]

2. In a letter of Colonel Boudinot, he writes of the British Commissioners: "We were very sociable, but had previously obtained the character of our opponents, and were convinced that they depended much on out-drinking us. We knew that Col. Grayson was a match for them, and therefore left all that part of the business to him, They sat down often with Grayson while we were preparing to go off; 'till they could scarcely sit upright. Just before sundown they were put on their horses and went for the city."

Appendix . No. 1.

The Commissioners appointed by his Excy Genl Washington to confer, determine & agree upon a Treaty & Convention for the exchange of Prisoners of War, and for all matters whatsoever that may be properly contained therein.

Having examined the Papers on the part of Genl Sir Wm Howe to his Commissioners and compared them with their own, observe a difference, which in their apprehension, is very essential and important.

General Washington in his Commission expressly declared it to be given in Virtue of full Powers to him delegated. Gen[l] Sir W[m] Howe in his Commission makes no acknowledgement of any authority by which he acts.

It appears to be the Intention of the respective Generals, mutually expressed in their Powers to do an extensive & permanent Act, which shall not only effect a settlement of past differences & a general Exchange of Prisoners for the present, but shall extend to the establishment of a regular and explicit Cartel in the future. The objects of this Cartel will not be wholly of a Military nature, but will include matters of very interesting civil concern. It is apprehended that the Power of entering into a Treaty of such importance is not naturally inherent in military command, and that it cannot be exercised by either of the Generals as an official Act, merely in virtue of their military capacities, but must be founded on special Authority according to reason & universal Practice ought to be declared, otherwise it will not appear nor have the least efficiency or operation. That if this authority does not exist, the negotiation can have no sufficient foundation. It must rest solely on the footing of personal Confidence. The publick faith cannot be considered as pledged for the performance of any engagements in consequence of it, and then may of course be overruled at pleasure.

Could the credit of individuals be supposed great enough, in preservation of personal honor, to prevent the interference of superior authority, their influence could not at any rate extend beyond their own Command, and should the Causalities of war remove them, their successors would not be in any manner bound by their engagements.

In fine it is conceived, there would be a manifest impropriety in conducting a Business of this nature on personal ground, as such a measure would be destitute of that Validity which the solemnity of a publick Act alone can give, and which the magnitude of the objects it is intended to comprehend indispensibly requires. Personal confidence or the mutual credit of individuals, is too slender & unsubstantial a basis for concerns of so great variety & extent as the Treaty in contemplation must necessarily involve.

New Town, April 10, 1778.

     WILLM. GRAYSON,
     ROBT. H. HARRISON,
     A. HAMILTON,
     ELIAS BOUDINOT.

To COL. CHARLES O'HARA,
COL. HUMPHREY STEVENS,

CAPT. RICHD. FITZPATRICK.
Appendix No. 2.

The Commissioners appointed by his Excy Sir Wm Howe to take into consideration all past transactions relative to the Exchange of Prisoners, to adjust the differences that have so long subsisted in regard to them, to remove all difficulties that may arise in carrying into execution a general Exchange of Prisoners with both parties at this time, and finally to establish a regular & explicit Cartel for the future.

Having recd the objections made to the Commission under which they act, from the Commissioners appointed to meet them for similar purposes by General Washington, are much concerned to find they are likely to prove an obstruction to the execution of so desirable a purpose they conceive the Powers delegated to them by their Commission to be sufficient and simple for effectually accomplishing the purposes therein contained, and hereby declare themselves ready & desirous of immediately entering upon a Treaty with the Commissioners appointed by General Washington for carrying into execution the different objects of their Commission.

New Town, April 11, 1778.
Chas. O'Hara,
Humphy. Stevens
Richd. Fitzpatrick

To Col. Grayson,
Lt. Col. Harrison
Lt. Col. Hamilton,
Elias Boudinot, Esq.

Appendix No. 3.

The Commissioners appointed by his Excellency General Washington to confer, determine & agree upon a Treaty & Convention for the exchange of Prisoners of War, and for all matters whatsoever, that may be properly contained therein—
Are inexpressly concerned that the Commissioners on the part of Gen$^l$ Sir Wm Howe should think it necessary to make the objections stated in their Powers, and supported as they apprehend, by the most conclusive reasons, an insurmountable obstacle to the progress of a negotiation intended to answer the most benevolent and estimable purposes. As Gen$^l$ Sir W$^m$ Howe, must be supposed fully empowered to enter into the Treaty, his commission imports, they can conceive no sufficient reason for not declaring his Powers, and would flatter

themselves that nothing could be easier than to remove the cause of their objections, and to proceed on the business on admissible terms. They are ready and solicitous to treat on fair, proper & equal ground such as will give efficiency to their proceedings and place a publick Act on the foundation of publick authority.
NEW TOWN, Ap 11, 1778.

> WM. GRAYSON,
> ROBT. H. HARRISON,
> ALEXR. HAMILTON,
> ELIAS BOUDINOT.

To Col. Ch. O'Hara,
Col. Humphy Stephens,
Capt. Richd. Fitzpatrick
Appendix No. 4.

By his Exc$^{cy}$ Geo. Washington Esq$^r$ Gen$^l$ & Commander in Chief of the Forces of the United States of America.

To Col. William Grayson, Lieut. Cols. Robert Hanson Harrison & Alex$^r$ Hamilton and Elias Boudinot Esq$^r$ Commissary General of Prisoners.

Whereas a proposition was made by me on the 30$^{th}$ day of July 1776 to his Exc$^y$ Sir W$^m$ Howe, and acceded to by him on the first day of August following, stipulating an Exchange of Prisoners, officer for officer of equal rank, soldier for soldier and Citizen for Citizen. And whereas differences have arisen in the construction & execution of this Agreement, and it has been found by experience to be inadequate to all the desirable purposes for which it was in tended, not being sufficiently extensive & definite to comprehend the diversity of circumstances incident to the State of Captivity, or to ascertain the various modes of relief applicable to all.

In order to adjust all such differences, to prevent others in future, so far as may be practicable, and to fix the Exchange and accommodation of Prisoners of War, upon a more certain, liberal & ample foundation, you are in virtue of full Powers to me delegated, to meet such Commissioners of suitable rank as are or shall be appointed on the part of Gen$^l$ Sir W$^m$ Howe, and who shall come duly authorized to treat on the subject at German Town on the 31$^{st}$ day of March Inst., with them to confer, determine & agree upon a Treaty & Convention for the Exchange of Prisoners of War, and for all matters whatsoever which may be properly contained therein, on principles of Justice, Humanity & mutual advantage, and agreeable to the customary rules

& practices of War among Civilized Nations. For all which this shall be your sufficient Warrant and your engagements being mutually interchanged shall be ratified and confirmed by me.

Given under my Hand & Seal at Head Quarters at Valley Forge this — day of March 1778.

Go. WASHINGTON.

By his Exc$^{ys}$ Command,
JOHN LAURENS, A.D.C.

Appendix No. 5.

By his Exc$^y$ Sir William Howe, Knight of the most Hon$^{ble}$ Order of the Bath, Gen$^l$ & Commander in Chief of all his Majesties Forces within the Colonies laying on the Atlantic Ocean from Nova Scotia to West Florida inclusive, &c., &c.

To Col. CHARLES O'HARA,
CoL. HUMPHRY STEPHENS,
CAPT. Richd. FITZPATRICK.

In pursuance of an Agreement entered into with Gen. Washington for the Appointment of Commissioners on his Part and on mine to meet at German Town on Tuesday the 10th day of March 1778 with full Powers to take under their consideration all past Transactions relative to the Exchange of Prisoners, to adjust the differences which have so long subsisted in regard to them, to remove all difficulties that may arise in carrying into Execution a general Exchange of the Prisoners of both Parties at this time, and finally to establish a regular & explicit Cartel for the future—

I do hereby nominate & appoint you Col. Charles O'Hara, Col Humphry Stephens & Captain Rich$^{d"}$ Fitzpatrick Commissioners on my part for the purpose af$^{sd}$ and you or any two of you are accordingly to repair to German Town on the Day abovementioned and there to treat, determine & agree with a like number of Commissioners of suitable rank on the part of Gen$^l$ Washington vested with similar Powers to those herein contained, upon all Matters whatsoever relative to Prisoners. For all which this shall be to you Col. Charles O'Hara, Col. Humphry Stephens & Cap$^t$ Richd Fitzpatrick or to any two of you a sufficient Warrant, and your Engagements so concluded upon, will upon condition of their being mutually interchanged be finally ratified & Confirmed on my part.

Given under my Hand & Seal at Head Quarters at Philadelphia the 5 day of March 1778.

WM. HOWE.

By his Exc[ys] Command
ROBT. MACKENZIE, Sec[y].
(Appendix.)
Copy of rough Propositions made by Gen[l] Howe's Commissioners for Consideration, with our answers.

A General Exchange of Prisoners to take place according to the following form viz, officer for officer, soldier for soldier, as far as number and rank will apply. *AGREED.*

In Case there should not be an equality in the rank of Officers to be exchanged

Lt. General equal to 1 Major Gen & 1 Brig[r] Gen[l]—or to one Brig[r] Gen[l] & two Colonels.

Major Gen[l] equal to 1 Brig[r] Gen & 1 Col., or to 1 Col & two L[t] Cols.

Brig[r] Gen[l] equal to 1 Col. & 1 L[t] Col., or to 1 L[t] Col. & 2 Majors.

Colonel equal to 1 L[t] Col. & 1 Major, or to 1 Major & two Captains

L[t] Col. equal to 1 Major & 1 Captain, or to 3 Captains.

*Agreed to the 1st part of the alternative, the principle to be pursued thro' out thus*

| | | | |
|---|---|---|---|
| *Ensign* | *1* | *Lieut* | *2* |
| *Cap[t].* | *3* | *Major* | *5* |
| *L[t] Col.* | *8* | *Col* | *13* |
| *Brig[r]* | *21* | *Maj Gen* | *34* |
| *Lt Gen* | *55* | *Cap[t] Gen* | *89* |

Major equal to 2 Captains or 4 Subalterns.
Captain equal to 2 Subalterns.

In Case it should at any Time, from a deficiency of Officers, be found necessary to exchange them for men the following propositions are submitted to consideration.

| | | |
|---|---|---|
| L[t] Gen[l] equal to | 1500 | rank & file |
| Major Gen[l] | 750 | " |
| Brig[r] Gen[l] | 375 | " |
| Colonel | 187 | " |
| L[t] Col. | 93 | " |
| Major | 46 | " |
| Captain | 23 | " |

Subaltern    12    "
Sergeant      3    "

*The ratio of this calculation to be governed by the preceeding, and the value of an Ensign in privates to be considered hereafter.*

In Case it should be found expedient to stipulate a certain Rate of Exchange to be paid in Money for Prisoners, when there happens to be no Prisoners on one side to return,—proposed that each man not disabled by wounds or otherwise from bearing arms, be rated at —— Sterling, and the Ransom for Officers to be apportioned accordingly, agreeable to the foregoing Proposition.

*Referred for consideration.*

Commissioned Officers to be treated with respect & admitted to such Liberty upon Parole, as the nature of the situation may permit.

*The gen$^l$ Idea to be adopted with a more enlarged explanative.*

Military Officers acting upon the Staff to be considered only according to their Ranks in the respective Armies.

*Agreed to the gen$^l$ Principle & those who have no rank to be provided for.*

Persons in civil Employment to be exchanged for their equal, or otherwise as may be agreed upon at the time of Exchange.

*The proposition to be more fully explained.*

Deserters not to be included in the Cartel.

*Agreed to & to be defined.*

Prisoners in general to be exchanged as soon after Capture, as circumstances may admit.

*Agreed to & the time to be fixed*

Returns of Prisoners and the Places of their Confinement to be transmitted by the respective Commissaries to each other on the 1$^{st}$ day of every month specifying the Causalities since the preceeding return.

*Agreed.*

Permission to be given by both Parties for the purchase of Provisions, and small necessaries at the market prices.

*Agreed in aid of their rations.*

Clothing & Money to be supplyed by each Party, to their respective Troops, and passports to be given accordingly.

*Each party to have permission to send clothing & money to their prisoners.*

Surgeons with Medicines to visit their Prisoners in their different Stations, at stated periods & upon previous notice.

*Agreed upon proper restrictions.*

Hospitals—regulations for them. The protection of the sick & wounded, and those attending upon them, to be considered by the Commissioners.

*Agreed—to be explained.*

Provisions—The quantity, quality & price of the Ration p day to be ascertained as well as the manner of supply & the mode of payment.

*Agreed.*

Accounts to be settled by Commissioners at stated periods and the balances to be paid accordingly.

*Agreed.*

The troops now in Captivity & such as may be taken before these Articles are void by mutual consent, are to be exchanged bona fide agreeable to them.

*Agreed—to be further explained.*

Source: *Pennsylvania Magazine of History and Biography* 24, no. 3 (1900), 291-305.

A formal exchange was not agreed on between Washington and Howe, although many prisoners on both sides were released by June 1778.

## John Patten, Certificate for Stephen Southall

April 1, 1778

This is to Certifie that Stephen Southall is Appointed to a 2d. Lieutenancy in the 2d. North Carolina Battalion and is to be respected as Such.

John Patton, Colo.

Source: Record Group 93, M 859, Roll 45, Document 14427, National Archives.
Southall had been an Ensign in the Fifteenth Virginia Regiment. Officers moving between the lines of different states rarely occurred.

## Samuel French, Ordnance Report to George Washington

Ordnance & Military Stores with the Army from the First of March to the 31st of March 1778 Showing the Balance Remaining on Hand the First Day of April 1778

104

|  | TOTAL AMOUNT of LAST RETURN | RECEIVED THIS MONTH Mar. 31 | DELIVERED THIS MONTH Mar. 31 | AT CAMP April 1 | AT RHEIM TOWN April 1 |
|---|---|---|---|---|---|
| Musket Cartridges | 42012 | 42616 | 46342 | 30354 | 7932 |
| Muskets | 364 | 300 | 287 | 377 | 41 |
| Bayonets | 354 | 187 | 310 | 231 |  |
| Bayonet Belts | 182 | 352 | 447 | 87 |  |
| Cartridge Boxes | 78 | 203 | 171 | 110 |  |
| Flints | 10857 |  | 1405 | 9433 |  |
| Pounds of Slow Match | 120 |  | 40 | 20 | 60 |
| Budge Barrels | 3 |  |  | 1 | 2 |
| Drudging Boxes | 8 |  |  |  | 8 |
| Tube Boxes | 3 |  |  |  | 3 |
| Lt. Horseman Swords & Belts | 77 |  |  |  | 77 |
| No. of Drag Ropes | 15 |  |  |  | 15 |
| Carbine Swivels | 83 |  |  |  | 83 |
| Gunners Belts | 25 |  |  |  | 25 |
| Tin Cartridge Boxes | 748 |  |  | 46 | 702 |
| Belts for Cartridge Boxes | 331 |  |  |  |  |
| Pouches | 65 |  |  |  | 65 |
| Horns | 129 |  | 10 | 6 | 113 |
| Bullet Moulds | 20 |  |  |  | 20 |
| Spears | 70 |  |  |  | 70 |
| Lint Stocks | 43 |  |  | 39 | 4 |
| Portfire Sticks | 11 |  |  | 10 | 1 |
| Sheep Skins | 17 |  | 2 | 3 | 12 |

| | | | | | |
|---|---|---|---|---|---|
| Brushes and Pickers | 1980 | | | | 1980 |
| Quarts of Sweet Oyl | 63 | | 1 | 62 | |
| Empty 5 ½ inch Shells | 50 | | | | 50 |
| Rheams of Paper | 404 | | 24 | 79 | 301 |
| Rheams of Common Paper | 20 | | | | 20 |
| Pounds of Powder | 2675 | | 1802 | 873 | |
| Pounds of Musket Ball | 3690 | 2003 | 4367 | 1326 | |
| Round Shot Fixed 3 Pdr | 386 | | | 95 | 291 |
| Round Shot Fixed 4 Pdr | 48 | | | | 48 |
| Round Shot Fixed 6 Pdr | 459 | | | 182 | 277 |
| Round Shot Fixed 12 Pdr | 152 | | | | 152 |
| Grape Shot Fixed | | | | | |
| 3 Pdr | 235 | | | | 235 |
| 6 Pdr | 315 | | | | 315 |
| 12 Pdr | 96 | | | | 96 |
| Case Shot Fixed | | | | | |
| 3 Pdr | 439 | | | | 439 |
| 4 Pdr | 240 | | | 32 | 340 |
| 6 Pdr | 906 | | | 32 | 850 |
| 12 Pdr | 63 | | | | 63 |
| Sponges and Rammers | | | | | |
| 3 Pdr | 22 | | | 3 | 19 |
| 4 Pdr | 22 | | | 6 | 16 |
| 6 Pdr | 26 | | | 5 | 21 |
| 12 Pdr | 4 | | | | 4 |

| Item | | | | | |
|---|---|---|---|---|---|
| Paper Cartridges Filled | | | | | |
| 3 Pdr | 106 | | | | 106 |
| 4 Pdr | 56 | | | | 56 |
| 6 Pdr | 68 | | | | 68 |
| Loose Iron Ball | | | | | |
| 3 Pdr | 300 | | | | 300 |
| 6 Pdr | 210 | | | | 210 |
| Fuses Fixed | | | | | |
| 5 ½ In. | 235 | | | | 235 |
| 8 In. | 64 | | | | 64 |
| Wad Hooks and Ladles | | | | | |
| 3 Pdr | 1 | | | 1 | |
| 4 Pdr | 3 | | | 1 | 2 |
| 6 Pdr | 9 | | | 3 | 6 |
| 12 Pdr | 2 | | | | 2 |
| Paper Cart's Empty | 200 | | | | 200 |
| Fifes | 82 | 302 | 59 | 244 | |
| Tubes | 802 | | 122 | 404 | 330 |
| Portfires | 431 | | 30 | 61 | 340 |
| Rifles | 20 | 13 | 25 | 8 | |
| Gun Barrels | 15 | | 15 | | |
| Pounds of Sulfur | 135 | | 4 | | 131 |
| Spunge Tacks | 1976 | | 150 | | 1826 |
| Light Horse Cartridge Boxes | 44 | | | | 44 |
| Drum Cords | 44 | 38 | 34 | 48 | |
| Pounds of Thread | 9 ½ | 27 | 36 ½ | | |
| Sets of Drum Sticks | | 181 | | 181 | |
| Gun Worms | | 545 | | 545 | |
| Screw Drivers | | 1802 | | 1802 | |
| Files | | 42 | 17 | 25 | |

| | | | | | |
|---|---|---|---|---|---|
| Shells for 8 Inch Howitzers | | 24 | | 24 | |
| Drum Snares | 96 | 230 | 59 | 267 | |

Stores Damaged Unfit for Service

| | | | | | |
|---|---|---|---|---|---|
| Cartridge Boxes | 29 | 280 | 200 | 109 | |
| Musket Cart. | 33080 | | 9000 | 10400 | 13680 |
| Bayonet Belts | 64 | | 51 | | |
| Rifles | 26 | | 26 | | |
| Lbs of Powder | 120 | | | | |
| Lbs of Shot Fixed 4-12 lb | 14 | | | 120 | 14 |
| For 5 ½ inch Howitzer Case Shot | 145 | | | | 145 |
| For 5 ½ inch Howitzer Shells Fixed | 57 | | | | 57 |
| For 8 inch Howitzer Shells Fixed | 13 | | | | 13 |
| For 8 inch Howitzer Shells Empty | 2 | | | | 2 |
| 8 Inch Howitzer Case Shot | 4 | | | | 4 |

To His Excellency Gen. Washington
Signed Saml. French, Commissary of Military Stores

Source: Record Group 93, M 859, Roll 68, Document 21045, National Archives
Reamstown was and is a small town in Lancaster County, Pennsylvania.

## Josiah Lacey to Mrs. Isaac Coller

To Miss Coller　　　　　　　　Camp Valey Forge. Apriel 2d. 1778
　　Dear Madam—This is a Disagreeable Task to me that I am Calld upon to Pen these Lines that must Bring Suchey Mallincolley News to you Nothing Less Dose these Bring than the Mallincolley Sound of Death—your Husband Departed this Life this Mornig about 8 oClock and was Decantly Buried this Evening this no Doubt must be Heavy News to You and your Children—But may God of his Inifinet Mercy Surport you under you afflictions and tryals and give you Grace and wisdom to Consider from whence those afflictions Come and Cause you to Say with Holy Job the Lord Gave and the Lord taketh way and Blessed be his Name—I Heartyly Condole with you on the Loss of a Husban which no Doubt was Dear to you and your Children But Sence he is no more I hope you may yet Finde Such Necessary assistance as you will Stand in need of Both of a Spirittual and Temperal Nature and that You may be Carried Safe through This Troublesom world and at Last Land in the world of Shineing Bliss is the herty Prayer of your unknow Friend and Humble Servt.
　　　　　　Josiah Lacey
N.B. Mr. Coller Died with the Small Pox

Addressed: To Wife of Isaac Coller
　　　　　Danbury Bethel Society Connecticut
Pr. Favor of Sergt. Scribnor

Source: Inventory Number 22298, Priced at $8,750 by Seth Kaller Inc., 914-289-1776. On sethkaller.com website May 19, 2013.
Isaac Coler or Coller, was a Private in the Fifth Connecticut Regiment. Lacey a Captain in the same unit. Letters of condolence such as this are very rare from the American Revolution period.

## Richard Parker, Certificate for William Sandford

I do certify that Capt. Wm. Sandford of the 2nd Virga. Regiment made Oath to his acct. of Money recd from the United States, and that Mr. Maddison Pay master to the Regiment being upon furlough prevents his settling them finally
　　　　　Rd Parker Colo 1st. Virga. Regmt—　　　　Apl 5th 1778

Source: Record Group 93, M 859, Roll 110, Document 31235, National Archives.
Sanford's resignation appears as effective on April 6, 1778. Richard Parker had been Lieutenant Colonel of the Second Virginia, and was promoted to be Colonel of the First Virginia, effective February 10, 1778. Ambrose Madison was the Paymaster.

## John Allison to Peter Muhlenberg

Sir $Ap^l$. $6^{th}$ 1778—
    The Bearer $Cap^t$. Camp is Just return'd from Furlough, he informs me his Affairs in Virginia Is in such a situation as by no means admit of his continuing in the Service, If you think proper to recommend him to his $Exc^y$. for a Resignation, he is clear of any Debt contracted with his Country since he join'd the $Reg^t$.—
        Am Sir $y^r$ $Ob^t$. $Hhb^l$
        J. Allison
To $Gen^l$. Muhlenberg
Note shows he "resign'd $7^{th}$ April 1778"

Source: Record Group 93, M 853, Roll 12, Volume 169, Commissions and Resignations, 1776-1780, f. 231, National Archives.
John Allison was a Lieutenant Colonel in the First Virginia State Regiment. John Camp was a Captain in that regiment.

## Louis Lebique Duportail to Horatio Gates

Sir                     Camp valley forge 6 april 1778
I sent you the memorial upon the mineers which I had the honour to speak to you about. you will see in is dated in the month of january and if then I hastened the execution of it, you thinck that it is more necessary now.
I sent you an other menorial for the appointements of the engineers. it is fit that these things are settled and I beg you to be so good as to be about it.
I am with great Respect sir your humble & most obed servant
        Le Chr. Duportail
Sir please to present my Compliments to Mrs Gates
I beg you pardon if I send you a letter for major villefrance I fear that letter don't parsent to him by another way.

Source: Robert C. Norton Collection, The Western Reserve Historical Society.
Duportail, a Frenchman, was Brigadier General of Engineers. Major General Gates, the victor of Saratoga, was serving as President of the Board of War.

## Richard Kidder Meade to Nathanael Greene

D$^r$ Sir   Monday Morng 6th. April 1778

    I am commanded by his Excellency to desire that you will furnish Genl. Lee with a Good Waggon & Team to transport his Baggage up the country—you will also be pleased to furnish two of the best Horses you have. both Waggons & Horses to be sent here early to morrow morning.

    With respect I am Your mo. Obdt
                R K Meade   ADC

Source: Gratz Collection, Case 4, Box 10, Historical Society of Pennsylvania.
Major General Lee had been captured in 1776. He had been exchanged and was coming out from Philadelphia.

## Frederick Weissenfels to Tench Tilghman

Sir—   Camp Valley Forge apr 6$^{th}$ 1778

Lieut James Miller of the 2d. N:Y: Battalion, the Bearer hereof—having a Desire to Resign his Commission. I would Recommend him to his Excellency for his acceptance.

    he has Served with me upwards of two year, [*sic*] During Which time he alwais behaved becoming an officer and a Gentelman, he is not indebted to the States nor the Regiment, but has made a Setlement agreable to order I am with Respect

    Sir, Your most obied humbl Serv$^t$:

Source: Record Group 93, M 859, Roll 23, Doc. 7455, National Archives.
Weissenfels was Lieutenant Colonel of the Second New York, Miller was a First Lieutenant. His resignation was accepted and effective on April 7.

## James Wesson to George Washington

Camp Valey Forge April 6th: 78

This may Certify that Lieut. Thomas Lock, of my Regiment, is not Indebted either to the Continent, or the Regiment, and has my Approbation for A Discharge—
James Wesson Colo
To His Excellency Gen$^l$. Washington

Source: Record Group 93, M 859, Roll 6, Document 1681, National Archives.
Lock or Locke's resignation from the Ninth Massachusetts Regiment was effective on April 26, 1778.

## Henry Young, Status of the Seventh Virginia Regiment

Camp Valley Forge April 6th 1778
As all the Officers of Capts Webbs, Poseys, Crocketts, Spencers, Hills & Lipscombs Company's are absent and all the Privates except 18 are discharged, on Furlough, at Hospitals &c. No particular account can be given of them as to their Numbers, time of discharge, terms or Service or other Casualties—
The above is true to the best of my Knowledge
Henry Young Capt.

Source: Record Group 93, M 246, Roll 104, f468, National Archives.
These few lines on the strength of the Seventh Virginia Regiment, emphasize how weak some of the units were, particularly those from Virginia and North Carolina.

## Tench Tilghman, Discharge for John Wilkins

Headquarters Valley Forge   The 7th of April 1778.
Captain John Wilkins, of Col. Spencer's Regiment, having desired to leave the service on account of the particular situation of his family and private affairs, his resignation is, upon that account accepted.
By his Excellency's Command,
Tench Tilghman

Source: *Manuscripts*. (Fall 1971), 274.
Wilkins' resignation from Spencer's Additional Continental Regiment was effective of April 8, 1778.

## William Cook, Diatribe Against William Alexander

*To* the Printer *of the* Pennsylvania Packet,
   SIR,
IN your paper of the 21st of January last, an advertisement of a very extraordinary and unprecedented nature appeared, signed by order of Major General Lord Stirling, by the Lordship's Aid de Camp, which must have greatly surprised the Public. Perhaps all the annals of the world cannot produce an instance of a Field Officer of the first rank being ignominiously advertised in a public news-paper before he had been previously condemned by a fair trial, and rendered obnoxious to his country, and a punishment so severe, and ruinous to his character. Lord Sterling is the first who has dared to attempt so flagrant an injustice. Such a procedure must have incensed all who are friends to the credit of our army, and given ground for ridicule to our enemies.

   I conceived myself aggrieved, and sent in my resignation; a privilege I thought every officer, in that case, had a right to do, and therefore made no doubt of its being accepted. If I was guilty of any misdemeanors, it was known where I might be found. I went to my home, whence I was liable to be summoned to answer any charges which might have been exhibited against me; instead of which I was publicly advertised as a criminal. I appeared and submitted to a trial—But lest the insinuations which his Lordship intended to destroy the character of a man who never injured him, and who made his duty as an Officer and Patriot his peculiar pleasure, should have the designed ill effect, I beg leave, through the channel of your useful paper, (the same in which my supposed disgrace was published) to lay the opinion and sentence of the Court martial before the Public; to whose candour I hope it will appear that his Lordship's behaviour to me has been cruel and unjust.
   I am, Sir,
      Your humble servant,   W. C.

*The following is the determination of the Court-martial.*

   "IT appears to the Court, having maturely considered the first instance of disobedience which Col. Cook is charged with, the evidence given respecting it, and Col. Cook's reasons, that Col. Cook did not go with his regiment when the brigade to which Col. Cook belongs did march toward the enemy, but they are of opinion, on account of Col. Cook's being unwell at the time, the greater part of the regiment being unfit for service and staying in camp, and the part of the regiment that went being sufficiently officered, they excuse him from censure; at the same time think he should have mentioned these circumstances to Lord Stirling, who commanded the division.

"The Court having considered the next instance of disobedience of orders that Col. Cook in charged with, the evidence and Col. Cook's defence, are of opinion that he, after having been refused leave of absence, did, without leave, leave camp, and did not return until near two months after he went away, being a breach of the General Orders of the 22d of December last, and contrary to good order and military discipline, and do sentence him, on account of the circumstances of Col. Cook's case, and on account of the good character he has sustained as an officer, only to be reprimanded in General Orders: They do acquit Col. Cook of giving leave of absence to officers of his regiment, and reporting them absent without leave, by which they were brought to their trial, by a Court martial, and acquitted. The Court adjourned till Monday next.

LACH, M'INTOSH, President."

"The Commander in Chief approves the sentence, and hopes the disgrace to an officer of Col. Cook's rank, of being found guilty of the charge of quitting camp without leave, will be a sufficient reprimand.

"The preceding is a true copy of the original,
N Gilman, Ad. Gen."

Colonel Cook, as well to do himself justice, as to satiety the impartial world, has published the foregoing proceedings of a Court Martial respecting his trial, from all which the candid reader may fully see the flimsey reasons upon which his Lordship founded his scandalous advertisemetn. And to what do these mighty charges amount to when all is done? Colonel Cook is only reprimanded in general orders. His Lordship's conduct, upon the whole, brings to my mind the fable concerning the birth of the mountains when they were in labour, and mankind, with anxious expectation waited for some wonderful, some monstrous production. What was the issue? A little mouse came creeping forth. *Parturiunt montes, nasectur rediculus mus.* A curiosity something similar to this has his Lordship raised in the minds of many, by his blustering advertisement. No doubt many have thought that even death itself was too small a punishment for a person obnoxious to such charges" When great things are threatened great things may be expected. But sure I am, those Members of the Court who have seen the ungentlemanly advertisement, and I believe they had all seen it, must be greatly surprised to find these mighty charges so much diminished, that had Colonel Harrison but remembered positively the receiving and reading Colonel Cook's resignation, in all probability the Court would have acquitted him. But why did not his Lordship express in the public papers the same charges that were exhibited to the Court? Nay; perhaps he thought, and indeed very justly too, that the most effectually way to destroy a good character is to give a sly broad hint, and then leave the reader's own imagination to suggest the rest.

Colonel Cook now submits to the candid public, who may judge impartially for themselves, whether the manner in which his Lordship has treated him, does not redound more to his Lordship's dishonour as a gentlemen, than to Colonel Cook.

Source: *The Pennsylvania Packet or the General Advertiser*, April 8, 1778.
Cook was Colonel of the Twelfth Pennsylvania, and his resignation was official on March 7, 1778. The advertisement referred to can be found in volume five of this series. A letter from Lord Stirling detailing his charges against Cooke is in volume 1. The Court met on March 10, and the results were posted in General Orders on March 14, 1778. The Latin phrase can be translated as: Mountains will be in labour, and an absurd mouse will be born.

## Robert Spencer to George Washington

Camp Valey Forge April 9$^{th}$. 1778
These are to certify that Capt$^n$ Britton of Col$^o$ Spencer's Reg$^t$. is not (to my knowledge) Indebted to the Regiment or the United States—
    Your Excellency's most Obed$^t$. Hble Servant
        Rob$^t$. Spencer P.M.

Source: RG 93, M 859, Roll 57, Document 17983, National Archives.
Captain William Brittin was allowed to resign, effective on April 10, 1778.

## Nathaniel Chipman to Elisha Lee

Valley Forge, April 10, 1778.
Dear Sir,—I have received letters from many of my old friends, but from you, Fitch and Coggswell, whom I esteemed my most intimate

friends, not a line. Letter after letter have I sent to no purpose—they may have indeed miscarried, though the opportunities were very direct. I am informed by letter from A—, that you are still teaching a school at Middletown.

How are times in Connecticut? What the run of politics? What plan of operations have your chimney-corner generals struck out for the next campaign? They have doubtless something in agitation. I saw an item of this in a letter from a gentleman of your acquaintance; I will give it you in his own words, as near as I can recollect them. "It is a disgrace to humanity, to Britons and Americans, that two such powerful armies, on whom the fate of Europe and America depends, should lie inactive. What can Howe, what can Washington mean? What stupidity! It is not enough that we carried the campaign through almost half the winter? No, we must still keep the field in defiance of frost and snow, or what at that season is still worse, rain and hail, though one half the army was disbanded and the other half worn out with fatigue. Nothing less will suffice than the siege of Philadelphia in the depth of winter. How mean, how despicable must such persons appear to men of the least reflection. Persons who never saw an army, or read of a battle, except in a newspaper, who, for intelligence, depend on common report at three hundred miles distance, and yet would persuade the world that they could direct the movements of an army better than an experienced general on the spot, who is minutely informed of every circumstance relative to both armies. That men, who pretend by be rational, should speak in this manner, is indeed 'a disgrace to humanity.'"

There is another thing that raises my indignation still higher. I learn that it is a common topic of conversation in Connecticut, and, indeed, through New England, that General Washington will not fight. "Let Gates," say they, "take the command, and we shall see an end of the war." General Gates has done well; he has done gloriously; I have as high a sense of his merit as any man. But the truth is, Burgoyne failed himself, and Gates conquered him. Besides, Gates was in a situation to command what assistance he pleased, and that the flower of the continent. What shall we say of Washington here at the head of fifteen, or at most twenty thousand men, for his army never exceeded that number, and one third of them Pennsylvania militia, who for the most part never dared to face an enemy. I have seen when our regiment was closely engaged, and almost surrounded, seven hundred of them quit the field without firing a gun. On the seventh of December, the army of the enemy, exclusive of those left to garrison Philadelphia, and the neighboring posts, amounted to eleven thousand effective men. From this you may judge of their strength at the opening of the campaign. There is not another state on the continent where so many traitors are to be found, as in this, and yet General Washington baffled all the stratagems of a wary, politic, and experienced general, and has several times fought him not unsuccessfully. All General Gates has done does not render it even probable, that in General Washington's situation he would not have been totally defeated. The army, to a man, except those who conquered under Gates, have the highest opinion of General Washington. They love, I had almost said, they adore him. While *he* lives, be assured, they will never brook the command of another. I cannot but observe here, that nothing has been more detrimental to us, than publicly exaggerating our strength, and diminishing that of the enemy; you will readily perceive the consequences. When the campaign will open I know not. The troops spend their time in discipline, in which they made great proficiency. We have for our inspector general, Baron Steuben, who has been aid-de-camp to the king of Prussia, and lieutenant-general in his service.

Source: Daniel Chipman, *The Life of Hon. Nathaniel Chipman, LL.D. Formerly Member of the United States Senate, and Chief Justice of the State of Vermont* (Boston: Charles C. Little and James Brown, 1846), 23-26.
Chipman was Second Lieutenant in the Second Connecticut Regiment. Lee was a Captain in the Fourth Connecticut.

## The Marquis de Lafayette to Horatio Gates

Camp near valley forge 10h April 1778

Dear Sir

I arrivd two days ago in this army and left general Connway at albany who will forward the coming down of some of the regiments garrisoned there—according to the instructions I have recieved before my departure—there has been a letter sent to albany by the board of war from a french oficer mr Segond, That gentleman is recomenanded to me, and I have wrote to Congress my desire of his being employd in our army—Count de pulaski will I believe make him an oficer in his legion which I think will be a very useful corps on account of the activity and military temper of her chief.

There is also at York a gentleman of my family who had left sick in carolina and by the neglect of some I need not to mention was

never sent for till this time—he has been excepted from the gen[coutule] of [17 Juliay] the french oficers sent by mr deane as he has been considered as one in my family what in fact he is—he was to be a Captain eighteen month ago, and I do not ask from Congress any particular thing for him but what they will judge proper—I am glad you have promised to general portail the plan of your last campaign because I will beg leave to take a copy of it
   very sincerely I have the honor to be
   Sir Your most obedient Servant

Source: Horatio Gates Papers, New-York Historical Society.
Segond was appointed a Captain in Pulaski's Legion about April 15, 1778. Capitaine, the second officer referred to, was appointed a Captain on April 16, 1778, to rank from December 1, 1776.

## Oliver Spencer to George Washington, Spencer to Tench Tilghman

Sir            Camp V. Forge April 10th 1778
  The Bearer Cap Jno. Maxwell of my Regt is induced to resign, on Account of the Difficult Situation of his Family. your Excellency's acceptance of his resignation will be Esteemed a favour—
  Im your Excellency's Most Obed$^t$. Hble Servt
    Oliver Spencer, Col.

Source: Record Group 93, M 859, Roll 58, Document 18283, National Archives.

Dear Sir         Camp Valley Forge April 11th 1778
The Bearer Cap$^t$. Maxwell has Settled his recruiting Acct. with me, & as to any other matters relative to the States he is not indebted, but rather on the Contrary,
  I am Sir Your Most Obed$^t$:

Source: Record Group 93, M 859, Roll 58, Document 18282, National Archives.
Captain John Maxwell's resignation was effective on April 11. Spencer was Colonel of Spencer's Additional Continental Regiment.

## Hugh Maxwell to Bethiah Maxwell

    Camp at Valy Forge. Saturday evening, April 11th, 1778.

My Dear,

When I consider up the Dealings of Providence towards you and I ever since we have had the pleasure of Being acquainted with Each other I am almost lost in wonder and astonishment—Not that we have ever Been Rich in the worlds good; but always Blessed with a Competency, So that if ever there was any thing wanting it was on our parts. that is thankful Hearts and Contented Minds—Besides our Health, our food, our Cloathing, and all that we have, let it be ever so much of this worlds good, will signify but little—without Contentment. If you Have Bread and Butter and Coffee and Tea and Cups and Saucers: yet you Know if you have not Sugar you cannot Make a pleasant Breakfast. Well it is Just So with Contentment it Sweetens all our Enjoyments and gives them a proper Relish.

If ever we were unhappy I think it is Being So Long Separated from each other and my long absence from our Dear little ones—But as—I am now in the line of my Duty—and—called to the unpleasing task of a Soldier, so we must look to that God—to govern our family and soon put an End to this Distressing war and Return me to you to take a Share of your Burdens and Rejoice with you—above all things for peace to this Dreadfully Distressed Country.

Do my Dear let us for once Supose the war is over! and peace established upon Honourable terms to america—We Shall not Begrudge all the Distresses and hardships we have suffered—so our Enemies may be at peace with us—That those Blessings may Soon take place—is the constant prayer and ever Shall be of him that with his Love to you and all our children Subscribs him Self your
    Hugh Maxwell

Source: Hugh Maxwell Papers, U.S. Army Military History Institute, Carlisle, Pennsylvania.


**Ebenezer Crosby to Daniel Newcomb**

      Flying Hospital, Camp Valley Forge April 12th. 1778—
Dear Sir,

I should have done myself the pleasure of writing you before this, had I not been prevented, first by Illness, and afterwards by a determination to leave Camp and return home, and only waited for the roads to become passable; but having entirely recovered my health while thus waiting, and being very desirous to see the event of the ensuing Campaign, I, a few days since, laid aside my former resolution, and with it all expectations of seeing you and my other Friends at Boston Hill—God only knows when.—I have nothing of a private or public nature to write, that will be either interesting or entertaining to you. As for our Army, which I must say some thing about, it is small but tolerable healthy, better clothed and on a much better and more respectable footing than ever before.—Large reinforcements are on their march from the Southward, some of which are expected in Camp in a few days. It is impossible to know the number of the enemy, but they must be weak, or certainly knowing our situation, as they did, they would have come out and put us to the utmost distress and danger, when we were not able to fight them with any prospect of success, or to retreat without leaving all of our artillery and baggage behind, for want of horses, having kill'd hundreds and rendered, I might say thousands, unfit for service during the winter thro' the great scarcity of forage—If our reinforcements arrive soon enough for the army to take the field before Genl. How is reinforced, there will be the greatest prospects of a successful Campaign, if not, I fear there will be but little done; as he will be able then to hold Phila. but cannot with his present force.—A Committee from Congress, one of whom was Mr. Daney, has been setting here great part of Winter, their chief business has been the new modeling the Army. They are gone to make their report to Congress, & it is generally thought the army will be put upon an establishment similar that of the British—

Please to give my Compliments to all Friends, & particularly to Dr. Greenleaf, if at home, and tell him, as the same causes prevented my writing to him before, as did to you, & as he told me he expected to go a privateering this Spring, I shall not write now 'till I hear from him.—I hope you will give me the pleasure of receiving a line from you, which shall be greatfully acknowledged by, Dear Sir, your much obliged Friend & Humble Servt.

Ebenr. Crosby—

To Mr. Daniel Newcomb
Addressed: Mr. Daniel Newcomb Boston—Favd. by Major French

Source: Newcomb Family Papers, Newcomb-Johnson Box 1, (7), The Huntington Library, San Marino, California.
Crosby was a Surgeon in the General Hospital. In 1779, he transferred to the Commander-in-Chief's Guard, and resigned in 1781.

## Benjamin Names, Receipt for Reenlistment Bounty

Recvd of Capt. Andw. Fitch ten Pounds Lawfull Mony as a bounty Given by the State of Connecticut to those who inlist in the Contanattal Army

Valy Forge
Ap$^l$. 12$^{th}$ 1778

Recvd pr me Benjamin X Names
his mark

verso Benj$^n$. Names
Rect £10-                         No 15

John Reed Collection, Valley Forge National Historical Park.
Names appears on a March 1778, muster roll for Fitch's company in the Fourth Connecticut Regiment as "Musterd not fit for the Service."

## Walter Stewart to Charles Stewart

Dr. Col                                              Sunday Morng.
    You will much Oblige me by furnishing my Servant with a little Salt to put up some butter making for me in the Country
    I shall send my Boy to your Quarters tomorrow Morning by Six OClock And Am Yrs sincerely
              W Stewart
In a different hand: Deliver'd ½ a Bushell salt
        April 12, 1778

Addressed: Col Chas. Stewart    Issuing Commy. Genl.

Source: Houghton Library, The Stewart Papers, bMS AM 1243, Number 277, Harvard University.
Walter Stewart was Colonel of the Thirteenth Pennsylvania Regiment. Charles Stewart was Commissary General of Issues, which meant he was in charge of the issues of food and spirits to the Continental Army.

## Nathaniel Chipman to Elisha Lee

Camp, at Valley-Forge, April 1778.
Dear Sir,—I had just sealed my letter No. 3, when yours of the 25th instant came to hand. I have prevailed on the post to wait for this. I have

in a former letter given you a particular account of my adventures since I saw you; but I suppose the letter miscarried. I have not now time to enter into details. As to the situation of the armies, Howe is in Philadelphia, and we are encamped and strongly fortified twenty miles above, on the banks of Schuylkill. I can give you no account of their intentions, since, whatever may be the reason, I have not of late been admitted to the cabinet. The officers of the army are at present in a great dilemma, whether in contempt of poverty and the unmerited reproaches of their ungrateful constituents, they shall still continue in the service of their country, or quit, and join with the rest of the world in the pursuit of riches. Depend upon it, if something is not done, most of them will resign, and that soon. I have no expectation of seeing you in the country till the close of another campaign. I have a letter from Swift. Please make him my compliments, and tell him I shall not fail of answering him by the first opportunity.

Source: Daniel Chipman, *The Life of Hon. Nathaniel Chipman, LL.D. Formerly Member of the United States Senate, and Chief Justice of the State of Vermont* (Boston: Charles C. Little and James Brown, 1846), 26-27.

## William Davies et al., Certificates for Gross Scruggs

By the resignation of Col. Marshall on the 9th Decr. 1777, Cap. Scruggs became entitled to a Majority, and is next in Seniority to Major Hopkins.

April 16. 1778.                William Davies.

Source: RG 93, M 859, Roll 110, Document 31249, National Archives.

This is to certify that I received all the Cloth & Trimings from Major Scruggs, which he got out of the Virga. State Store—for which I will answer—

                                Edwd. Duff
April 22$^{nd}$. 1778—          Surgn, 5$^{th}$. Virga. Regt.

On reverse: "Resignation 23d. April 1778 Major Scrugs Virginia—"

Source: Record Group 93, M 859, Roll 110, Document 31250, National Archives.

This certifieth that Majr. Scruggs is nothing indebted to the regiment—
April 22th. 1778    Andw: Russell Capt:
                    Comdt: 5th: V: Regt:
                    Wil Pride Qr. Mr.
                    Lipscomb Norvell P. M.

Source: Record Group 93, M 859, Roll 110, Document 31251, National Archives. Edward Duff was Surgeon, Ensign William Pride was serving as Quartermaster, and Lipscomb Norvell was Paymaster of the Fifth Virginia Regiment.
Gross Scruggs of the Fifth Virginia Regiment, was on furlough in January and February 1778, and apparently never returned to the army.

**William Bayley to Jean Bayley**

Valey forge in Pennsylvania About twenty miles Above Philadelphia April 16th 1778

Honoured Mother

I take this Opertunity Rite to You Hoping these fue Lines Will find You and Yours Injoying your and their Healths I Would inform You that I With the Rest of this Armey Have Had the small Pox and through the Great Goodness of God have had it Very favourable and Since I have bin Sick with a feaver but through God's mercy am Got Better—

I Should be Glad if You Would Send me Word in Your Next—Letter Weather these Shoos & Stockings Was Your Gift or the Towns if it Yours I have a Pair of Shoos & Stockings due from the Town I have Nothing more of News at Present and so must Conclude

Remembring my Love to my Brothers & Sisters Relations and inquiring friends

  So no more at Presant from your
    Dufifull Son  William Bayley
Addressed: to John Bayley

Source: Andrew Hawes Papers, Coll. 64, Box 2, Fl. 15, Maine Historical Society.

**Benjamin Fishbourne for Anthony Wayne, to Thomas Wharton Jr.**

Dear Sir, Camp,      Mount Joy, April 16th, 1778.

Capt. Irwin & Lieut. Vanlear, belonging to the Ninth Penns[a] Regiment, being now sent on the Recruiting service, they will waite of you for your Instructions; as these Gentlemen do not belong to General Wayne's Division, but to Lord Sterling's, you will please to note the same, they are of the Line of Penns[a], and will come under your Notice in the same manner as the former.

Col. Butler, to whom these Gentlemen belong, also requests Informing you that he has other officers from his Regiment on the same service. If they should want Cash for that purpose you will supply them. The Colonel writes, directing them to call on you for your orders.

I am your Excellencies Most obedient, Hu'ble Servant, For the
 Genl. & Self. By order of Genl. Wayne.
  Ben. Fishbourne, A. D. C.

Source: Samuel Hazard, ed., *Pennsylvania Archives* 1st ser., vol. 9, (Philadelphia: Joseph Severns & Co., 1854),
Captain Benjamin Fishbourne was an Aide-de-Camp to Wayne. Wharton was President of the Supreme Executive Council of Pennsylvania, then in Lancaster. He was in effect the governor of the state.

## Charles Stewart to Samuel Gray

Sir,         Commissaries Office 16th April, 1778.
 I am not a little surprised at the miscarriage of my Letter to you of the 17th. February, and now send you a copy. Could I suppose Letters by post subject to stoppage, I would have sent you a Coppy long since.
 Yesterday at Head Quarters yours of the 16th March was given me by Colonel Tilghman one of His Excellencys Aids de Camp—If your Returns do not come to hand in three or four days, I shall be obliged to proceed to Congress without them. Col Jones has nearly completed those of his Department, and his want of Money is so pressing, that he can wait no longer, without a supply. In hopes of getting the Monthly Returns from the several Deputy Commissaryes General, so as I might make a General Return, and an Estimate of the Monthly Expence of the Issuing Department, I have put of [*sic*] the journey as long as possible. I will after consulting with Coll Dyer, on the intended bounds of the District, in the Eastern States, apply to Congress if necessary, and have them fixed, I hope to your liking, and am,

Your Most Obedient Servant
Cha$^s$ Stewart C. G. of Issues.
Samuel Gray Esq$^r$.
D. C. G. of Issues, Fishkill.

Source: Peter Force Collection, Ms. 19,061, Series 7E, Item 137, Charles Stewart Papers, Roll 44, Library of Congress.
Gray was a Deputy Commissary General of Issues at Fish Kill, New York.

## Joseph Ward, an Appeal to the Generous and Brave

To the GENEROUS and BRAVE.

YOU only are the men to whom your country can look in the day of trial for assistance, and you are the instruments Heaven hath employed for her deliverance; therefore permit me to address myself to you in few words; a few to the wise is sufficient. In this month I left the camp of our southern army, and I have the pleasure to assure you, that notwithstanding the fatigues of the last campaign, and the hardships of the winter, the spirit of patriotism and valour glowed in the bosoms of the officers and men, all wishing for the arrival of the necessary reinforcements to extirpate the enemy, and put a glorious period to the war. Long and inactive campaigns are equally painful and injurious to the brave soldiers, and to the people at large; and millions of reasons now urge you to decisive exertions; there *was* a time for delay, but *now* is the time for action, and the united efforts of the *generous* and *brave* in these states will in a very few months deliver this country from the hostile rage of savage Britons. I speak confidently, because Heaven hath owned our cause, and never will forsake us, until we forsake our cause. The enemy's force is now small compared with what it hath been, and by pouring in early reinforcements to our army, they may be crushed before any assistance can arrive from Britain. This I know is the design of our General, and the wisdom of his design must strike every mind.

Some perhaps will suppose it unnecessary to send so large a reinforcement as the General may call for; and others make objections to sending men to this or that place; but we must confide in the wisdom of our General, we have sufficient reason so to do; and had all his calls been complied with, the last year would have seen an end to the enemy. And if his requisitions are complied with this year, I will pawn my honour and my life, that this year will see the enemy driven from every part of these united states.

All our misfortunes originate in indolence, we are ever too late in our business, let us be instructed by experience and now act the part wisdom dictates. Let us despite that timid unmanly spirit which dwells only in little souls, and harbours a thought of *dependence*. Act like yourselves, now rouse at the call of WASHINGTON and your *Country*, and you will soon be crowned with glory, independence and peace—This inestimable prize is before us, let us press on until we secure it.

Present ease and interest we must part with for a time, and let us rejoice at the sacrifice; like parting friends, we shall soon reimbrace with extacy of joy.

What words can paint the solid joys, the delightful contemplations, the high-born pleasures that will forever feast the patriotic mind! He that wishes for HAPPINESS let him *now* put forth all his strength for the immediate salvation of his country, and he shall reap immortal pleasure and renown.

It is good for us the anticipate the joy that will fill our minds, when we shall behold the reward of our labours, when we shall see our country flourish in peace, when grateful millions shall hail us the guardians of our country; and an approving conscience competes the transport of our bosoms and lights up the eternal sunshine in our souls!

*April* 16, 1778.                    A SOLDIER.

Source: *The Boston-Gazette, and Country Journal*, April 20, 1778.
This was written by Joseph Ward, Muster Master General.


**Elias Boudinot to John Winslow**

Sir                                    Camp Aprill 17th. 1778—
Your several Letters of the 8th. & 10th. Ins$^t$. safely came to hand—As to Ensign Oakley you may depend on his being returned if I can find him, if not shall do every thing that is just & equitable on the Settlement of the final Exchange—Mr. Marriner I know nothing of, if he is a military person, you may depend on the same Treatment with regard to him, as I shall do all I can to prevent any dishonorable Conduct in our Prisoners—

I do readily agree to the Exchange you mention of Lt. Whitworth for Lt. Duval and shall enter it accordingly—I have exchanged Lt. Middagh on Long Island with Mr. Ferguson for Lt. Stratton now at Philadelphia—

Am Sir Your Hble Servt
Elias Boudinot
Com Gen¹ of Pris

P.S. I send enclosed a Letter for Lt. John Priestly containing one half Joe

Source: Firestone Library, Princeton University.
Winslow was the British Deputy Commissary of Prisoners at New York City.


### Peter Stephen Du Ponceau to Nathanael Greene

Sir:  Camp, Valley Forge, April 17, 1778.

Baron Steuben would be much obliged to you if you would be so good as to give an order to major Craig to furnish him with two common tents, and that marquise which Col. Lutterloh had before his departure, which he has ceded to the baron. Moreover, sir, you would oblige him very much by ordering your deputies to furnish him with three wooden bowls, and four or five wooden trenchers. Meanwhile the baron presents his compliments to you.

I have the honour to be sir,
Your most obedient And very humble servant,
P. S. DU PONCEAU, A. D. C.
To the Hon. Maj. Gen. Greene.

Source" Robley Dunglison, "Biographical Sketch of Peter S. Du Ponceau," *American Law Magazine*. vol. 5, no. 9 (April 1845), 9.
Captain DuPonceau was an Aide-de-Camp to Baron Steuben


### Hugh Maxwell to Bethiah Maxwell

My Dear,  April 19, 1778.

I am Never Weary of writing to you any More than I was ever weary of Talking with you in those pleasing Days wherein I enjoyed your company. Five or Six Days ago I Sent you a long Epistle. I Hope you will receive it Safe. It is now Sunday five o'clock afternoon a Very fine Day—I Supose you Just Returned Home from Meeting with your Family around you—I can form an Idea in my mind of you all and fix in my Fancy Just how I think you Look and from my Heart lift up a Hearty prayer—for you all by Name—and Deliver us from this callamity of war for we are Brought Very low well the time will come—

the Men are affraid to Send letters for Fear of the Small pox going Home in them and you must be Very carefull that your Letters are well Smoked before you let any Body Handle them that Never had it. I Sent my last letters by Lieut Allen of Ashfield—in them Sent what I thought was proper for you to Do with your Farm but after all you are the best Judge of what is Nessesary. There has nothing turned up Since that that gives me any Encouragement that I can get home Soon but I dont think it will be long till there dos and you may Depend on my taking the first oppertunity to See you. Let me Beg of you my Dear to Settle your mind in Patience—you know your trouble afflicts me and that it would give me great pleasure to Know that with the courage and Fortitude of a Heroine which is a Female Hero you Suported your Self in all your Trials.

In Hopes Soon to See you and Bring my love to you and to all my Dear little ones I Subscibe my Self your Loving
Hugh Maxwell

P.S. cleanse Mrs. Davidsons Letter well of the Small pox by Smokeing it well. Shiner and Cutting is very well but think best not to Send letters at present. you may Depend that our Money is in higher Demand and Better credit—I mean 20 Dollars of it will purchase more in the city of Philadelphia than in any part of New England and that English and west india goods are Sold cheaper for paper money in Philadelphia or New York cities than in Boston and to Day we Hear that the court of Great Britain has Made Some proposals to America for peace—I wish they may make Such proposals as we could agree to I Should think my Self that my post Script is long but there is an Ending to it. H.M.

Source: Hugh Maxwell Papers, U.S. Army Military History Institute, Carlisle, Pennsylvania.

## Elias Boudinot to Robert Livingston, Jr.

Sir  Camp Aprill 20. 1778 –
A long absence from Camp has been the reason of an Answer to your favour of the 8th March being so long delayed—

It would give me great Pleasure to receive the Supply of flour & what you mention but I cannot possibly take upon me to give more than the regulated Prices without an Order from Congress –

The sufferings of the Prisoners would make me do almost any Thing in my Power to relieve them, but here my hands are tyed—All I have yet purchased in Jersey has been at the regulated Prices, and no more is given in this State—

I am Sir with great Respect
>ELIAS BOUDINOT
>Com: Genl of Priss.

Robt Livingston Esqr

SOURCE: Gilder Lehrman Collection, GLC 03107.03371, On deposit in the New-York Historical Society.
Livingston was Chancellor of the State of New York. In 1789 he administered the Oath of Office to George Washington.


## Andrew Dunlap to Leonard Bronck

Dear Sir          Head Quars, Valley Forge   April 23d, 1778.

I embrace this as a favourable Opportunity to inform you that I am safely arrived at the above mentioned place where I found our regiment, I have seen your old acquaintance Mr. Allen, Adjutant to Coll. Jackson's Reg't. at this place, he desires to be remembered to you.

I can with pleasure inform you that I am well, hope these may find you and father's family the same together with all old acquaintances.

Should be happy if I could send you some news, but what we have is so immaterial this is not worth notice. You will do me a favour to give my compliments to Betsy Tryon, Rachel Dedrick & Fanny Tryon and their respective families

>Am sir your Affectionate friend,
>Andrew Dunlap

Addressed: to Capt. Leonard Bronck, Coxsackie.

Source: *The Spirit of '76* (January 1900), 6, no. 5, 84.


## Samuel Tenny to Peter Turner

Dear Doctor              From our Den, April, 23rd. 1778—

I am to acknowledge the Receipt of yours of the 4th April & make you as good a Return as the very short Time allow'd me for writing will permit.—As I esteem a sincere Friend as a kind of second self, I heartily rejoice in the good Fortune you are so happy as to meet with at Home; & wish for a continuance of it. Could I be a Sharer it it, according to your generous Wish, I dare say the Happiness of us both would be encreas'd by the Partnership But this the Fates deny. While you are in the peaceable Enjoyment of all the Conveniences & Delicaces of Life that an Epicure could wish, and add to these the Conversation of agreable Friends & the rapturous Embraces of your charming Eliza, I—poor I—eat the Scanty Allowance of a common Soldier, drink a little vile Whiskey once in a while, & if by Chance I see a pretty Lady riding thro' Camp, gaze like an Astronomer at a Comet, & think myself as happy, as the Times will allow—Oh, my Friend, this is not living,—Tis barely existing, & God knows when Times will mend. One Thing I am determin'd upon, & may Poverty never intervene to counteract my Intentions; & that is, if I live thro the War, to spend the same Number of years & months I have been in the army, in all the Luxury of Living, This I think is the only way to get the Ballance that will be due.—

We have nothing remarkabl. to communicate. Little Corneille has been lucky enough to make his Escape & join us—upon which Parish set out to join you; with 20 Days Furlough; perhaps he is with you by this.—

I sincerely wish for your Company, but chearfully submit to the Fortune that keeps us apart because it is favourable to you.—Please to make my best Compliments to your Eliza, & all Friends: & let my Assiduity in writing, rather than base professions, convince you of the Sincerity & Affection with which I wish to be esteem'd,

Dear Sir, your Friend & hl Servt.
S. Tenny—

Source: Peter Turner Papers, Box 1, William L. Clements Library, University of Michigan.
"Little Corneille" is apparently Surgeon's Mate Elias Cornelius of the Second Rhode Island Regiment, who had been taken prisoner on August 22, 1777, and appears on the muster rolls at Valley Forge beginning in April. John Parrish was Surgeon's Mate in the Second Rhode Island, transferred to the First Rhode Island in April 1778.

## Tunis Van Waganer to Leonard Bronck

Dear Sir                               Head Quarters April 23d. 78
Received your kind favor of the 2nd inst. and am very glad you and relations are well. We hear that Col. Van Schaik's Reg't is on their march for this place and our reg't is ordered to the Highlands. If that is the case you may expect to see me next Pingster.

Am very glad to hear that you are in such a good posture of defence in the Highlands. As to news here we have none of Consequence. Am under many obligations to you for favoring me with a disposition of the ladies in your quarter, am very glad that in your opinion they are disposed to favor gentlemen with their agreeable company, but I am sure you aught to condole with me for the difficulty I undergo, that is, absent from them all, while you and the rest of your neighboring young gentlemen are enjoying the sweets and ease of a private life. Tho I think if I was there this moment I should find out whether they were the genuine thing or not, or I much mistaken. And as to them longing for matrimony with those that are agreeable I join you in sentiments and are of opinion that a great many young men are rather dilatory, or they would relieve some of the suffering ladies.

I don't say this as a reflection on you, it is only an observation on some others of my acquaintance. You may read those two clauses to Jacob Van Vechten.

Am glad to hear that you was with my favorites, as you style them, am glad you entertain so high an opinion of them. I sympathize with these former as well as with yourself for the loss of her mother and you may be sure that I am happy to think that I am not out of memory tho absent and shall expect to hear further from Sir,
          Your affectionate driend
                and humble servant,

Source: *The Spirit of '76* (January 1900), 6, no. 5, 84-85.
Van Waganer was a Second Lieutenant in the Second New York Regiment.

## John Chessborough, Advertisement for Missing Horse

                          Camp, Valley Forge, April 24, 1778.
STRAYED or STOLEN from the subscriber, Assistant Commissary of Issues to the North Carolina brigade, a light bodied grey MARE,

about fourteen hands high, five years old this spring, trots and paces, but inclines most to the latter, has not any brand that is perceivable, but is remarkable for the mounting lock, or that part of the mane next the saddle being much whiter than any of the rest—any person securing the said mare so that the owner may get her again, shall receive EIGHT DOLLARS reward,
                    from JOHN CHEESBOROUGH.

Source: *The Pennsylvania Packet*, April 29, 1778.

## John Gibson, Certificate for Hardin Perkins

April 26th. 1778. This may Certify that Lieu$^t$. Hardin Perkins of the 6th. Virginia Regiment, is not Indebted to the Regiment to Knowledge             Jno. Gibson Co$^l$
                             6 Virg Reg$^t$

Source: Record Group 93, M 859, Roll 110, Document 31340, National Archives. Gibson was Colonel of the Sixth Virginia Regiment. First Lieutenant Perkins, of the same regiment, was allowed to resign on April 26, 1778.

## Friedrich Wilhelm Augustus von Steuben to Henry Laurens

Honble Sir                    Camp Valley Forge April 26th. 1778.
    I have had the honor to write to your Excellency on Acct. of Capt Landais a brave and Experienced Officer in the French Service. I am very glad that you are able to Judge yourself of his merit and Abilities, and I am sure that you will Soon be convinced that he does not fall Short of the picture I have made of him.
    When you have heard him and read the papers he will produce to you, you will think it a real advantage for America to possess Such a deserving officer. The Interest I take to any Thing that regards your Nation, makes me wish that this officer be employed So as to afford Honor to him and Advantage to the Country But I am persuaded that his own Merit will be a Stronger Recommendation for him, than any thing I could say to your Excellency in his favor, I shall therefore leave it to your Prudence to Judge of his Abilities and to deal accordingly
        I have the honor to be Honorable Sir Your Excellencys

Most Obedient & Most humble Servt
Steuben

Source: Henry Laurens Papers, Roll 9, South Carolina Historical Society.
Landais had commanded the ship which brought Steuben to America. Congress gave him the command of the frigate *Alliance* in which he had a very erratic record. He is best known for firing into John Paul Jones's *Bon Homme Richard* at the Battle of Flamborough Head.

## Albigence Waldo, April 26, 1778

VALLEY FORGE
A poem by Dr. Albigence Waldo.
Second Line, in Camp.
Valley Forge, April 26th, 1778.

PRAISE OF THE CAMP AND ITS FOUNDER, WASHINGTON.
    'Tis not each aspiring dome
That graced the streets of ancient Rome.—
Not Troy's high walls, that rais'd the eyes
With tow'ring spires toward the skies.—
Not London's pride—that painted Doll,
Though once our happy Capitol—
Can equal, as the world must own,
This spacious Camp of WASHINGTON!
Such columns and high towers as those,
Which art and grandeur did compose
With spacious Mosques, and Domes of yore
Where labor'd works of year before,
Where Women painful "vigils kept,"
And sometimes pray'd, or whor'd, or wept.

    Not gradual thus, with slow device,
Did this fair Camp in order rise,
Ere two revolving Moons were past,
From a thick wood and ruthful waste,
Regular—numerous huts do rise,
Lay wide a prospect to the skies,
And when the eyes the whole pursue
Camps, Forts, Picquets, Breastworks rise in view,

Green hills, green forests, field and vales,
Plantations, plains, and flow'ry dales,—
Various pleasures these prospects bring
Now Phoebus ushers in the Spring.

But here to sing the General's praise,
With WASHINGTON to grace my lays,
Would strain my muse beyond its pow'r,
And ev'n true praise itself devour,
Yet still I must and will impart
A verse or two to shew my heart.

Oh, WASHINGTON! what soul like thine,
If aught below can be divine,—
'Tis thou!— 'in every instance try'd
Above all passion, pain, or pride,
Or pow'r, or rage of public breath,
Vile Lucre,' or the dread of Death.
Not one that knows thee but must love—
Those that but see thee will approve!
The World and Angels do commend
The heav'n-born Universal Friend!
Oh, could I reach the true sublime!
Transmit his worth to the latest time!
In son'rous verse sublimely raise
His virtues and deserved praise,
Quartos and folios I'd write upon
And shew the world a WASHINGTON!

But let me shrink into myself,
Least from Parnassus some vile Elf
From tall Pergassus tumble me
And make me but too plainly see
I ne'er was born nor made a Poet,
Make all that know me, and Celia, know it,
Therefore I'll softly walk along
And humbly sing my narrative song.

A FAIR DAY, AND THE DIVERSIONS OF THE ARMY.

Now from the East the morning ray
Beams genial mildness on the day,
Warm zephyrs gently fan the plain
The clouds are fled and the skies serene,
The dancing nymphs and sportive swains
Are lightly skipping o'er the plains,
The day serene—joy sparkles round
Camp, hills and dales with mirth resound,
All with clean clothes and powder'd hair
For sport or duty now appear,
Here squads in martial exercise,
There whole Brigades in order rise,
With cautious steps the march, and wheel.
Double,—form ranks,—plattoons,—at will.
Columns on columns justly roll,
Advance, retreat, or form one whole,
Now evolutions, grand go through
When all the varying glitters shew,
Of guns and bayonets, polished bright,
Which dazzle the spectators' sight
Here bashful modesty must hide
Its face, and give full scope to pride.
Here the grand strut, and stately mien
Advances from their humble screen,
For if the soldier fails t' exert
His utmost pomp and pride of heart—
He's from the column set aside
Till learn'd in military pride

Next diff'rent Sent'nels there and here,
To guard our flanks, and front, and rear,
Picquets at distance watch the foe
While Scouts are marching to and fro.

Then diff'rent companies are found
Gather'd on various plats of ground
Wher'er the elastic Ball will hop,
Or on clean, even places drop,
When the strong Butt's propelling force
Mounts it in air, an oblique course.

One Choix at Fives are earnest here,
Another furious at Cricket there.
At Fives th' experienced active hand
Will have the Ball at his command,
Which mounts, rebounds, remounts, at will
Till each one curse him for his skill.—
At Cricket, him who bowls with force
Evades the Batt's half circling course,
Which, if not nimbly urged on
The Ball may strike the Cricket down.
A third—at batt—contend alike
Who best can catch, or best can strike.
A fourth at bowling rack their skill
Who best can toss the bowl at will,
Who its rotations can confine,
That one fair bowling lay the nine.

   Others, less fond of these diversions,
Walk round in useful conversations,
Or to some silent hut repair
That grog affords and homely fair:
Here Spanish Poles amuse the mind,
Now from each gloomy thought refin'd.
And close attention does afford
Least the first monarch rule the board.

   Now Phoebus plunges in the sea
And the gray ev'ning shuts the day,
All parties to prepare for musings
Repair to huts and drink the loosings.
There, loud talking soon begins
Of who plays best, and who most wins.
Of politics, or frothy matter
That sudden raises gen'ral clatter.
Then of cowards, fools, rascals, rattles,
Of duels, heroes, wars and battles,
Of fornicators, witches, scolds,
Fatigues and hardships, heats and colds,
Of beauty, women, wine, and love,
Of thund'ring armies and of Jove.

Huzza! the chorus loudly cry,
Responsive vales Huzza! reply.
Toasts for the Cause, for sweethearts, wives,
Long peace, long health, and happy lives.
Huzza! again, loud rings the chorus,
For Heav'n and Washington are for us:
'Then all being hush'd,' by wine or rum,
They sound an equal gen'ral hum.
So distant Cannon loudly roar
When first in air th' explosions bore,
Till waves of sound grow weak and thin
And sink away in gradual din.

## A STORMY DAY, AND THE HARDSHIPS ATTENDING IT WHEN THE ARMY ARE IN TENTS.

  From the propitious day serene,
My rugged fancy shifts the scene
From sports, and drinking, (in due form,)
Now views the horrors of a storm.
See, yonder black'ning vapors rise,
Sudden o'erspread the lurid skies.
Some scatt'ring rays the shroud pervade
Disclose the melancholly shade,
Dread horrors spreading round us here
While heav'n's artillery draws near,
The pond'rous clouds with water pent
By bursting peals will soon be rent.
Now livid flashes dart around
And spread in clouds or pierce the ground,—
Now peals on peals of thunder roll,
With trembling horrors fill the soul!
While bursting clouds pour down in floods,
On hills, in vales, on plains and woods.

  Th' astonish'd herds with sudden fright
Fly to some covert first in sight.
Houses that ancient labor rear'd
Or simpler modern arts prepar'd
Secures th' inhabitants from rain
Or all the blasts of Eolus' train.

But not so in the field of Mars,
The scene of hardships, storms, and wars.
Though huts in windter shelter give,
Yet the thin tents in which we live,
Through a long summer's hard campaign,
Are slender coverts from the rain,
And oft no friendly barn is nigh
Or friendlier house to keep us dry,
When'er the movements of the foe
Oblige an army to forego
All sleep,—and nights in fatal damp
Make forced marches or encamp
In some foul field or fenny places
Where nightly dews o'erspread our faces,—
Or floods of rain from heav'n descend
And drive us all to our wits' end.
Here, some amid the gloomy night
Move tents and baggade to some height,
And on wet clothes, wet blankets lie
Till welcome sunshine makes them dry,
Others despising storms and rain
Still in the flat or vale remain,
There sleep in water, mud, and mire,
Or drizzling stand before a fire
Composed of stately piles of wood,
Yet oft extinguished with the flood.

Th' unhappy sick, destin'd by fate
To languish in this hopeless state
Forlorn, half cover'd, shiv'ring wet,
Not one dry place to lay or set,
Their groans from weakness, faintness, pain,
Mingling with noise of wind and rain
Augment the scene, and make the whole
With pitying anguish fill the soul.

And yonder soldier, doom'd to stand
By his superior's just command,
Out-braves the force of storm and wind

With firm and persevering mind.
In open field—with wakeful eye
To watch each lurking enemy,
To guard the camp by day and night
From each assault or sudden fright.
Such equally demand regard
And claim their Country's just reward.

  If pain or sickness rack the soul,
The stranger chiefly can condole
And lend to us his friendly aid
His house afford;—perhaps a bed,—
The Wife's or Parents' tender care!
Is not to be expected here.

A BATTLE, AND THE HARDSHIPS CONTINUED.

  Now slightly view the distant battle
Where drum, and arms, and armies rattle.
See yonder boasting foes advancing
With fiery steeds on each wing prancing.
View their fell rage, their dreadful glitter
As if a hundred worlds they'd fritter.
Th' affected pride of Albion's race
Grins terribly in every face.
With cautious boldness they proceed,
Experience seems to wing their speed,
And now in solid columns form,
Dread omen of a deadly storm.

  Then see Columbia's sons parade
With nobly calm and martial pride.
Firm virtuous rage—benevolence—
Distinguish every countenance.
Determined, they rush to the place
With wond'rous military grace,
Where the fierce foes disdainful come,
And there in equal columns form.

  Then the thundering armies meet,

Each heart with furious rage does beat,
For death or vic'try all prepare,
And now loud volleys rend the air.
Here smoke in spacious volumes rise
That seem to shroud th' affrighted shies,
While darting fires flash through the volumes
And leaden deaths break ranks and columns.
Yonder, amid those balls and flashes,
The bayonet's fatal thrusts and clashes
Of glitt'ring swords—behind—before—
Empurple th' earth with human gore.
Columns on columns urge their way,
Increasing terrors each display,
While winged balls fly swift around
Lays hundred welt'ring on the ground.
Volleys on volleys incessant rend
The trembling air—loud shrieks ascend—
And dismal groans from mangled men
Augmenting the terrific scene
Till the proud foes are vanquish'd quite
And sudden taken themselves to flight.
Now shouts of vic'try shake the ground
And all th' adjacent vales resound
Then from the hostile bloody plain
Those who survive amidst the slain,
Are each one safe convey'd away,
And sable night shuts up the day.

 Such are the hardships, toils, and pains;
And such the pleasures of campaigns.
To these just as the laboring marches
In summer's heat, when the sun parches,
Through sandy plains and clouds of dust
With the extremes of heat and thirst,
Till some fair spring we come athwart
And careful quench our parching drought.

 Here oft the thoughtless soldiers try
T' extinguish thirst too suddenly,
Who by full draughts of the cool rill

Their heated juices instant chill.
Hence dire diseases here begin,
Or sudden deaths close up the scene.

  Yet, not in Summer, we, alone
Do joyless march in heat of sun,
But also in bleak Autumn's days
And colder nights—when no delays
Admit refreshments to be giv'n,
Nor aught to cover us by heav'n.
The frozen ground our fated bed,
On rails or logs we rest the head,
Or like a herd of friendly swine
Together numbers of us join
And parallel stretch ourselves along
With heads to tails, a medley throng.

  And when some days we've not a bit
Of wholesome ailment to eat,
And every friendly bottle drean'd,
From which 'tis hardship to be wean'd.
Night comes on us in this condition
Yet still we march with frank submission,
Bleak fields oft make us jump behind
Some neighb'ring tree to 'scape the wind.
Near day the whole are bid to halt,
Take rest—without bread, meat, or salt.
A gentle sighing's heard around
We faintly tumble on the ground,
Strive to compose ourselves to sleep
'And pray the Lord our souls to keep.'

  Such toils with dread I now review
Since I'd a portion of them too,
The home-stuff'd, gay, licentious, proud
Who feast amidst a pleasing crowd
Of friends, relations and females
Enjoy their pleasures by 'details,'
Think little of the pains there are
In these unpleasing scenes of war.

## COMPLAINT OF THE WANT OF FEMALE PLEASURES, ETC.

Celia! think not we roam abroad,
Enjoy the pleasures of a lord,
And feast on Women, Wine, and Love,
Which virtue never will approve.
No! here our minds pensively roam O'er the past scenes enjoy'd at home,
That give superior pleasures, too, Than ev'ry scene we here go through.
   Though friends are firm and lasting here,
A pleasure that is ever near,—
Through Honor and our Country's love
With hopeful favors from above
Are strong incitements to endure
Those toils, such noble joys t' insure.
Yet a mighty void remains,
The soul is still represt with pains
Such as myself here never find
The softer pleasures of the mind—
The pleasures that in Women are,
That gently smooth the 'brow of care.'
   What! though there are, in rags, in crape,
Some beings here in female shape, In whom may still be found some traces of former beauty in their faces,
Yet now so far from being nice
They boast of ev'ry barefaced vice.
Shame to their sex! 'Tis not in these
One e'er beholds those charms that please.
   But happy for sire Adam's race
Eve still has daughters who have grace
And native purity retin'd
That adds sweet lustre to the mind.

   How sweet the thought of being possess'd
Of a fair one, with virtue bless'd
Whose soul is moulded to our own,
Whose tend'rest love is ours alone,
In whose soft bosoms when reclin'd
We taste the pleasures of the mind;

He converse ev'ry gloom suppresses,
Her pity banishes distresses,
And like a pleasing morning ray
Lights up the soul to open day.
Her gentle smiles becalm the mind
And make the veriest savage kind,
Dispel each angry rugged feature,
Convert a man t' a human creature,
Prepare the soul to hold converse
With beings of superior race.
Such is the pow'r of female sweetness,
Virtue, elegance, and neatness,
And such the spouse indulgent Heav'n
To favor'd Alphonso have giv'n.

### CONCLUSION.

Thus, Celia! I have brief related
Th' unpleasing scenes to which we're fated.
Accept it as a real proof
Of my affection and my love.
Nor think that I, who am so lazy,
Would e'er have wrote so much to please ye
Was not my friendship for you more
Than e'er a husband's was before.

My muse can now no further pass
But end with lines from Hudibras,
To make you willingly dispense
With each bad rhyme and more bad sense,
To take my meaning as intended
With truth and plain narration blended,
Which here shall stand as my Preface
Although put in uncommon place,
Make all apology for this
New narrative ling-letter—viz:
'Those that write in rhyme still make
The one verse for the other's sake—
For one for Sense, on one for Rhyme
I think's sufficient at one time.'

Source: *The Historical Magazine, and Notes and Queries, concerning the Antiquities, History and Biography of America.* Vol. 7, series 1 (September 1863), 272-274. The first part of the poem was published in Book Five of this series.

**Adam Allen Receipt**

Camp Valey Forge 27th Apl. 1778 Recd from Ephraim Blaine the under mentioned Sums Vizt

| | |
|---|---|
| Capt. Van Sweringham his own Horse | £ 6. "—" |
| Ditto One For Baggage | 3..18—" |
| Captn. Findlays | 3. 18—" |
| Lieutn. Ambersons | 3..18—" |
| Lieutn. Neely | 3..18—" |
| | £21" 12—" |

on Acct. of Horse hire from the Kittaney to Carlisle—

        his
Adam X Allen
     mark

Source: Peter Force Collection, Series 8D, frame 2217, Library of Congress. This may have been Adam Allen of the First Pennsylvania Regiment.

**Francis Barber to Richard Kidder Meade**

Sir

I obtained a Captain's Commission dated the twenty sixth of last October for the Bearer Captain Anderson of the Third Jersey Regiment, which he accidentally lost.—I request you will confer a Commission of the same date upon him.

    I am, Sir, your very humble Servt.
        F. Barber Lt Colo. 3rd Jers: Reg
          April-28th: 1778
Lt Colo. Mead

Source: Record Group 93, M 859, Roll 12, Document 3971, National Archives.
Joseph Inslee Anderson served to the close of the war.

## James Mitchell Varnum to John Sullivan

Sir                         Camp Valley Forge 28th April 1778

    Since my last, wch I hope has reach'd you, two pestiferous Blasts have been raised by the invisible Influences of Toryism. Colo Carleton called upon, & drawing many Circles and other astrological figures upon the Bridge, at length allayed their Fury.—Whether he is possessed of the Staff found by Camillus after the Conflagration of Rome by Berennus King of the Gauls, with wch Romulus divided the Heavens, Or whether the Neads of Scotland have reascended to Earth, and inspired the neutal Powers of his Mind with magic Art; Or whether some of the supernal Genii agitate him, is uncertain; But all agree that there is something misticle in his Operations.—In Camp, we fare much better than heretofore; Recruits come in very cleverly from Virginia: The Doctors at the Hospitals are graciously pleased to send us a considerable Number, & Old Scammell says the Enemy dare not attack us. At any Rate, we do not imagine they are inclined to disturb us much, as Lord North and the Devil have made a League to appear in the borrowed Garb of Ithurial, & sooth America into political Security 'till their Reinforcements can arrive from Europe.— It is incumbent on us to clapperclaw them in the Interim. If the States assert themselves we shall do it: If not, let them be Slaves.

    General Lee is exchanged.—Baron Du Calb is going the France, & Monsieur le Congrie have said nothing, as yet, about the Arrangement of the Army. This Delay, horrid Delay, keeps us relaxed; but Baron Stupend is very advantageous in disciplining the Troops.—

    The Enemy are pretty quiet, and in great Uneasiness. Lord & Gen$^l$ Howe are going home. Sr G. Amherst & Adl Keppel are to succeed them; & his most Satannic Majisty is to be Lord Lieutenant of North America, with two Foutre le Changs for Secretaries &c.—

    You have no Letters from the Post Officer here, that I can discover. I have inquired frequently. I hope you will honor me with a Correspondence.—Whither you do or not, I shall continue to fulfill my part of the Ingagement; & at the End of the War, either at an earthly or etherial Tribunal, shall bring an Action of the Causus Assumsit against you for all Delinquencies.—

Monsieur D Lisle has published a damned, rascally Piece in the last Jersey Paper, blackguarding the Army &c &c—I have fixed & sent one Dose for him, & shall visit him with two more, and then a Sermon I shall soon publish, & send you a Copy; But is to Be kept a Secret.—For is it a common Maxim, though not true, "that good cannot come from Evil.—Capt Sullivan's Chest is still with me; I shall take the best Care of it, & send it with my Baggage. When that happens I will write you according to his request.—I am only waiting to know precisely the Doings of Congress, to determine me whither I shall send a part, or the whole of my Baggage to Rhode Island.—If the Enemy remain at Rhode Island, it will be in your Power, I imagine, to influence the Troops of that State being sent there; Had it not been from the Sentiment of Governor Cooke they would have been sent undoubtedly, as the matter was pretty well fixed—Should they not remain, I expect to meet you at a middle Distance, or somewhere else—Genl Washington shines with additional Lustre, and is the Adoration of the Army.

The Struggle between Duty to the public, & domestic Affection give me great Inquietude; But as Toryism is almost vanquished, I expect soon to be able to impartially to decide, & follow the Result of a mature Judgment, so as to feel no Stings of Conscience in the Result.

Be pleased to mention me, with great affection & Esteem to your Family, & accept of the sincere Service of your ever faithful & devoted Friend—

Source: Sullivan Papers, New Hampshire Historical Society.
Major General John Sullivan had been in charge of building the bridge across the Schuylkill River after the army arrived at Valley Forge. In late March 1778, he left Valley Forge to assume command of a force in Rhode Island in an effort to push the British out of Newport.

## Clement Biddle to Moore Furman

Dr Sir                                       Moorhall 29 April 1778

Inclosed is List of the persons Employ'd in my Department in Jersey except Sussex.—I shall write to each of them to take their Directions & to be subordinate to you—You will please to direct the Light horse Accounts since 1st. March to be paid off—much is due on them—

Genl. Greene informs me you have an Order for a Sum on your Treasury—dont let the Forage Branch suffer & any that you use of it thereror shall be replaced or Carried to my debit here—

I beg you to use to utmost delegince in having the quantities mentiond in the List layd in varying the places as you judge best to answer the General plan—Troops will be daily coming from the Eastward & it is probable that the Enemy move to the North River in which Case the Forage would be wanted for our Whole Army & Not a moment should be lost to prepare it—

    I am DSir Yr. mo: Obed Serv
      Clement Biddle
       CGF

On Public Service By Express
To Moore Furman Esqr.
D Q M Genl Pitts Town

Source: RG Dept. of Defense, Subgroup: Adjutant General's Office (Revolutionary War), Numbered Manuscripts, Roll 13, Mss. No. 4665. New Jersey State Archives.

Quantities of Hay & Grain proposed at the following places with as much Straw as could be got—to be constantly kept up.—

|  | Bushl Grain | Tonns hay |
|---|---|---|
| Pompton | 3000 | 75 |
| Morris Town | 3000 | 75 |
| Fleming Town | 6000 | 150 |
| Pitts Town | 6000 | 150 |
| Suckasunny | 6000 | 150 |
| Hackets Town | 5000 | 125 |
| Alexandria | 6000 | 150 |
| Coryells ferry | 2000 | 50 |

    Moorhall 29 April 1778
    Clement Biddle  CGF

List of Persons employ'd in the Forage Department in the State of New Jersey—except Sussex—

| District or | Persons employd | Forage Masters— |
|---|---|---|

| District or Magazine | Persons employd to Purchase | Forage Masters— |
|---|---|---|
| South of the road from Trenton to Woodbridge to supply Brunswick Princeton Trenton & Allen Town— | Coll Elisha Lawrence—named by him— | |
| Springfield & | Revd Mr. Caldwell | Springfield retained by Revd Caldwell |
| Elizabeth Town | Mr. M. Williamson | Mr. Williamson at Elizabeth Town— |
| Raway Woodbridge &c | Mr. De. Marsh is well Acquainted & a good hand—not now in Employ—he has a press erected— | |
| Pompton— | Peter Kinnant | Mr. [blank] is named Forage Mr there |
| Suckasuny— | Chr. Banker | Chr. Banker FM. Mr Fitzrandolph has Assisted—if he continues he must take the Oath to the States— |
| Brunswick— | Mr. Jno. Staats is there by order of QMG | |
| Morris Town— | C. Banker & Mr. Jno. Pomeroy for Issues— Caldwell for hay Suckasunny, Grain Springfield Hay | |
| Fleming Town | Wm Lowrey— | Wm Lowrey— |
| Alexandria— | John Sherrard— | Jno. Sherrard— |
| Coryells Ferry— | Emanuel Coryell | E Coryell |

Source: RG Dept. of Defense, Subgroup: Adjutant General's Office (Revolutionary War), Numbered Manuscripts, Roll 12, Mss. No. 4409. New Jersey State Archives.

Dr Sir  Moorhall 29 April 1778

I wrote to you this Morning by Express—Mr. Wm. Lowrey Son of our Friend Thos Lowrey has Acted for some time not only in the purchasing of Forage but as Quarter Master at that post—his Conduct therein has been such as to deserve Commendation—his Accounts have been Regular & the business well managed—

Your attending to him as far as can be done in the New Arrangement I shall esteem as a particular favour Conferd on Dr Sir

Your mo: Obed. Servt
Clement Biddle

Addressed: To Moore Furman Esquire
D. Qur. Mr. Genl. Pitts Town

Source: RG Dept. of Defense, Subgroup: Adjutant General's Office (Revolutionary War), Numbered Manuscripts, Roll 13, Mss. No. 4666, New Jersey State Archives.
This flurry of documents indicates the some of the planning to support the Continental Army if it had to move into New Jersey after the British.

## The Marquis de Lafayette, Appoints John Cropper

Division orders at Valley forge Camp
the 29th April 1778
Colonel Cropper will Command the eleventh Virginia regiment in gen woodfords' brigade, till further orders,

the M. de lafayette   m.g.

Source: *Calendar of Virginia State Papers and Other Manuscripts, 1652-1781* (Richmond, 1875; reprint, New York: Kraus, 1968), 1:299.
Lieutenant Colonel John Cropper was in the Seventh Virginia Regiment, but the weakness of so many of the Virginia units caused them to be combined. See Henry Young's report of April 6, 1778, above.

## Humphry Thompson to Unidentified

*To the* PRINTER *of the* PENNSYLVANIA PACKET.

SIR,

*Inclosed I send you an original letter from serjeant Humphry Thompson—as it discovers a truly original genius, and, in point of pomposity of stile, equals any of the famous Burgoyne's letters. I trust you will not hesitate to give it a place in your Paper.*
AN OFFICER IN THE ARMY.
*Camp, Mount-Joy, April* 29, 1778.

*Exuberant Genius,*
AS the malignity of the vulgar incomparably transcends human comprehension, and their groveling insinuations will climaxicate the minutiae of human frailty, you cannot want faculty to investigate the ebullition of that incentive that has so inundated a character whose lucidity appeared in the moral world equal to any planetical phoenomenon.
A. M. 5777 alias P. N. C. 1777, I have the honour to make one of that terrific accumulated body of freeman encamped at Middle Brook, whose unparalleled achievements, and unequalled prowess in arms, would obliterate the character of a Macedonian army, and whose terror not only put a stop to the depredations of an army of veterans, but drove them from the confines of that patriotic province, and made them take shelter within their lignean batteries, on the surges of a boisterous and tempestuous current.—At that time the famous politicians of the epocha were divided in their opinions, and the question was, whether they had totally withdrawn their fleets and armies, or the Fates had desired them to plough the Atlantic twice ten years, Ulysses like, to receive the retribution of their national crime? maturely pondering the arguments *a priori & a posteriori*; I coincided with the former. Amusing myself, and highly pleased that the Diety was tired of punishing the iniquities of the American world, the curtains of the evening began to encircle me, and the shades of Erebus grew more sable, when one of the daughters of Venus intercepted me in my perambulations, whom I discovered to be sauntering about in tasteless existence—[ ]*h me miserum! de qua perfectione decidi*—My meretricious faculties were alarmed, *en verite*; the organs of my corporal system were entirely shocked; and, for a short time, every muscular motion forgot to vibrate; the fair discovering in me an uncommon structure, was prompted to extend her balmiserous hand and raised me from my torpid supinity; by which time she was environed with other graces not less agreeable in pulchritudenary

Features—I was assisted into a carriage drawn by quadrupeds and vehicled into a *Virgin Province* at that time unknown to me—All this time my ideas, simple and compound, centered in my Diana, as a principal and virtual focus.

I had no avocations, nor did my country strike my auricular nerves—no expansion of my common sensorium—all was love! all was joy extactic and compleat!

Posthumous to my departure from the theatre of human carnage, I was enveloped in a dulcid, lethargic stupefaction of reiterated voluptuosity for three diurnal periods, and, as I conceive, entranced in the *saporific calm of Paphian joys*—but the fatigues of repetition, destroying and annihilating my virile powers, I was reduced to a state of *compos mentis*—

I [s]ay, after again emerging into the world upon my examining my calendar, I was astonished to find that the lunar periodical revolutions were numerically equal to the muses, and upon hearing of the enemy's return to the Continent, I am again determined to make a glorious epiphany.

By this time, Sir, I trust the antecedant cogitations have expaciated you to form something definitive and conclusive respecting the character of a child of misery and an offspring of misfortune, and that you will be moved to reconcile me to you causidical brother Colonel B——g, from whom I have unfortunately revolted.—Through your benign mediatorial influence, I hope to be renovated in his estimation, and that my quondam defections may be entirely and sempeternally absorbed in the chaos of perpetual oblivion.

I am, Most Exuberant Genius, with pedestal humiliation, and retrograde speculation,

    Your torquated friend and distressed
    Humble servant,
    HUMPHRY THOMPSON, Serjeant.

*From my sequestered Museum, near the*
 *Lancaster Road, April 23, 1778.*
*To Colonel ——, in General W——'s Division.*

N. B. If Serjeant Thompson will return to his regiment by the 27th of June next, his quondam defections will be buried in oblivion.

Source: *The Pennsylvania Packet or the General Advertiser*, May 27, 1778.
The writer has not been identified.

## William Alexander to John Stevens

Camp Valley Forge April 30, 1778

In addition to the very unexpected accounts we have lately had from England, of L. North's propositions, &c, Mr. Robert Morris has received a letter from the patriotic Governor Johnston Member of Parliament in which he tells him, that France is about to offer very advantageous Terms to America, and advises us not to be in a hurry to Conclude anything, for that Great B. will soon offer us terms still higher. In short, I am almost led to believe that if we appear stronghanded which the Commissioners arrive, they will give us Independence Itself rather than not accommodate matters; for they are hard run by the French, whom they cannot avoid going to war with, and are afraid we shall be in Alliance with Defensive & Offensive. I sincerely wish all our Battalions were filled,—that & only that will Secure us Success in the Negotiations.

Lady Stirling & all the Girls join in their love to all your family with your affectionate Humble Serv't
Stirling

Source: Archibald Douglas Turnbull, *John Stevens, an American Record* (New York: Century Co., 1928), 63-64.
Stevens was William Alexander's brother-in-law and was then in the New Jersey legislature.


## Elias Boudinot, Visit to Germantown

MEETS THE BRITISH COMMISSIONER AT GERMANTOWN, TO EXCHANGE THE HESSIAN PRISONERS, AND THE CONVERSATION THAT TOOK PLACE THEREAT.

In the Spring of 1778 about the month of May or beginning of June, I was appointed by Genl. Washington to meet a Commissioner on the part of the British, at Germantown to Exchange the Hessian Prisoners in our Custody—On my arrival I found the British Commissioner was the same General Robertson, who had brought out a Gentn. with him, who had been an acquaintance of mine, a very sensible, prudent, Genteel Man—After doing our Business and dining together—This Gentn asked me if I would walk in the Garden with him I readily agreed. when there he asked me if I had any objection to a confidential Political Conversation—I said I could have none.—He told me that the British exceedingly regretted our unhappy dispute—That they were convinced, it could end in no substantial good to either party—That they were now convinced of the propriety of healing the breach.—That if any person would undertake to settle the unhappy dispute, he was authorized to promise them anything from a Dukedom to Ten Thousand Sterling pr annum. To this I replied as before to Genl Robertson, that offers of that kind could have no effect on men who were acting from Principle, That America wanted Peace & Quietness.—That the British had invaded us, and it was on her part to say what she wanted.—He said he came authorized in the fullest manner, to offer a Carte Blanche, it should be signed by proper Authority and I might fill it up myself.—I told him that I was too well acquainted with the British Govt. & of the nature of the dispute, not to know that such an offer was merely delusion & that it could only tend to decieve, for they never designed nor could do any such thing—He in the most positive Terms assured me that it was all real and nothing could give more pleasure to the Govt. than to have it agreed to—I answered that I did not doubt his honesty in the business but well knew that he was imposed upon.—He however consulted so strenuously on the rectitude of their intention, That he would venture his life upon their agreeing to any Terms that I would dictate. In reply I said I would try him & thereby bring the matter to the test,—That I would fill up the Carte Blanche with only our Term—"That we should be allowed our Single free Bottom to every part of the World"—His countenance fell and with much apparent distress, said Sir, you are right, it is impossible.—Well sir, said I, it is not all the Power of Great Brittain and all that she is worth, will ever bring America to submit without having a free Trade to every part of the World, with as many ships as she can command, and therefor this project is vain—He acknowledged his Error begging my pardon for the trouble he had given me, and the freedom he had used,—and we returned into the House—After some little time Genl Robertson came to me and curiously asked me who I thought would be Govr. of Pennsylvania.—I told him it lay between Mr Robt Morris and Mr Joseph Read—that one of them would be chosen, but which I knew not—we then soon parted

Source: Elias Boudinot, *Journal of Historical Recollections of American Events During the Revolutionary War*, (Philadelphia: Frederick Bourquin, 1894), 23-25.

## William Alexander to John Stevens

                                  Camp Valley Forge, May 1st, 1778.
I wrote you two days ago by Lawrie Jun'r. Every hour almost since bring is extraordinary news from Europe. France and Spain have declared our Independence and have entered into a very honorable Treaty of Alliance with our Ambassadors, a French fleet in on its way to America in defiance of Great Britain; that is one side of the question. It is on the other certain that the Commissioners are coming out from Britain with full powers to treat with us, even unto independency. This sudden change in their behaviour is owing to their having discovered that France was going into Treaty with us, and the fear of loosing us induces them now to give whatever we shall ask, to be in alliance with them.

    Thus unexpectedly are two of the mightiest nations of Europe become Courtiers to the people of America and our efforts to bring this to pass will no longer be called a Rebellion but a Glorious Revolution.

    Communicate the Contents to Govr Livingston.

Source: Archibald Douglas Turnbull, *John Stevens, an American Record* (New York: Century Co., 1928), 64.

An alliance with France had been concluded in Paris in February. This news reached Valley Forge on April 30, and was celebrated on May 6.

## Robert Hanson Harrison to Elias Boudinot

D$^r$ Sir

    Major Burnet having one foot in the stirrup, I have not time to say more than a word or two. I give you joy. France has recognized us free & independent &c &c. Britain is in greater confusion than she has ever been since the Revolution—parties all over the Kingdom—Stocks fallen 10 PCent—a general bankruptcy apprehended—An invasion dreaded, France having marched about 50,000 men into the provinces of Normandy & Britany. The King of Prussia & Emperor at the Head of large Armies, their arrangements not known, This account brought by the Frigate La Sensible of 36 guns belonging to his most Christian Majesty which arrived about 20th Ulto at Falmouth Casco Bay after a passage of 35 days. The dispatches would reach Congress last night. The Bellefonte frigate was dispatched with 'em 6 weeks before & after being out near that time was forced to return having sprung her masts—Majr Burnet will give you further particulars. Hence proceed Lord North's benevolent intentions toward us & his change of language.

I received a letter from Mr Loring but not Syllable, nay not a vowel or consonant, about Genl Lee. It is upon the subject of the old prisoner account & requesting an early meeting of Two disinterested Gentlemen to adjust it. I wish you & he could liquidate matters, but I wish more that you would push to Congress—Do hasten there I know you are materially wanted

My Compliments to Mrs [Boudinot] & Miss Sukey and the Ladies [in] their Neighbourhood of my acquaint[ance.]

   Adieu $Y^{rs}$. Affecty
     Rob: H: Harrison

May 2 1778

Source: Dreer Collection, Soldiers of the American Revolution, Vol. 2, Historical Society of Pennsylvania.

## Return of the North Carolina Brigade

### McIntosh's Brigade

**Field Officers**

| | | | |
|---|---|---|---|
| Colonels. | 2 | Lieut. Colonels. | 2 |
| Majors. | | | |

**Commissioned Officers.**

| | | | |
|---|---|---|---|
| Captains. | 11 | 1st Lieutenants. | 8 |
| 2nd ditto. | 12 | Ensigns. | 2 |

**Staff**

| | | | |
|---|---|---|---|
| Chaplains. | 2 | Adjutants. | 2 |
| Pay Master. | 2 | Qr. Master. | 3 |
| Surgeons. | 3 | Mates. | 1 |

**Non Commissioned**

| | | | |
|---|---|---|---|
| Sergt. Major. | 3 | Qr. Mr. Sergt. | 3 |
| Drum Major. | 3 | Fife Major. | 2 |

Sergeants.   52   Drums and Fifes. 46

**Rank and File.**
Present Fit for Duty.   385
Sick Present.   275   Sick Abst.   77
On Command.   109   On Furlough.   14
Total.   860

**Wanting to Compt.**
Sergeants.   7   Drums and Fifes,   11
Rank and File   1060

**Since Last Monthly Return.**
Dead.   46   Discharged.   4
Deserted.   2

**Joined.**
Sergts.   2   Rank and File.   32

Valley Forge, Pennsylva. May 2nd 1778.
Extract From a General Return of the Continental Army Under the Command of His Excellency George Washington Esqr. Genl. and Commander in chief of the Armies of the Independent States of America.

Source: *State Records of North Carolina*, 13:410.
This return shows the North Carolina Brigade even weaker than it was on February 29, as shown above.

**William Williams to Thomas Wharton Jr.**

White Horse, May 2, 1778
Sir: During my confinement as a prisoner of war, several promotions took place, among which number I expected to have been placed. Since my escape, I found I was neglected; I mentioned it to his Excellency General Washington, who told me it should be rectified, and that it was General Wayne who gave in the report of the officers for promotion.

I sometime after called on General Wayne for the reasons; he told me he knew of no other, that it was not customary to promote those who were prisoners. Sometime since I waited on his Excellency General Washington, to know if there was any likelihood of my being restored to my rank, he again informed me that it was thro' General Wayne I was left out, and desired me to inform General Wayne to let him know the reasons why there was not a vacancy left in the promotions for me. (I have since wrote to General Wayne to that purpose;) his Excellency, at the same time, informed me that the State has taken upon to settle the rank of the army; upon this information, I trouble your Excellency with my situation, that I cannot serve in my present commission on account of a number of junior officers, who would command me. I have the satisfaction to inform your Excellency, that I have not been charged, since I have been in the service, with the least neglect of duty or disobedience of orders, and I am conscious I never turned my back on the enemy without orders, nor never feared to face them when I had orders. I was the second captain in the First Pennsylvania battalion, and by different rules for promotion, numbers of junior officers now command me. I shall be happy when my country has no further occasion of my services, yet am willing to serve, but would not chuse to hold a commission at the will of an Individual.

Source: Thomas Lynch Montgomery ed. *Pennsylvania Archives*, 5th. series (Harrisburg: Harrisburg Publishing Co., 1908), 775.
Major Williams, of the Second Pennsylvania Regiment, had been captured at Germantown and escaped on April 20, 1778. It was the policy of the Continental Army not to promote captured officers, as their exchange for equals would be more costly. This led to much controversy when they were exchanged or escaped. On June 28, 1778 he was promoted to Lieutenant Colonel of the Third Pennsylvania.

## Jeremiah Olney, Certificate for Bethuel Curtis

Camp Valley Forge 3rd May 1778.
To Whom Concern'd
    This Certifies that Lieut Bethuel Curtis is not Indebted to the State, or Continent, to my knowledge.
               Jereh Olney Lt. Colo

Source: *Publications of the Rhode Island Historical Society*, new series 2, 4 (January 1895), 223.
Olney was Lt. Colonel of the Second Rhode Island Regiment. Second Lieutenant Curtis was discharged the same day.

**Lachlan McIntosh to William Alexander**

My Lord—
    The bearer Major Duval informs me your Lordship has a Vacancy for an Aid De Camp & is very desirous of having the Honor of Serving in your Family.—If it should be agreable, I can assure your Lordship that I have experienced him to be a Young Gentleman of Honor & true Spirit—he is of a reputable Family in Virginia, Served Some time an Officer in my Brigade in Georgia, & Resigned when I came from thence with a View of Seeing more Service in Camp.—
    I have the Honor to be.—Your Lordships
        Most obt. Hble Servt.    Lachn. Mc.Intosh
            Camp Valley Forge 4th. May 1778
Rt. Honl. The Earl of Stirling

Source: William Alexander Papers, The New-York Historical Society.
Captain Daniel Duval of the Second Georgia Regiment was appointed temporary Brigade Major of the North Carolina Brigade on February 26, 1778. Alexander did not utilize Duval but he came an Aide-de-Camp to Steuben.

**Friedrich Wilhelm Augustus von Steuben to Henry Laurens**

Honorable Sir                                      Camp 7th May 1778
    I have to acknowledge the honor done me in communicating to me the importance intelligence received from Europe, and be assured I take a most sensible part in the Happines of your Country
    At the same time I congratulate you on the conclusion of a Treaty of Alliance with the Court of France; a Treaty as honorable as advantageous to both Powers—I esteem myself extremely happy in being in America at so interesting an Epoch & feel a sensible pleasure in seeing the Independance of America established on so Solid a Basis I may not perhaps have an Opportunity of drawing my Sword in your Cause but no matter <u>Be Free & happy</u> and I shall never regret the Voyage I have undertaken to offer you my Services

I have the honor to be with the greatest regard
Your Excellency's Obedt. humble servt
Steuben

Source: Henry Laurens Papers, Reel 9, South Carolina Historical Society.

## Unknown to Silas Deane

May 7, At Camp

No words to express the universal joy the good news sent over by his brother has diffused to all the hearts of patriots. Yesterday had solemn rejoicings at camp for which purpose the army was under arms. After part of the articles of the Treaty were read to the troops, thanksgiving followed and a discourse in praise of His Most Christian Majesty and those who brought about this happy work; other details of the celebration; effect of this treaty on the war. Rejoices at his now acknowledged rank in France and wishes to see him in Paris as soon as the writer shall think himself useless in the station he is.

A. L. 2 p. XLIV, 22
————  ———— to Silas Deane

Source: I. Minis Hays, ed. *Calendar of the Papers of Benjamin Franklin in the Library of the American Philosophical Society* vol. 4 (Philadelphia: APS, 1908), 258.
Deane was the first diplomat sent abroad by the United States, and was one of the commissioners who negotiated our alliance with France. At the time of this letter he had been recalled to the United States. The rejoicing referred to the *feu de joie*, a major celebration of the alliance. See the next document.

## Philip Van Cortlandt to Pierre Van Cortlandt

Camp Valley Forge May 7-1778

I have the pleasure of Informing you that I had the Honour Yesterday of being present at & partaking with the Officers and Soldiers of Our Army the Joys of the greatest Day Ever yet Experienced in our Independent World of Liberty. A feu de Joy was Fired in the Following Manner After the Troops were Arrived at their posts which was on the high grounds formed in two lines in Order of Battle. A Signal Gun being Fired at the park was followed with a Discharge of Thirteen

Cannon—Fire'd on Our left near Schulkill a Running Fire of musquetry then began On the Right of the Army and so on from Right to left untill the whole Army had Fire'd Then a Signal Gun and all the Army Gave Three Huzza's for the King of France, Then Repeated in the Same manner 13 Cannon a Running Fire and Huzza's for the Friendly Powers in Europe the Same Fireing took place with three Huzza's for the Free and Independent American States—We then March'd Our Men to their Respective Parrades and Dismis'd them Waited on his Excellency where all the Officers of the Army had the Honour of Dining under Sheds Cover'd with Tents for that purpose—Our Army is in Exceeding fine Spirits and a universal Joy Crown'd the Day. we hear from Mr. How by Deserters which Comes in Every Day from them that the Report in Philidela. is that Congress has Agreed to Lord Norths proposals—and that there will be no more Fighting this is done I Suppose to prevent Desertion I have no more News to give you at present must therefore beg of you to make my Kind Love and Respects to Mamma Brothers & Sisters and
    Accept the Same from Yr. Dutifull Son
    Philip Cortlandt

 May 10th 1778—
Not having had an Oppertunity of Sending this letter until now gives me an oppertunity of adding to it and to Observe how frail Mankind are and it is the will of God but of Short Duration—When I Came to Camp which was the last of April I found all my Officers in Good Health Capt. Riker among the Number who is now out in Eternity he was taken sick the 2d. of May went out of Camp the 3d Died the 8th and was Buried the 9th I herewith Inclose a letter to Mr Bradford his Brother in Law that his Sister May be acquainted with the Death of Husband I had him Interred with the Honours of War in the Burying Yard of Valley Presbyterian Meeting About 3 Miles from Camp
 I Recd. your by Lieut. Fairlie Arrived the Day before Yesterday Am much Obliged by Your by Your Advancing him Fifty Dollars—Am Very Sorry to hear of the loss of the Cattle what a Pack of Villains them Basley's are In my Opinion there is not One of them to be Trusted
 Deserters from the Enemy are Daily Coming in they say their Officers tell them the Fireing in Our Camp was Occasion'd by a Party of their's Attacking our Camp.—It is Expected that we Shall all keep Our present Situation at least four Weeks longer
    My best Respects &c. from Yr. Dutifull and

Affectionate Son
Philip Cortlandt

Source: Van Cortlandt-Van Wyck Papers, New York Public Library.
Van Cortlandt was Colonel of the Second New York Regiment. Captain Abraham Riker, whose death is mentioned above, is one of the few men whose place of burial is specifically stated. There is a marker to him at the Riker-Lent Burial Ground, Astoria, Queens County, New York.

## John Laurens, Resignation of Matthias Hite

Head Quarters 8th May 1778.
Captain Matthias Hite of the Eighth Virginia Regiment has obtained leave from His Excellency the Commander in chief to resign his commission— John Laurens
Aid de Camp

Source: John Reed Collection, Valley Forge National Historical Park.

## Christian Febiger to William Alexander

May it please your Lordship: May 9st: 1778:—
    Your Lordships Message of the 7st: instant was by some Mistake not handed me untill Yesterday, when on my Way to Generall Courtmartial, on which I have been this forthnight:—on my receiving your Lordships first message I immediately inform'd the Commandant of our Brigade who order'd another Officer to take the Command of the Fatigue party, and I thought that, that Officer had inform'd your Lordship of the Same. I likewise inform'd Major Munroe some Days ago that I was on Courtmartial:
    I therefore humbly request your Lordship would excuse my Neglect, as if I had conceiv'd your Lordship was uninformed of the Circumstances, I shou'd immediately have reported:
    I am with Sincere Respect your Lordships
    Most obedient and most humble Servt:
Christian Febiger
Colo. 2d: V: Regt:

Source: William Alexander Papers, The New-York Historical Society.

Colonel Febiger of the Second Virginia Regiment, was born in Denmark. Apparently Alexander had ordered Febiger to command a fatigue party, but was unaware he was serving on a court-martial.

## Nicholas Fish to Richard Varick

My dear Varick    Camp Valley Forge May 9th 1778—
I was some time before honored by the Rect. of Your Favor of the 28th. March, which appears to have been written previous to the Arrival of my Answer by Col Cortlandt, to your former Letter—In Your last You speak of Your Intentions of retiring from the Service of Your Country, which I should have been at a Loss to have accounted for, had I not known the inactivity of Your Station in the Army, which to be sure to a Person of your active Disposition could not be the most agreeable, and which I suppose determined Your Resignation—
You mention the appointmt. of our Friend Mr. Scott to the Office of Secretary of State of New York—In fact I scarcely know whether to rejoice or otherwise in the Appointment. True it is, that this is an Office of considerable Profit, but in my opinion far inferior in point of honor, to his Merit and Pretensions; and besides if I am not mistaken in our Constitution, he will in consequence loose his Seat in the Legislature, in which Case his acceptance of the Office will occasion a public Loss & Injury; upon the whole therefore, I could wish he would spurn at the Offer, & remain simple Senator until the Arrival of that Period when he will be seated in the chief Majestracy of the State—
Doubtless You have heard the Cause, and probably the Particulars of our Rejoicings in Camp on the 6th inst. We were for one Hour employed in returning Thanks to the Supream Governor of the Universe for the signal Display and Manifestations of his approbation, of our just and righteous Exertions in Defence of this infant Empire, and supplicating a continuance of his Favors—At ten o'Clock a.m. the Signal Gun for assembling the Troops into Brigades was fired—at 11 agreeable to the previous Disposition the Signal was given for the whole Line to move in Columns of Brigades to their Ground, where We past a Review by his Excellency the Commander in Chief. At one o'Clock p.m. a Continental Salute of 13 Cannon was given and immediately succeeded by a feude joy of a running Fire from right to left thro' the whole Line, & concluded with three Cheers

of the Line, with the following Expression 'Long live the King of France'—The same Process was repeated and concluded with three Cheers and 'Prosperity to the united States of America'—The Afternoon was selebrated by all the Officers of the Army in the most rational and jocund amusemnts. at Head Quarters, and the Day concluded with universal Happiness & the strictest Propriety.

But here I must stop, here my Prospects are sullied. Permit me dear Varick to ask Your Sympathy and Condolence on the melancholy Event of my Mothers Death, the News of which has just reached me since I have been writing, and tinctured my most happy Moments with Misery & Gloom. ... My Pangs would be keen beyond Decription (as I am told that during her illness my absence gave her infinite Distress) were I not fully convicted of the Propriety of my Conduct, which ever was founded upon the pure Principles of Duty and Love to my Country."

N. F.

Addressed: To Lt. Col. Richard Varick at Poughkeepsie

Source: Sotheby's Auction House, The JAMES S. COPLEY LIBRARY: MAGNIFICENT AMERICAN HISTORICAL DOCUMENTS: FIRST SELECTION, New York |14 Apr 2010, 02:00 PM | N08653, lot 51, Sold for $22,500.

Fish was Major of the Second New York Regiment. Varick was Deputy Muster Master General with the rank of Lieutenant-Colonel. He later served as Washington's confidential secretary.

## Thomas Jones to Jacob Anderson

Sir      Commissaries Office, Camp Valley Forge May the 9th. 1778

M$^r$. Dill whose family lives near Pottsgrove will if he Chuses be fix'd again at that Post in a few days as he was at that Post before, I intend to give you a Post at Middletown, on the Susquehanna in Lancaster County, to which place I would have you prepare to remove as Soon as Mr. Dill goes to Potts grove, in your way would have you call here to Receive the Sallary due &c. I am sir

    Yr. Mo. Obt. Servt.
     Thomas Jones    D. C. G. of Issues

Source: Record Group 93, M 859, Roll 122, Doc. 34987, National Archives.
Anderson and Robert Dill were Assistant Commissaries of Issues.

## Stephen Stevenson, Deserter Notice

*EIGHTY DOLLARS* Reward.
DESERTED from the Ninth Pennsylvania regiment, the 24th of April last, the following men, viz. *Joseph Kennedy*, about 20 years of age, fair complexion, and black hair; he formerly lived in Warrington township, York county. *Elisha Davis*, about 5 feet 5 inches high, about 18 years of age, black complexion and black hair; he formerly lived in Warrington township, York County. *William Bell*, about 23 years of age, about 5 feet 10 or 11 inches high, of a redish complexion, and is a stout well made fellow; formerly lived near Hunter's-Town, in York County. *Thomas Reed*, about 30 years of age, 5 feet 8 or 9 inches high, darkish complexion, and black hair; formerly lived in Cumberland county. And *Solomon Brown*, aged 21 years, about 5 feet 7 or 8 inches high, redish complexion, black hair, and is a stout well set fellow; he is a German, and formerly lived in Reading township, York county. They all belong to Major Francis Nichols's company. Whoever takes up said deserters, and confines them in any goal, or delivers them to Lieut. STEPHENSON, shall have the above reward, or Sixteen Dollars for each man.

Source: *The Pennsylvania Gazette*, May 9, 1778; May 16, 1778; May 30, 1778.
Stephen Stevenson was a First Lieutenant in the Ninth Pennsylvania Regiment.

## Josiah Lacey, Blanket Receipt

Camp Valley Forge   May 10th. 1778—
Reced. of Willm. Redfield States Commissary one State Blanket For John Wakely of my Company.
    Recvd. Pr. me
        Josiah Lacey Captn.

Source: Goldberg Auctioneers, Auction 38, Lot 460, November 18, 2006, Http://images.goldbergauctions.com/php/search1c.php?sale=38&item=104792.
Wakely or Wakeley, a private in the Fifth Connecticut Regiment, was discharged on June 2, 1778. Lacey was a Captain in that Regiment and William Redfield is listed as a Sergeant.

## Leonard Miller, Ration Receipt

Camp Valley Forge May 10th. 1778
These may Certify that I the Subscriber have Recd. of Capt. Haynes Twelve Dollars in full for the Remaindr. Due on the within Rect. Signed by Majr. Cranston for Rations more than was Due to him Paid by me Leonard Miller Qmr

Docketed: Quarter ms. Millers Rect.

Source: Record Group 93, M 859, Roll 7, Document 2203, National Archives.
Major Abner Cranston had died on May 29, 1777. Cranston, Captain Aaron Haynes and First Lieutenant Leonard Miller were all in the Thirteenth Massachusetts Regiment.

## James Glentworth, Oath of Allegiance

I *James Glentworth, Lieut. of 6th Pennya. Reg.* do acknowledge the UNITED STATES of AMERICA to be Free, Independent and Sovereign States, and declare that the people thereof owe no allegiance or obedience to George the Third, King of Great-Britain ; and I renounce, refuse and abjure any allegiance or obedience to him ; and I do *Swear* that I will, to the utmost of my power, support, maintain and defend the said United States against the said King George the Third, his heirs and successors, and his or their abettors, assistants and adherents, and will serve the said United States in the office of *Lieutenant* which I now hold, with fidelity according to the best of my skill and understanding.

*James Glentworth.*
Sworn at the Valley Forge Camp
this 11th day of May, 1778, before me
STIRLING, M. G.

Source: *The Pennsylvania Magazine of History and Biography*, 1, 2 (1877), 174.
First Lieutenant James Glenworth of the Sixth Pennsylvania Regiment served until June 1783. Congress had resolved on February 3, 1778 "That every officer who holds or shall hereafter hold a commission or office from Congress, shall take and subscribe the following **oath** or affirmation...." Glenworth and hundreds of other officers were taking the oath around this time.

## Charles Pettit to Davis Bevan

Sir                                        Moore Hall 12 May 1778

Whatever Artificer's Work M$^r$. Weiss may think necessary for the Accomodation of the Public Stores under his Care, you will please to order to be done on his Requisition

                        Chas. Pettit AQM Genl
To Mr. Davis Bevan, Sup. A.

Source: Record Group 15, M 804, Roll 2523, National Archives.
Pettit was an Assistant Quartermaster General. In the General Orders of May 5, Bevan was "appointed by the Quarter Master General to superintend the Artificers and to deliver out boards, Plank &c.—in future therefore when boards or Plank are wanting or Artificers are necessary to Do any Jobbs in the Army an order signed by a General Officer, Officers commanding Brigades or Brigade Quarter Masters and directed to Mr Bevan at Sullivan's Bridge will be duly attended to."

## Clement Biddle to Moore Furman

Dr Sir                                        Moorhall May 14. 1778—

The bearer Mr. Mathew Ernest was recommended to head Quarters & from thence to me to provided for in the Forage Department—his Age rendered him unfit for Camp service but I have him an Appointment & sent him to the Revd. Mr. Caldwell to fix him at some place in Jersey where he came recommended from—no place being fixed for receiving Forage by Mr. Caldwell he has again Called on me & I take the Opportunity by him to inclose you Mr. Caldwells Letter to me which you will please to peruse & I have referd him to you for Directions relative to what he has therin—I also send you by Mr. Ernest Nine thousand Six hundred Dollars on Account & hope to hear favourable Intelligence of your forming the Magazines.—

Inclosed is an Account of what Iron was deliverd at White marsh by my Order to the Qur Mr Genls. black Smiths.

        I am Dr Sir        Your mo: Ob: Serv
                Clement Biddle
                    CGF
I request as a favour as Mr. Ernest came recommended from Your State that he may be fixed at some of the forage Hous
please to order some Forage for present Use to Coryells ferry

Addressed: On public Service To Moore Furman Esqr.
D Qur Mr Genl. Pitts Town Jersey

By Mr Ernest who is to pass   C. Biddle

Source: Record Group Dept. of Defense, Subgroup: Adjutant General's Office (Revolutionary War), Numbered Manuscripts, Roll 13, Mss. No. 4668.

## Alexander Church, Receipt for Steuben's Horses

Receivd May 14: 1778 of Baron Steuben four horses into the Continental Yard all Branded **C A**
Alex$^r$. Church
Camp Valey Forge

Source: Chaloner and White Mss, Box 6, Historical Society of Pennsylvania. Church was Superintendent of Continental Horses with the army.

## The Marquis de Lafayette to Henry Laurens

dear Sir Valley forge                     Camp 14th may 1778
I have just now receiv'd your favor by Clol gimat and instantly beg you would offer to the Consideration of Congress the affair of Clol Armand—that gentlemen has incurr'd great expenses from his own to raise an independant Corps—he flatters himself he could bring into the field before long 400 good men, was he entitled by an order of Congress to enlist hessian desterters or prisoners—he has already inlisted a great number of frenchmen and will not take one english desertor—he wish'd that his old corps be given back to him, and they he may be annexed to some state in order to get the bounty by inlisted man—but, sir, I have explained that matter very fully in a letter wrote three weeks ago, and will only confine myself in telling that ardently I wish to send soon good news to that gentleman; as he is exposed every day to an immense deal of expenses by his zeal and impatience of being soon in the field.

    may I beg in this letter the gentlemen of Congress who have done with french papers to be so good as to deliver some to you for me—it is almost the only way of satisfying my curiosity for every thing which has happened since some time in my most beloved country.

I beg you would transmit to me the account of the affairs I took the liberty of reccommending to you when decided by Congress in behalf of french gentlemen—theyr confidence deserved my exertions, and the pleasure of being useful to my countrymen is one of the greatest I may feel.

I hope the Gentlemen of Congress have not been displeased with the letter of my uncle the Mis de noaïlles to his britannick majesty, and the effects it has produced—with the highest regard I have the honor to be
   Sir Your most obedient servant
     the Mis de Lafayette
Endorsed: Marquis delafayette
  14 May 1778 Recd. 16th— Ansd. 17th.—

Source: Henry Laurens Papers, South Carolina Historical Society.
Charles Armand-Tuffin, Marquis de la Rouërie, had been commissioned a Colonel, without a command, by Congress on May 10, 1777. He persuaded Washington to allow him to raise a partisan corps consisting of as many as two hundred Frenchmen. On June 11, Washington gave him command of Ottendorf's independent light infantry corps. On June 25, 1778, Armand corps, which the Board of War called "The Free and Independent Chasseurs," was taken into Continental pay by Congress. After Pulaski's death in the fall of 1779, his Legion and Armand's corps were consolidated under Armand as Armand's Legion, which consisted of both infantry and cavalry. On March 26, 1783, Armand was commissioned a brigadier general

**James Mitchell Varnum to George Washington**

Sir—       Camp Valley Forge 14th May, 1778.
 Lt. Turner is recommended for a Discharge, with an Allowance of Time sufficient for him to go Home in—
      J. M. Varnum
His Excellency
Gen$^l$. Washington.—

Source: Record Group 93, M 859, Roll 2, Document 665, National Archives.
Lieutenant Isaac Turner was discharged from the Second Connecticut Regiment, effective on May 16, 1778.

## Thomas Clark and Lachlan McIntosh, Certificate for Thomas Jones

Camp Valley Forge May 15th. 1778

These are to Certify that Mr. Thomas Jones (a Second Lieutenant in the 7th. North Carolina Battalion) may be spared from his Battn. without prejudice to the Service of the United States—and has my permission to resign his Commission, if agreeable to Genl. Mc.Intosh—it appears that he is not indebted to the Public or Soldiery,

              T. Clark Col 1st N. C. B

Agreed
    Lachn. Mc.Intosh B.G.

Source: RG 93, M 859, Roll 45, Document 14417, National Archives.
Jones appears as "Discharged" on the June 1778 muster roll. Clark was Colonel of the First North Carolina Regiment.

## Johann de Kalb to Henry Laurens

Sir                       Camp at Valley forge May 16th. 1778

I had the honor to write to your Excellency the first instant by Major Brice and the 7th. by the Post the former on some apprehensions of mine on account of the Treaty concluded with France, the articles not being known then, which the publication thereof has entirely stilled. The latter was to give you joy to that happy Event Entreating you at the same to forward a Packet for France, I would request the same favour for the two here inclosed but all three by different conveyances, being of the same contents.

War being declared in Europe your Enemies in all appearances will withdraw part of their Troops in America if not the whole, I do not think them able to do otherwise, It would be only burning their Candle at both ends at a time. But notwithstanding the favorable aspect of affairs, I could wish the States would not be remiss in preparations for the continuance of the War, but to exert themselves to the utmost in filling their Regiments and Stores of all kinds.

By the inclosed I request Mr Thomson to send me an Extract relating to Chvr. de [blank] who was repeatedly promised by the States, a Cols. Commission. If your Excellency would interfer in this matter, and have the same confirmed by Congress, you would do a piece of justice to both these Gentlemen, the one of fullfilling his Engagement, the other of obtaining a favour and it would in a high degree oblige

    Your Excellency's Most
      obedient and most humble Servant
        The Bn. de Kalb

This instant I receive the honour of your letter dated 3d. May.

Source: Henry Laurens Papers, Reel 9, South Carolina Historical Society.

## Lachlan McIntosh, Oath by Allegiance for Adam Boyd

I, Adam Boyd, Chaplain in the 2d N. Carolina battalion, do acknowledge the United States of American to be Free, Independent Sovereign States, and declare that the people thereof owe no allegiance or obedience to George the Third, King of Great Britain; and I renounce, refuse and abjure any allegiance or obedience to him; and I do swear—that I will, to the utmost of my power, support, maintain and defend the said United States against the said King George the Third, his heirs and successors, and his or their abettors, assistants and adherents, and will serve the said United States in the office of chaplain—which I now hold, with fidelity, according to the best of my skill and understanding

    ADAM BOYD.

Sworn to, Valley Forge Camp, 16th May, 1778 before,
    LACHN. McINTOSH, B. G.

Source: *The State Records of North Carolina*, ed. Walter Clark (Winston: M.I. & J.C. Stewart, 1896), 8:418-19.

## Charles Pettit, Fords on the Schuylkill

*Names of the Fords on Schuylkill.*

| Miles from Reading. | Depth of Water. |
|---|---|
| Kern's Ford, | 9 Inches. |
| Frederick Mickel's Ford | 12 Inches. |
| Henry Bingman's Do., | 15 Inches. |

|     | Location | Depth |
| --- | --- | --- |
|     | Stock Falls, | from 10 to 15, Rockey. |
| 2   | Callopey Stream, | 18, Rockey. |
|     | Lewis's Ferry, | 2 to 15, Very Rockey. |
|     | Cow and Calf, | 12 Inches. |
| 6   | Lewis's falls, | 5 to 7, Long and Rockey. |
| 7   | Postion, Murry Island, | 10, 15 Inches. |
|     | Leonard Lappoe's shoals, | 8, 12. |
| 8   | Green tree ford, | 5, 6. |
| 9   | Baichel shoals, | 8, 12. |
| 11  | Jacob Hewit's Ford, | 8. |
| 14  | Campbell's Ford, | 6, 7. |
| 15  | David Davis's Ford, | 7, 8. |
| 17  | White Horse ford, Gerlin's | 12. |
|     | Abraham Wanggert's Ford, | 15. |
| 21  | Jacob Floyd's Ford, | 14. |
| 23  | Pott's grove ford, | 12. |
| 24  | Mr. Baichell's, | 6. |
| 26  | "   " Pott's Dam, | 5. |
| 27  | Bombohook Ford, | 6. |
| 29  | John Heisler's Ford, | 12. |
| 30  | Daniel Matt's shoals, | 10. |
| 31  | Edw. Barker's Ford, | 6, Small Rocks. |
| 31¼ | Barker's shoals, | 6, 7. |
| 33  | Geo. Ross's Fishdam, | 12. |
| 34½ | Erasmus Laver's Shoals, | 6, Rockey. |
| 35-6 | Frederick Sower's shoals, | 6, Do. |
| 35½ | Lawrence Hipple's Ford, | 6, 10. |
| 37  | Ming's Island, | 8, 10, Level Bottom. |
| 38  | Adam Hallman's long shoals, | 7, 12. |
|     | Black rock, | 4 to 20 feet. |
| 40  | John Buckwalter's Fishdam, | 6, 15 Inches. |
| 43  | Gordon's Ford, | 7, 15, French Creek. |
| 44  | Moore Hall, | 9, 10 Inches. |
| 45  | Richardson's Ford, | 7, 13, Rockey. |
| 45½ | Pennypacker's | 7, 12. Fishdam. |
| 46½ | Pawling's ford, | 7, 12. Stoney. |
| 49  | Sullivan's Bridge, | 8, 12, Stoney. |

Source: *Pennsylvania Archives*, 1st. ser. (Harrisburg, 1853), 6:514-15.

This accompanied a letter Pettit wrote to Thomas Wharton, Jr., President of the Supreme Executive Council of Pennsylvania on May 16, 1778, requesting improvements to the Schuylkill river to facilitate transportation of supplies to the army. The proposed work never took place.

## Samuel Mansfield to John Lamb?

Dear Sir                          Arty. Park 17th May 1778

    This will be handed you by Capt Lieut. Thompson Wharein I Send you a Coppy of the account of the Cloathing that I Recivd in Boston and the Distribution of Them allso the account of Sum Blankets That I Recivd. of Mr Todd Newhaven.—
    Pleas to remember me to Capt. Brown & the other Officers.—
    I am Sir Your Most Obedt. Huml. Sert.
                Saml. Mansfield

Source: John Lamb Papers, New-York Historical Society.
Mansfield was a Captain in the Second Continental Artillery. Lamb was Colonel of that regiment. No address, probably to Lamb. Tood was likely Michael Todd, as he is mentioned in other correspondence in this collection.

## Abraham Sheppard, Certificate for James Wilson

I do hereby Certify that Capt: James Wilson of my Regiment is neither indebted to the United States of America nor the Officers or Soldiers of the X North Carolina Battn. under my Command to the best of my Knowledge; and that he has my Consent to resign his Commission. Given under my Hand at the Camp, Head Quarters, Valley Forge 17th May 1778
            Abrm: Sheppard
            Col X No. C. B:

Source: Record Group 93, M 859, Roll 45, Document 14437, National Archives.
Sheppard was Colonel of the Tenth North Carolina Regiment. A note on the back reads "Capt James Wilson 10th. No Carolina Regt. resignd 18 May 1778."

## Charles Fleming, Certificate Regarding Thomas Lipscomb

Ensign Thomas Lipscomb                        May 19th. 1778
    to the United States of America D$^r$.

To 3 pr. Shoes at diff$^t$. times at 2 dollers.
Then Received of Ensign Thomas Lipscomb six dollers in full of the above Account—
 I do hereby certify that it does not appear that Ensign Lipscomb stood indebted to the United States of American further than for the abovementioned Shoes Given under my hand this 19th. day May 1778. Cha$^s$. Fleming
Cap$^t$. Comm$^t$. 7$^{th}$. Virg$^a$. Reg$^t$.

Source: Record Group 93, M 859, Roll 110, Document 31228, National Archives. Ensign Thomas Lipscomb's resignation from the Seventh Virginia Regiment was accepted on May 20, 1778.

**William Davies, Certificate for Burwell Green**

I do hereby certify that Ensign Burwell Green was appointed Ensign to the 14th. Virginia regiment on the thirtieth day of August 1777, and that he has had no opportunity of having the date inserted in his commission, since he came to camp.
May 20. 1778, William Davies Col. 14th. Vir. Regt.

Source: RG 93, M 859, Roll 110, Document 31195, National Archives. Green's resignation was accepted, effective on June 18, 1778.

**Peter Muhlenberg to Robert Hanson Harrison**

Sir
 Lieut. Waples of the 9th. Virga. Regt. waits on His Excellency to sollicit his permission to resign. Mr. Waples has obtained a Certificate from the Commanding Officer of the Regt. Certifying that he is not indebted to the States; The present situation of that Regt. is such that it cannot be injured by the Resignation of Mr. Waples.
  I am Sir Your Most Obedt. Servt.
   P Muhlenberg
Colo. Harrison—

Source: Record Group 93, M 859, Roll 110, Document 31282, National Archives. A note on the reverse shows that Second Lieutenant Samuel Waples was allowed to resign on May 22.

## John Smith to Charles Scott

Sir,                              Valy Forge May 23rd. 1778
The Reason I have for Resining my Commission is, I have Affairs unsettled at home,—and my presence there is Absolutely Necessary; therefire I hope Sir, You will Except of it,
    I am Sir, with much Esteem Your very Huble. Serv$^t$.
                John Smith L$^t$. 4$^{th}$.
                         Virg$^a$. Reg$^t$.
To Briga$^r$. Gen$^l$. Scott

Source: Record Group 93, M 859, Roll 110, Document 31263, National Archives. His resignation was accepted effective May 25, 1778. See Benjamin Lawson's certificate of May 22, 1778, for Smith in Book Five of this series.

## John Woodson, Advertisement for Missing Horse

STRAYED or STOLEN, From the Forage yard of Gen. Green's division, some time in April last, A Likely roan or mouse coloured HORSE, three years old in May, about fourteen and a quarter hands high, shod all round, has a thick bushy mane and switch tail. From every circumstance he is believed to have been stolen by a set of waggoners from Northampton County, under the command of Henry Heartman, Waggon Master: The subscriber expects that Mr. Heartman will search among the waggoners that were under his direction when he left camp; if he should neglect to comply with this request, and the horse be found in a future day with those waggoners, (as the subscribe intends making all possible enquiry) Mr. Heartman shall answer it as an encourager of thieving, as such an instance could not have happened without his being privy to it. A reward of FIVE POUNDS will be given for the horse,
        and on conviction of the thief TEN POUNDS.
             JOHN WOODSON,
                Brigade Quarter Master to Gen. Muhlenberg.

Source: *The Pennsylvania Packet*, 23 May 1778.

## Burges Ball, Certificate Regarding Captain Thomas Parramore

May 24th 78

I hereby Certify that Cap$^t$. Parramore of the 9th. Virga. Regimt. is not indebted to ye. Regimt. or ye. United States.

        Burges Ball Lt Col.       9th Virginia

Source: Record Group 93, M 859, Roll 110, Document 31238, National Archives. Thomas Parramore, a Captain in the Ninth Virginia Regiment, was allowed to resign on May 26, 1778.

## Michael Crous, Receipt for Cattle

French Crick Bridge May 24 1778

Recev'd of Coln. Henry Champion D Cy P. E. Depet by the hand of Ephraim Ackley Eighty four head of Beef Cattle for the Use of the Continental Army Branded **C A H C**
N.B.      pr me (Michael Crous)
        A C of P

Source: Peter Force Collection, Ephraim Blaine Papers, Roll 77, f2249, Library of Congress. French Creek is a few miles west of Valley Forge, where the Army's cattle herd was kept. Colonel Henry Champion of Connecticut, played a critical role in purchasing and supply beef to the Continental Army.

## Eli Catlin to George Washington with an Endorsement by Philip B. Bradley, May 25, 1778.

May it please Your Excellency—

    For some particular reasons with which your Excellency is acquainted, I am under the necessity of soliciting leave to <u>resign my Commission</u>

    I am, Your Excellency's Obedt hum Servant
Camp at Valley Forge 25th. May 1778   Elis Catlin Cap$^t$

This is to certify that Capt Catlin is not indebted to the Regiment for any Continental moneys that he has received
                pr Philip B. Bradley Col$^o$.
Valley Forge May 25 1778

Record Group 93, M 859, Roll 2, Document 682, National Archives.
Captain Eli Catlin was allowed to resign from the Fifth Connecticut Regiment. His resignation was effective the same day. Bradley was Colonel of the same regiment.

## Burges Ball, Certificate for William Henderson

May 29th 1778.

I hereby Certify that Cap$^t$. Henderson of the 9th. Virg$^a$. Regimt. is not indebted to the Reg$^t$. or to Y$^e$. United States.

  Burges Ball

Source: Record Group 93, M 859, Roll 110, 31241, National Archives.
Ball was Lt. Colonel on the Ninth Virginia Regiment. William Henderson of the same regiment was allowed to resign on May 30, 1778.

## Board of General Officers

At a Board of General officers held Valley Forge May 29th 1778—agreable to a General order May 28th have made the Following Report:

  The Claims of Lt. Colo. Regnier, and the other Lt. Col. of the State of New York Respecting their Standing in Rank being considered, the Board are of oppinion, that Lt. Colo. Regnier, will take Rank of these Getelm: upon Court Martials Detachments and all Dutys from the Line, but that they Command him, in the line of the State, for notwithstanding Lt. Colo. Regnier, his Rank as Lt. Colo. wass antecedent to theirs in the line, yet his apointment in the State was Posterior.

  His Excellency Ratifies the Report.

Source: *Public Papers of George Clinton: First Governor of New York* (Albany: State of New York, 1990), 3:374.
Pierre Regnier de Roussi had been commissioned a Lieutenant Colonel of militia by General Richard Montgomery in November 1775, and in January 1776, Benedict Arnold appointed him Lieutenant Colonel of the First Canadian Regiment, which was later disbanded. De Roussi pleaded his case to Congress, which resolved that he was entitled to the rank and pay of a lieutenant colonel and referred him to Washington for employment. Regnier de Roussi became lieutenant colonel of the Fourth New York Regiment on March 26, 1777.

## James Giles, Receipt for Arms

Received Camp Valley Forge May 30th. 1778 of Colonel Swifts Regt. by the hands of H Daggett QMr, Nineteen Good Muskets—five bad Muskets—Nineteen Bayonet Belts, thirteen Cart'ge Boxes, fit, and [six] unfit for Service—
    James Giles Condr. M. S.

Source: General Collection Manuscript Miscellany, Group 1518, Item F-1, Henry Daggett Papers, Beinecke Library, Yale University.
Giles was a Conductor of Military Stores. Daggett was Quartermaster of the Seventh Connecticut Regiment.

## Ephraim Morgan, Receipt for Clothing

                        Camp Valey ford 1st. June 1778
I Ephraim Morgan a Non Commisoned officer In the Continental army In the first Battalion from the State of Connecticut, have Received of the Select Men of Preston in Said State, by the hand of John Bordman the following articles (viz) one pare of Lining Breaches a Lining Shirt & a pare of Stockings
    Recd pr me
                Ephraim Morgan—

Source: Photocopy, Valley Forge National Historical Park.
Text and signature in different hands. Some New England towns supplied their soldiers with clothing. At this time the Connecticut soldiers were the best clothed in the army.

## The Marquis de Lafayette to Henry Laurens

dear Sir                       Valley forge Camp 7th june 1778
I beg that you would be so good as to trouble the honbl Congress with a new request of mine, which I am much Concern'd for—the chevalier de Cambray who now waits on Congress brings me letters from several of my most intimate friends, where he is particularly recommended to me—that Gentlemen has also a letter from doctor franklin, and a certificate of some services he had the happiness of Rendering to the state of North Carolina—he will expose himself to

you his services and pretentions—I schall confine myself in assuring you that any thing which will be done for him I'll take as a particular favor—I make a Rule for me of Recommanding any french gentlemen who desires me to do so, and whom I think worthy of the attention of Congress—but Ms de Cambray is one of those whom I owe to my friends and my feelings to be very particular upon.

with the highest Regard I have the honor to be
  dear Sir  Your most obedient servant
    the Mis de Lafayette
the honorable the President of Congress

Endorsed: Marquis delafayette 7 June 1778 Recd 8th.

Source: Henry Laurens Papers, South Carolina Historical Society.
Louiis Antoine Cambray was appointed a Lieutenant-Colonel in the Corps of Engineers.

## William Brent et al., Statement Regarding Robert H. Saunders

Messieurs DIXON and HUNTER,
 *AS it may at once give satisfaction to the curious and inquisitive, as well as disappoint the censorious, and prevent disagreeable explanations, I hope you will insert the enclosed, to oblige your humble servant,*
    ROBERT H. SAUNDERS.
LIEUTENANT *Robert H. Saunders*, of the first *Virginia* state regiment, having fell into a dispute with an officer of the same regiment, in which his character as a military gentlemen was called in question, lieutenant Saunders, [line missing] account, for which the officer arrested him, as being contrary to the articles of war. After lieutenant *Saunders* had continued in arrest six or seven days, the dispute was compromised, his friends having advised him to resign his commission, as he could not be justifiable by the articles of war in giving a challenge. And as he may probably be censured by his countrymen for resigning at the opening of a campaign, we think it necessary to declare that he has left the army in repute. Given under our hands, at *Valley Forge*, the 8th of *June*, 1778.
   W. BRENT, Lieut. Col.  J. ALLISON, Major.
   J. NICHOLAS, Capt.   AB. CRUMP, Capt.

Source: *The Virginia Gazette*, July 10, 1778.
The date Robert Hyde Saunders resigned is not known.


### Edward Roche to James Booth

Sir                        Valley Forge June 9. 1778
I intend to make application for a Captaincy in the Engineer Corps to be rais'd, and as I have little or no acquaintance with any of the Genl: officers here, find that a reccommendation from the State is necessary shall depend upon your Freindship to procure one from Genl: Rodney, I have not the Honour of being personally acquainted with him, but make no doubt he knows my Character, and will send a reccommendatory Letter to Genl: Washington—
If I do not git the above Comission, shall be oblidged to quit the Army, for by the Regulations of the Army the Pay Masters are to be appointed out of the Capts: or Subalterns of each Regiment—
Should you procure the above sd reccomendatory Letter send it up immediately. I send this by Capt: Anderson who is to send a man down from New Castle on purpose to deliver this If you can, send back my him—
I have inclosed a Copy of the Qualifications required, one I am deficient in, but I take it only extends to Frenchmen &c.
You know my abilities in the Mathematics & drawing and I hope you will represent them to the Genl:—
    We move tomorrow and Encamp about 3 Miles further down—
        I am Sir your Friend &c.
        Edwd. Roche

Source: RG 1800.066, Revolutionary War Letters, Folder 262, Delaware Public Archives, Dover, Delaware.
Roche continued as Paymaster of the Delaware Regiment, and in 1780 was captured at Camden, South Carolina. Booth was Secretary of State for Delaware.


### Elias Boudinot to Daniel Hughes

Sir,                           Camp June 10th 1778
    Immediately on rect. hereof you will be pleased to send forward by the best Rout you can all the Officers Prisoners of War under your Care—I mean belonging to the land Service

Let them come under the Care of some proper Person who will deliver then to Mr. Atlee at Lancaster, or if there is a shorter Route to this Place, let them be detained short of Camp till he can acquaint me of their Arrival—They must endeavour to avoid York Town on their way—

P.S. You are to observe that is the officers only who are to be sent in, who are to give their paroles for abiding with the officer you send with them to the lines & to come out whenever called for—

Source: Boudinot Papers, Historical Society of Pennsylvania.
Hughes was an Ironmaster in Maryland who was apparently acting as an Assistant Commisary General of Prisoners at Hagerstown, MD.

## Richard Taylor, Advertisement for Lost Property

LOST, on the 21st of May last, Between Newtown, Bucks County, and the Swedes Ford, A RED Morocco leather POCKET BOOK, with THOMAS G WATKIN, FROOM [sic], in capitals, on the cover. In the Pocket book were seven Thirty Dollar bills, and about Twenty five Dollars in smaller bills, two States Lottery Tickets, a Captain's commission, and sundry other papers. Whoever will deliver the said Pocket book and contents to the subscriber, of the first Virginia regiment, or Capt. FRANCIS TAYLOR, of the second Virginia regiment, at head Quarters, shall receive SIXTY DOLLARS reward. RICHARD TAYLOR, Captain.

Source: *The Pennsylvania Packet or the General Advertiser*, June 10, 1778.

## Matthew Clarkson, Certificate for Robert Forman

Auditors Office June 11, 1778

Robert Forman Esq. Pay Master to the ninth Virginia Regiment haveing setled his Accounts in this Office, whereon there appeared to be due to the United States the sum of One thousand and three Dollars and 62/72 parts of a dollar; has produced three receipts for the same from the Pay Master General of the same tenor and date,—his

accounts are therefore discharged in this Office agreeable to the Resolves of Congress in such case made and provided—
     Matth Clarkson
          Audr of Accts.

Source: Record Group 93, M 859, Roll 111, Document 31552.
A note on the reverse shows that Forman resigned on June 16, 1778. Clarkson was one of two men appointed by Congress in 1778, to serve as Auditors of the army's accounts. He later became Mayor of Philadelphia.

**Extract of a Letter**

Extract of a letter, dated June 11, 1778.

I returned from Camp last Tuesday. The enemy were positively to have left Philadelphia last Sunday, but for the arrival of the Commissioners. They were brought over by Commodore Elliot, Earl Carlisle, a young macaroni, with several mistresses, is quartered at Mr. Powell's, the late Mayor, the family having retreated into his back buildings; Governor Johnstone is at Mr. Charles Stedman's. Dr. Ferguson, their Secretary, asked safe conduct to York Town, but was told, it was needless. Some few vessels remain; the rest, between 3 and 400 in number, are below the cheveaux de frise, and extend to the Capes. The army are supplied with provisions sent up in boats. It is conjectured, that the obstacles which they may foresee in a march through New Jersey, will induce them to go by Water. I think the coming of the Commissioners will not do more than delay Gen. Clinton for some days.

Source: *Dunlap's Maryland Gazette Or the Baltimore General Advertiser*, June 23, 1778.
The so-called Carlisle peace commission, landed in Philadelphia on June 6. Composed of Frederick Howard, Earl of Carlisle, Member of Parliament William Eden, who was the brother of former Virginia Governor Robert Eden, George Johnstone, former Governor of West Florida it was empowered (along with Admiral Richard Howe and General Henry Clinton) "to treat, consult and agree upon the means of quieting the disorders now subsisting in certain of the colonies, plantations, and provinces of North America"—it failed to convince Congress to make peace.

## Richard Parker to Richard Kidder Meade

D$^r$ Sir

    Cap$^t$. Cummins of my Regiment has an inclination to Resign and as there will be from the late regulation more than a proportion of Captains and his engagements are such; that I recommend him for a resignation
June 11th 1778          I am Dr Sir Y$^r$. Very Obd [   ]
                                     Rd Parker
                                       Colo 1st: Va. Regm$^t$
To Colo. Meade

Source: Record Group 93, M 853 Volume 169, Commissions and Resignations, 1776-1780, Reel 12, f. 243, National Archives.
Alexander Cummins' resignation was accepted, effective on June 13, 1778.

## Elias Boudinot to Ezekiel Williams

Sir,                        Camp June 13 1778
    I have not time to answer your favor[s] which have duly come to hand and can only now desire you immediately to send in to NYork all the Officers Pris. of War now under your Care, taking their Paroles in the form sent you—You will be pleased to forward exact lists of a[ll] you send off as speedily as possible—
             Am in great Haste Yours &c

P.S. after sending off all the Officers—you will please to forward on in the same Manner the Privates under your Care, provided they do not exceed the number of 500—

Source: Boudinot Papers, Historical Society of Pennsylvania.
Williams was Deputy Commissary General of Prisoners for Connecticut.

## Henry Knox to William Knox

Dear Bill                       Camp 16th. June 1778
    The Enemy are expected to evacuate Philadelphia tonight—
The Two Lucys are well
    I am Your Humble Servant—

H Knox
Addressed: To Mr. Wm Knox Boston

Source: Henry Knox Papers, Massachusetts Historical Society.
William was Henry's brother.

## Burges Ball, Certificate for James McIlhany/McIlhaney

I hereby Certify that Lt. Mc.Ilhany who is entitled to a Captains Commn. since ye. 21st. day of Decr. in ye. 5th. Virga. Regt., is not indebted to ye. United States but very trifling wch. Lt. Bently of sd. Regt: will settle immediately.
June 18th. 1778.
      Burges Ball Lt. Colo. Comdt.
       5th. & 9th. V: Regts.

Source: Record Group 93, M 859, Reel 110, National Archives.
On the back appears the notation "Jas. McIlhaney resigned June 18, 1778." He was commissioned as a First Lieutenant on March 25, 1776, and the name appears as McIlhaney on the commission.

## William Davies, James Moon, and Peter Jones, Certificates for Burwell Green

                June 18. 1778.
 I do hereby certify that Ensign Burwell Green of my regiment does not stand indebted to the United States for recruiting money or other accounts, to the best of my knowledge.
     William Davies Col: 14th. Vir. Regt.

I hereby Certify that Burwell Green Ensign 14th Virginia Regimt is not indebted to the sd. Regimt or the United States, to the best of my Knowledge June 18. 1778
     James Moon PM. 14th Vir Rt.

Thereby certify that Burwell Green Ensg. 14th Virga. Regimt. has had no recruiting money to my Knowledge.
     Peter Jones Capt. 14th Virga Regt
     June 18th 1778

Source: Record Group 93, M 859, Roll 110, Document 31193, National Archives.
Green's resignation was accepted, effective on June 18, 1778.

## James McHenry to Walter Stewart

Sir                        Head Quarters Valley Forge 18 June 1778
     Your letter of yesterday came to hand last night
         I hope you will soon have the pleasure of entering this City
            I am Sir your very hble servt.
                 James McHenry            A Secy
P. S     M$^r$. Boudinott letter was handed to the General of which be plesed to inform him
     Colonel W. Stewart

Source: Peter Force Collection, Ms. 19,061, Series 7E, Item 138, Walter Stewart Papers, Roll 44, Library of Congress.
McHenry, who had recently been freed in a prisoner exchange, had been appointed Washington's Assistant Secretary. He was later Washington's Secretary of War and Fort McHenry was named for him.

## Jean Baptiste, Chevalier de Ternant, Opinion from Council of War.

                                               June 18, 1778.
My opinion relative to the matter agitated yesterday in the Board is as follows: 1. that the Intelligences received of the Enemy's motions are so uncertain & so far from being satisfactory about his Designs, that it would be highly imprudent to trust too far to appearances & undertake a march with the whole army, especially in several columns, whilst the Enemy has according to reports such a numerous Cavalry as to enable him to move rapidly & carry his point of attack either upon our position or upon one or two columns of lesser strength & to get the advantage of us by detail. Therefore I think it adviseable to send out between us & the Enemy a detachment of observation, which on our part will supply us with better & more positive intelligences, & on the other hand oblige the enemy to discover his intentions. That detachment consisting of 2000 troops supported by all the cavalry that can possible be gathered, will keep up an immediate, direct & constant correspondance with the small detachment under Gl. Maxwell & leave us no doubt about what is

detachment under Gl. Maxwell & leave us no doubt about what is passing….this detachment can at any time join the main army in case, it is likely to be engaged by any motion of the enemy; it will favour desertion which is an important object at this present juncture; & when the enemy has completed the evacuation of the city, & does not seem to mean any thing else but a retreat to New York, I think it likewise adviseable to follow that detachment which will be our advanced guard & make a sudden & rapid march into the Jersey, with the whole army, collected in one body, & without the baggage which may by sent by any road on our left, & thus will always be covered. The army by keeping together will be able to follow the enemy closer, to present his spreading, & laying waste the country, & lastly favour & protect desertion, which in this retreat of the enemy from such a place as Philadelphia, becomes an object of the greatest importance for the american army & will undoubtedly prove so if duly attended to…nothing from the knowledge I have of the country can prevent our joining afterwards the northern army if found necessary, or taking some advantageous post of observation, about Middleburg & keeping up an open'd correspondence with that army…celerity being the maine object of what the army is to undertake, I think it is indispensable to remove the sick &c., as soon as possible, & I should say immediately.

Source: Item 94, Joseph Rubinfine, "List 136: The American Revolution, A Catalog of Manuscripts," Joseph Rubinfine, 505 South Flagler Drive, Suite 1301, West Palm Beach, FL 33401, undated catalog, $2500.00.
Ternant was a sub-inspector to Steuben, and was serving without military rank. On September 25, 1778, the Continental Congress appointed him a Lieutenant Colonel and ordered him south as "inspector to the troops" in Georgia and South Carolina.

## Thomas Bradford's Narrative

After we were driven out of the city [Philadelphia] by the British, I went to our camp at Valley Forge and there received a commission dated January 10$^{th}$ 1778, as Deputy Commissioner of Prisoners. I performed the duties of this office till the evacuation of the city by the British, when I was ordered to take command of that post in Philadelphia, and I held it until about August 1783, having had several thousands of British prisoners under my charge, to forward for exchange, when the Board of War appointed a deranged Lieutenant of the Army to the office.

Source: Thomas Bradford Papers, British Army Prisoners Correspondence, 1777-78, vol. 1, Historical Society of Pennsylvania.

## Rowland Evans Complaint

Rowland Evans follows now with a third letter depicting more in detail his trials and discomforts suffered during this memo able winter with the armies so close at hand. The letter is neither postmarked, dated nor signed. Doctor Physick makes these entries on its top:
   Rowland Evans' Complaint to the Penns—Owner.
April 1, 1777, Rowland Evans' Lease and Term Commenced.
The letter then reads :—
   "September following. The British Army passed by the place and took about Three Hundred Bushels of Oats, tramped and ruined Five or Six acres of Buckwheat, besides potatoes, apples, etc., for which I never received any compensation. They likewise tore the bolting cloths in such a manner, that the Mill has grown much out of repute on account of the bad work she does.
   In the later part of the year 1777, the American Army took from me near Four Hundred bushels of Wheat which I designed to have paid my rent with and allowed me only 8-6 per bushel for it: also took hay to my great prejudice, having been obliged to send my cattle to Berks County to keep them from perishing.
   In May and June 1778, The Horse of the American Army were put on my wheat Meadow—The Wheat was computed twenty acres for which I was allowed 400 Bushels at 12-6 per bushel—the hay at £5 per ton—in Lieu of which I was obliged to purchase grain and hay at a most exhorbitant price.
   It is to be considered that when I first took this place, it was with view of doing Merchant work with ye Mills, as the exportation was then open, but as the Trade was stopt immediately after my time commenced I have no merchant work at all since April 1777, so that the Mill which used to be a valuable part of the Estate has been Scarce any advantage at all to me. having nothing but country Custom which was always Small by reason of the number of Mill's in ye neighborhood. and is now much smaller since the British Soldiers tore the bolting cloth."

Source: Dr. W. H. Reed, "Reminiscences of Audubon," *Historical Sketches, A Collection of Papers Prepared for the Historical Society of Montgomery County, Pennsylvania* (Norristown, Pa.: The Society, 1910), 189.

### John Robertson, Advertisement for a Missing Horse

TWENTY DOLLARS REWARD.
STRAYED or STOLEN from Camp at the Valley Forge, on the 18th of June last, a grey HORSE, about four feet eight inches high, eight years old, and branded on the near buttock R. a natural trotter. Whoever secures the said horse and delivers him to Mr. JONATHAN PRITCHARD, near the Yellow Springs, in Chester County, or to the subscriber with the army, shall receive the above reward.
JOHN ROBERTSON, Adj. 10th Virginia Reg.
2d Brigade.

Source: *The Pennsylvania Packet or the General Advertiser*, July 14, 1778.

### Cornelius Sheriff to the Inhabitants of Chester County

*Valley Forge, Aug.* 28, 1778.
THE inhabitants of Chester county, and those in the neighbourhood of the old encampment at the Valley Forge, that have public accounts to settle with the subscriber, contracted since the second of March last, are desired to attend at said place on Tuesdays and Fridays only, for payment.
C. SHERIFF, D. Q. M. G.

Source: *The Pennsylvania Packet and General Advertiser*, August 29, 1778; September 5, 1778.
Sheriff was a Deputy Quartermaster General. He was killed in 1779 when he fell off his horse.

### James Hopkins, Advertisement for a Missing Horse

THIRTY DOLLARS REWARD.
STRAYED from Camp a few days before the army left the Valley Forge, a bay Horse, fourteen hands high, eight or nine years old, trots very short and canters tolerable well; has a hanging mane, and is a little stiff in his off hind leg. Whoever gives information of said horse,

or brings him to Capt. JOHN PALMER'S, at the corner of Fourth and Arch-streets, Philadelphia, shall receive the above reward and all reasonable charges, paid by JAMES HOPKINS.

Source: *The Pennsylvania Packet or the General Advertiser*, October 27, 1778. Hopkins has not been identified

**John Mitchell, Payment for Horses and Hay**

ALL persons possessed of Receipts or Vouchers for HORSES taken by General Green or General Wayne, and the Officers under their command, in or about the month of March last; also all persons having HAY taken or destroyed by order of his Excellency the Commander in Chief, and having proper certificates, with appraisements of the value at the time taken or destroyed, are desired to present the same at my office in Chesnut-street for payment.
JOHN MITCHELL, D. Q. M. Gen.

Source: *The Pennsylvania Journal and Weekly Advertiser*, March 17, 1779.

**Albigence Waldo, Report on Inoculation**

While the American Army lay in Winter Quarters at Valley Forge in Pennsylvania, at the opening of the Spring, above four thousand, Officers and Soldiers, were Inoculated with the Small Pox, when they had little else but Beef and Flour for Regimen, & their preparation was almost universally that of Tartari Emetici & Jalap only, generally mixed and given together two or three times. The success was remarkable, & but few died, and those chiefly with a secondary fever which would mostly turn putrid principally owing to the uncommon fatigues of the preceding Campaign and unwholesome provisions for which this Campaign of 1777 was remarkable.
An Indian Soldier, who, among others, I inoculated at this time, while he was under the foregoing preparation, and thro' the whole course of the Distemper, rarely passed a day without being intoxicated with Spirits; notwithstanding which, he had the Distemper exceeding light, and recovered his former health in the usual time without any notable accident.—But his Companion, another Indian, who had the same

relish for Liquor, taking encouragement from the good fortune of his fellow, indulged himself but once in drinking too freely, and died the next day, at the time the pox were all thrown out upon the Skin.—Their Constitutions & former habits of body were nearly similar, and there was but little difference in their Ages.—Possibly the event of the latter might have proved the same with the other, had he indulged himself from the beginning; unless the fatal catastrophe of the latter was more owing to a peculiar habit & at that particular time of which the former was free.                A. W.—
1779

> Source: This is written on blank pages after the last chapter "Of Inoculation" in Samuel Sharpe, *A Treatise on the Operations of Surgery, with a Description and Representation of the Instruments Used in Performing them....* Ninth Edition (London:1769). The book was owned by Albigence Waldo, as his printed bookplate is inside the front cover. Trent Collection, Duke University Medical Center Library.

## Baptismal Record, Isaac Worley Till

Jsaace Worley Till Son to Hannah
a fre Nigroe woman in full
Communion with the Church
was born in Gen: Washingtons
Camp Valey forge ninteen months
ago & baptised on this 4th. Sabbath
of Augt. 1779

Source: "Wm. Marshall's Register of Births and Baptisms in the Scotch of Philadelphia for the Year 1768 to the Year 1801," *Journal of the Presbyterian Historical Society,*: 5 (1909-1910), 276.
This is the record of a truly unique event: the only birth recorded during the Encampment and that to a Black woman. She was the slave of a John Mason and was sometimes called Hannah Mason. At some point she married Isaac Till and they both worked for Washington. On June 23, 1780, Major Caleb Gibbs, paid her "eighty six dollars in full for two months wages at His Excellency General Washington's family." According to an obituary in John Fanning Watson's 1830 "Annals of Philadelphia," she is supposed to have been 102 or 103 when she died in 1825. If she was that old, her son referenced above would have been born when she was in her early 50s. Possible, but not likely. Watson also states that Lafayette visited her that year 1825 and helped her out financially.

## DOCUMENT CHRONOLOGY

James Mitchell Varnum to George Washington, December 22, 1777.
Francis Barber, Certificate Regarding John Conway, December 23, 1777.
William Bayley to Jean Bayley, ca. December 23, 1778.
Field Return of the Continental Army, December 23, 1777.
Jethro Sumner and Lachlan McIntosh, Certificates for Thomas Granberry/Granberry, December 24 and 25, 1777.
Anthony Wayne, "In Answer to Sundry persons in behalf of the Citizens of Phila.", December 24, 1777.
Extract of a Letter from an Officer, December 25, 1777.
Timothy Pickering Jr. to Clement Biddle, December 25, 1777.
Hugh Maxwell to Hannah Maxwell, December 26, 1777.
William Alexander, Pass, December 27, 1777.
Henry Dixon, Certificate for Thomas Granbery, December 27, 1777.
Extract of a Letter, December 27, 1777.
Nathanael Greene, Furlough for Samuel Waples, December 27, 1777.
Johann de Kalb to John Adams, December 27, 1777.
Johann de Kalb to the Comte de Broglie, December 27, 1777.
Charles West, Certificate for Joseph Baynham, December 28, 1777.
List of Stores Near Chester and Other Places, December 29, 1777.
Elias Boudinot to Henry Hugh Fergusson, December 31, 1777.
Numbers Wanting to Complete the Continental Army, Undated.
Extract of a Letter from a Captain of Light Horse, Undated.
Albigence Waldo, Certificate for Stephen Caleff, Undated.
Isaac Coit, Receipt for Clothing, January 1778.
Benjamin Ballard, Certificate for Retained Rations, January 1, 1778.
Robert, to his Mother, January 1, 1778.
Benjamin Coats, Pay Authorization, January 3, 1778.
Griffin Greene, Certificate Regarding Simon Smith, January 3, 1778.
Griffin Greene, Certificate Regarding Stephen Briggs, January 3, 1778.
Men Reenlisted in the Seventh Virginia, January 3, 1778.
Enoch Poor to George Washington, January 3, 1778.
Edward Stevens, Certificate for John Syme, January 3, 1778.
James Bancroft to Joseph Bancroft, January 5, 1778.
Johann de Kalb, to Anna Emily van Robais, Madame de Kalb, January 5, 1778.
Timothy Pickering, State of the New Jersey Regiments,

January 5, 1778.
William Davies to William Alexander, January 7, 1778.
Extract of a Letter, January 7, 1778.
Thirteen Artillery Men's Receipts, January 7, 1778.
William Alexander to Aaron Burr, January 8, 1778.
William Lee Davidson to Richard Caswell, January 8, 1778.
Elias Boudinot to Thomas Bradford,
    ca. January 11, 1778.
Michael Crous to Thomas Jones, Two Receipts for Cattle.
Richard Kidder Meade, Permission for Hugh Roe to Resign,
    January 14, 1778.
Thomas Jones, Ration Deficiencies of Third New Jersey Regiment,
    January 18, 1778.
Thomas Antoine, Chevalier de Maudit Duplessis to Henry Laurens,
    January 20, 1778.
Alexander Hamilton to Henry Emanuel Lutterloh, Lutterloh to James
    Young, January 20, 1778.
Jedediah Huntington to Mathew Irwin, January 20, 1778.
Gaston Marie Léonard Maussion de la Bastie to his Brother,
    January 20, 1778.
James McClure to David McClure, January 21, 1778.
Matthias Ogden to Jonathan Trumbull, Jr., John Pierce, Jr., to Ogden,
    January 21, 1778.
Extracts From Letters of Officers, January 22, 1778.
Andrew Dunlap to Leonard Bronck, January 24, 1778.
Charles Porterfield, Certificate for Daniel Reagan, January 24, 1778.
Tench Tilghman to William Alexander, January 24, 1778.
Jonathan Allen to Unidentified, January 25, 1778.
Timothy Bigelow to Nancy Bigelow, January 15, 1778.
John Fitzgerald to Hammond Beaumont, January 26, 1778.
A Lieutenant Colonel, Thoughts on the Army, January 29, 1778.
Elias Boudinot, Visit to Prisoners in New York, Undated.
Jonathan Todd, Jr., Receipt for Pay, Undated.
George Weedon to Richard Henry Lee, February 1, 1778.
Ephraim Blaine to Alexander Blaine, February 3, 1778.
The Marquis de Lafayette to Henry Laurens, February 4, 1778.
James Rix to Miriam Rix, February 5, 1778.
William Russell, Discharge for William Wroe, February 6, 1778.
Johann de Kalb to Henry Laurens, February 7, 1778,
An Officer to His Friend, February 7, 1778.

Thomas Jones to Unidentified, February 8, 1778.
Ephraim Blaine to John Lacey, Jr., February 10, 1778.
George Weedon, Discharge for James Hungerford,
 February 11, 1778.
Charles Scott, Discharge for David Grate/Great, February 12, 1778.
Thomas Jones, Return of Food Delivered at the Bakehouse,
 February 13, 1778.
Joseph Vose and William Shepard to George Washington,
 February 13, 1778.
George Weedon, Discharge for John Turnley, February 13, 1778.
Hugh Maxwell to Bethiah Maxwell, February 14, 1778.
William Russell, Discharge for David Street, February 14, 1778.
William Davies, Certificate for Le Roy Edwards, February 15, 1778.
Receipts by Robert Blair and John Chaloner, February 16, 1778,
William Davies to William Russell, February 16, 1778.
George Washington to Richard Howell, February 17, 1778.
James Chambers, Plantation Advertisement, February 18, 1778.
Samuel Tenny to Peter Turner, February 18, 1778.
Charles Scott to Samuel Gill et al., February 21, 1778.
John Wilson and Lachlan McIntosh, Certificate for Joshua Curtis,
 February 21, 1778.
Jedediah Huntington to Jabez Huntington, February 22, 1778.
James Monroe, Pass for John Wallace, Jr., February 23, 1778.
Rations Certifications by Jesse Baldwin, William Shute,
 and John Conway, February 28, 1778.
Return of the North Carolina Brigade, February 29, 1778.
Robert Hanson Harrison to Clement Biddle, March 3, 1778.
Lachlan McIntosh to Robert Hanson Harrison, March 3, 1778.
Samuel Bartlett to George Washington, with an Endorsement
 by James Mellen, March 4, 1778.
John Chaloner to Jacob Anderson, March 4, 1778.
Henry Daggett, Receipt, March 5, 1778.
Thomas Hughes, Certificate for James Hord, March 6, 1778.
John Paterson and Tench Tilghman, Discharge for
 Joseph Morse, March 7, 1778.
George Washington to Caleb Gibbs, March 9, 1778.
Samuel Jones, Pay Certificate for Horatio Turpin, March 11, 1778.
Walter Stewart, Discharge for Thomas Fleeman, March 12, 1778.
Joseph Ward to Richard Varick, March 13, 1778.
Joseph Jay, Deserter Notice, March 18, 1778.

John Bryce to James Johnston, March 21, 1778.
John Stokes and Charles Lewis, Certificates for Elisha Arnold,
    March 22 and 23, 1778.
Bounty Paid to Massachusetts Soldiers, March 23, 1778.
Samuel Goff, Payment from John Nixon, March 26, 1778.
William Woodford to Oliver Towles, March 27, 1778.
Robert Hanson Harrison to John Lacey, Jr., March 28, 1778.
Henry Bicker, Certificate for Philip Clumburg, ca. March 30, 1778.
Rowland Evans to Edmund Physick, March 30, 1778.
Nathanael Greene to Clement Biddle, March 31, 1778.
William Henry, Roll of Recruits, March 31, 1778,
Ebenezer Smith, Certificate Regarding Nathan Thayer,
    March 31, 1778.
Elias Boudinot, Prisoner Cartel Notes, March 31-April 11, 1778.
John Patten, Certificate for Stephen Southall, April 1, 1778.
Samuel French, Ordnance Report to George Washington,
    ca. April 1, 1778.
Josiah Lacey to Mrs. Isaac Coler, April 2, 1778.
Richard Parker, Certificate for William Sandford, April 5, 1778.
John Allison to Peter Muhlenberg, April 6, 1778.
Louis Lebique Duportail to Horatio Gates, April 6, 1778.
Richard Kidder Meade to Nathanael Greene, April 6, 1778.
Frederick Weissenfels to Tench Tilghman, April 6, 1778.
James Wesson to George Washington, April 6, 1778.
Henry Young, Status of the Seventh Virginia Regiment,
    April 6, 1778.
Tench Tilghman, Discharge for John Wilkins, April 7, 1778.
William Cook, Diatribe Against William Alexander, April 8, 1778.
Robert Spencer to George Washington, April 9, 1778.
Nathaniel Chipman to Elisha Lee, April 10, 1778.
The Marquis de Lafayette to Horatio Gates, April 10, 1778.
Oliver Spencer to George Washington, April 10, 1778,
    Spencer to Tench Tilghman, April 11, 1778.
Hugh Maxwell to Bethiah Maxwell, April 11, 1778.
Ebenezer Crosby to Daniel Newcomb, April 12, 1778.
Benjamin Names, Receipt for Reinlistment Bounty, April 12, 1778.
Walter Stewart to Charles Stewart, ca. April 12, 1778.
Nathaniel Chipman to Elisha Lee, April 1778.
William Davies et al., Certificates for Gross Scruggs,
    April 16 and 22, 1778.

William Bayley to Jean Bayley, April 16, 1778.
Benjamin Fishbourne for Anthony Wayne to Thomas Wharton Jr., April 16, 1778.
Charles Stewart to Samuel Gray, April 16, 1778.
Joseph Ward, an Appeal to the Generous and Brave, April 16, 1778.
Elias Boudinot to John Winslow, April 17, 1778.
Peter Stephen Du Ponceau to Nathanael Greene, April 17, 1778.
Hugh Maxwell to Bethiah Maxwell, April 19, 1778.
Elias Boudinot to Robert Livingston Jr., April 20, 1778.
Andrew Dunlap to Edward Bronck, April 23, 1778.
Samuel Tenny to Peter Turner, April 23, 1778.
Tunis Van Waganer to Leonard Bronck, April 23, 1778.
John Chessborough, Advertisement for a Missing Horse, April 24, 1778.
John Gibson, Certificate Regarding Hardin Perkins, April 26, 1778.
Friedrich Wilhelm Augustus von Steuben to Henry Laurens, April 26, 1778.
Albigence Waldo, Poem, Part Two, April 26, 1778.
Adam Allen Receipt, April 27, 1778.
Francis Barber to Richard Kidder Meade, April 28, 1778.
James Mitchell Varnum to John Sullivan, April 28, 1778.
Clement Biddle to Moore Furman, April 29, 1778. 2 letters
The Marquis de Lafayette, Appoints John Cropper to Command, April 29, 1778.
Humphry Thompson to Unidentified, April 29, 1778.
William Alexander to John Stevens, April 30, 1778.
Elias Boudinot, Visit to Germantown, May 1778.
William Alexander to John Stevens, May 1, 1778.
Robert Hanson Harrison to Elias Boudinot, May 2, 1778.
Return of the North Carolina Brigade, May 2, 1778.
William Williams to Thomas Wharton Jr., May 2, 1780.
Jeremiah Olney, Certificate for Bethuel Curtis, May 3, 1778.
Lachlan McIntosh to William Alexander, May 4, 1778.
Friedrich Wilhelm Augustus von Steuben to Henry Laurens, May 7, 1778.
Unknown to Silas Deane, May 7, 1778.
Philip Van Cortlandt to Pierre Van Cortlandt, May 7 & 10, 1778.
John Laurens, Resignation of Matthias Hite, May 8, 1778.
Christian Febiger to William Alexander, May 9, 1778.
Nicholas Fish to Richard Varick, May 9, 1778.

Thomas Jones to Jacob Anderson, May 9, 1778.
Stephen Stevenson, Deserter Notice, May 9, 1778.
Josiah Lacey, Blanket Receipt, May 10, 1778.
Leonard Miller, Ration Receipt, May 10, 1778.
James Glentworth, Oath of Allegiance, May 11, 1778.
Charles Pettit to Davis Bevan, May 12, 1778.
Clement Biddle to Moore Furman, May 14, 1778.
Alexander Church, Receipt for Steuben's Horses, May 14, 1778.
The Marquis de Lafayette to Henry Laurens, May 14, 1778.
James Mitchell Varnum to George Washington, May 14, 1778.
Thomas Clark and Lachlan McIntosh, Certificate for Thomas Jones,
    May 15, 1778.
Johann de Kalb to Henry Laurens, May 16, 1778.
Lachlan McIntosh, Oath of Allegiance by Adam Boyd, May 16, 1778.
Charles Pettit, Fords on the Schuylkill, May 16, 1778.
Samuel Mansfield to John Lamb?, May 17, 1778.
Abraham Sheppard, Certificate for James Wilson, May 17, 1778.
Charles Fleming, Certificate Regarding Thomas Lipscomb,
    May 19, 1778.
William Davies, Certificate for Burwell Green, May 20, 1778.
Peter Muhlenberg to Robert Hanson Harrison, ca. May 22, 1778.
John Smith to Charles Scott, May 23, 1778.
John Woodson, Advertisement for Missing Horse, May 23, 1778.
Burges Ball, Certificate Regarding Captain Thomas Parramore,
    May 24, 1778.
Michael Crous, Receipt for Cattle, May 24, 1778.
Eli Catlin to George Washington with an Endorsement by
    Philip B. Bradley, May 25, 1778.
Burges Ball, Certificate for William Henderson, May 29, 1778.
Board of General Officers, May 29, 1778.
James Giles, Receipt for Arms, May 30, 1778.
Ephraim Morgan, Receipt for Clothing, June 1, 1778.
The Marquis de Lafayette to Henry Laurens, June 7, 1778.
William Brent et al., Statement Regarding Robert H. Saunders,
    June 8, 1778.
Edward Roche to James Booth, June 9, 1778.
Elias Boudinot to Daniel Hughes, June 10, 1778.
Richard Taylor, Advertisement for Missing Property, June 10, 1778.
Matthew Clarkson, Certificate for Robert Forman, June 11, 1778.
Extract of a Letter, June 11, 1778.

Richard Parker to Richard Kidder Meade, June 11, 1778.
Elias Boudinot to Ezekiel Williams, June 13, 1778.
Henry Knox to William Knox, June 16, 1778.
Burges Ball, Certificate for James McIlhany/Ilhaney, June 18, 1778.
William Davies, James Moon and Peter Jones,
    Certificates for Burwell Green, June 18, 1778
James McHenry to Walter Stewart, June 18, 1778.
Jean Baptiste, Chevalier de Ternant, Opinion from Council of War,
    June 18, 1778.
Thomas Bradford's Narrative, Undated.
Rowland Evans Complaint, Undated
John Robertson, Advertisement for a Missing Horse, July 14, 1778.
Cornelius Sheriff to the Inhabitants of Chester County,
    August 28, 1778.
James Hopkins, Advertisement for a Missing Horse,
    October 27, 1778.
John Mitchell, Payment for Horses and Hay, March 17, 1779.
Albigence Waldo, Report on Smallpox Inoculation, 1779.
Isaac Worley Till, Baptismal Record, August 1779.

# INDEX

Ackley, Ephraim, 174
Acre, Ambrose, 16
Adam, John, 26
Adams, John, 8, 9; letter to, 7
  mission to France, 7-8
African-Americans, 71, 188
Albany, N.Y., 26, troops coming
  from, 116
Alexander, Kitty, 151
Alexander, William, 73, 123; diatribe
  against, 112; letters from, 23,
  151, 153; letters to, 20, 40, 157,
  160; witnesses Oath of
  Allegiance, 164; writes a pass, 6
Alexandria, N.J., forage at, 146, 147
Alisson, Robert, 9
Allen, Adam, receipt by, 143
Allen, Ethan, 51
Allen, Jonathan, 128; letter from, 41
Allen, Lieutenant, 127
Allen, Tho., 16
Allentown, N.J.; forage at, 89, 147
Allison, John, 177; letter from, 109
Amberson, William, 143
Anderson, Enoch, 178
Anderson, Jacob, letters to, 76, 162
Anderson, Joseph, 29
Anderson, Joseph Inslee, 143
Andrews, Wm., 16
Armand-Tuffin, Charles, Marquis de
  la Rouërie, 166
Arms, 77, 176
Armstrong, John, 33
Army, British, brutality of, 11-12;
  cannot conquer, 66-67; expected
  movements of, 183-84; expected
  to leave Philadelphia, 181;
  movements of, 6, 7, 11, 33; must
  be weak, 119; now smaller, 124;
  plundering murderers, 36;
  skirmishes with, 4, 36, 38, 39, 41,
  56-57; stronger, 18
  to leave Philadelphia, 180
Army, Continental
  discipline of, 116, 144; dressed
  like enemy, 73

engineers, 109, 178; Field
  Return, 2; friendly fire at
  Germantown, 34; good quality
  of, 18; in a miserable
  condition, 36; low numbers of,
  115; men needed to complete,
  10; much better, 119;
  mustering problems, 80-81;
  officers shabby, 62; poor
  morale, 61; problems with and
  recommendations for, 43-47;
  recruiting for, 24, 123; recruits
  needed, 61-63, 124-25; returns
  of the North Carolina Brigade,
  74-75; 154-55; short of men,
  10, 18, 19, 10; strength of, 20;
  suffering hardships and danger,
  5, 63
Arnold, Elisha
  certificates for, 82
Aston, Peter, 77
Atlee, William, 26, 179
Bailey, John, 41
Baldwin, Jesse,
  certificate by, 73
Baldwin, Mr., 42
Ball, Burges,
  certificates by, 174, 175, 182
Ballard, Benjamin,
  receipt by, 13
Ballard, Jeremiah, 29
Bancroft, James,
  letter from, 17
Bancroft, Joseph,
  letter to, 17
Banker, C./Chr., 147
Bankson, John, 82
Barber, Francis, 28
  certificate by, 1;
  letter from, 143
Barlow, John,
  deserted, 82
Barracks, temporary in a stable, 69
Barry, John, captures vessels, 81
Bartlett, Samuel, asks to resign, 76
Barton, Saml., 16

Battle of the Brandywine, 32-33
Bayley, Jean, letters to, 1, 122
Bayley, William, letters from, 1, 122
Baylor, George, feed for horses, 83-85
Baynham, Joseph, certificate for, 8
Beaumont, Hammond, letter to, 43
Belcher, William, 12
Bell, William, deserted, 163
Bently/Bentley, William, 182
Berks County, Pa., 185
Bevan, Davis, letter to, 165
Bicker, Henry, certificate by, 87
Biddle, Clement, 31, 32, 77; letters from, 145, 165; letters to, 4, 75, 88
Bigelow, Nancy, letter to, 42
Bigelow, Timothy, 83; letter from, 42
Birth at Valley Forge, 188
Black Regiment, 71
Blaine, Alexander, letter to, 57
Blaine, Ephraim, 77, 143; letters from, 57, 64
Blair, Robert. receipt by, 68
Blankets, 21, 53, 61, 67, 137, 163, 171
Bloomfield, Jarvis, 29
Bloomfield, Joseph, 28
Booth, James, letter to, 178
Bordman, John, 176
Bostwick, William, 29
Boudinot, Elias, 183
  letter to, 153
  letters from, 10, 24, 125, 127, 178, 181
  notes on prisoner exchange, 90-103
  prisoner exchange report, 151-152
  report on prisoners in New York., 48-55
Boughan, Richd., 16
Boughtnow, John, 23
Bowles, John, resignation of, 1
Boyd, Adam, Oath of Allegiance by, 169
Bradford, Gamaliel, 13
Bradford, Thomas, letter to, 24
  narrative, 184

Bradley, David, 16
Bradley, Philip B.,
  endorsement by, 174
Bradley, Timothy, 28
Bradley, Wm., 16
Brandywine, Battle of, 33-34
Brent, William, letter by, 177
Brice, John, 168
Bridge, Sullivan's, 144, 170
Briggs, Stephen, certificate for, 15
Brightwell, John, 16
Brittin, William, resignation of, 114
Broglie, Charles François, Comte de, 7; letter to, 8
Bronck, Leonard, letters to, 39, 128, 130
Brown, Captain, 171
Brown, Isaac, 11
Brown, Solomon, deserted, 163
Brown, William, letter to, 57
Brunswick, N.J., forage at, 147
Bryce, John, letter from, 82
Bucks County, Pa., 64
Burgoyne, John, 53
Burk, Thomas, 16
Burks, Saml., 16
Burnett, Robert, 153
Burr, Aaron, letter to, 23
Butler, Richard, 123
Butter making, 120
Caldwell, James, 147, 165
Caleff, Stephen, certificate for, 12
Cambray, Louis Antoine
  recommendation for, 176
Camp, John, resignation of, 109
Campbell, Capt., 51
Canada, plans to invade, 57, 59, 80
Cardwell, Wm., 15
Carlisle Peace Commission, 180
Carlisle, Frederick Howard, Earl of, 180
Carlton, Samuel, 144
Caswell, Richard
  letter to, 24
Caswell, William, 24
Catanch, William, 29
Catlin, Eli, resignation of, 174
Cattle, 26, 27, 174, 185

Cattle, branded, 174
Cavalry, American, 185
Chaloner, John, letter by, 76; receipt by, 68
Chambers, Catharine, 70
Chambers, James, advertises a plantation, 69
Chambers, Thorow Good, 16
Champion, Henry, 174
Chatham, Captain, 53
Chauncey, John, 11
Chessborough, John, Advertisement for a missing horse, 130
Chester County, Pa., 186
Chester, Pa., 7, 33; supplies at, 9
Chipman, Nathaniel, letters from, 114, 120, 192
Christiana, Del., 10
Christmas, 13
Church, Alexander, receipt by, 166
Civilians, accounts to be settled, 189; disaffected, 9, 11, 18; going to market in Philadelphia, 62; hard heartedness of, 67; pass for, 6; Pennsylvania has most traitors, 116; plundered by the enemy, 18; problems of, 87-88, 185; request aid, 3; robbed, 4; stupid rascals, 36
Clark, Thomas, certificate by, 168
Clarke, William, 29
Clarkson, Matthew, certificate by, 179
Clinton, Henry, 49, 180
Cloth, captured, 21
Clothing, 13, 59, 122, 171; army better supplied, 119 asked for, 67, mittens 1; received, 12; shortages of, 2, 20, 21, 40, 48, 58, 72-73
Clumburg, Philip, certificate for, 87
Clymer, Mr., 79
Coats, Benjamin, pay authorization, 14
Coggswell, Mr., 114
Coit, Isaac, receipt for clothing, 12
Colbourn, Andrew, 17
Coller, Isaac, death of, 108

Coller, Isaac, Mrs., letter to, 108
Colston, Samuel, 68
Committee of Congress at camp, 30-31, 40, 70, 73, 119
Congress, Continental, 144
Conway, John, certificate by, 73; certificate for, 1
Conway, Thomas, 60; at Albany, 116; disliked many officers, 63
Cook, Henry, 16
Cook, William, diatribe against William Alexander, 112
Cooke, Nicholas, 145
Cord, Abm., 16
Corke, Edward, 9
Cornelius, Elias, 129
Cornwallis, Lord Charles, 33-34
Coryell, Emanuel, 147
Coryell's Ferry, food at, 64; forage at, 146, 147
Courtland, Major, 49
Courts-Martial, 23, 112-114, 160
Cox, Richard, 29
Craig, Major, 126
Crain, Joshua, 16
Cranston, Abner, 164
Cricket, 135
Crockett, Joseph, 16, 111
Cropper, John, to command a regiment, 148
Crosby, Ebenezer, letter from, 118
Crous, Michael, receipts for cattle, 27, 174
Croxton, John, 16
Crump, Abner, 177
Cumberland County, Pa., plantation at, 69
Cummins, Alexander, resignation of, 181
Curd, John, 86
Curtis, Bethuel, certificate for, 156
Curtis, Joshua, resignation of, 72
Curtis, Marmaduke, 29
Daggett, Henry, 56, 176; receipt by, 77
Dana, Francis, 119
Darah, James, 68
Darby, Pa., enemy foraging near, 4

Darragh, Daniel, 14
Davenport, Claibourn, 15
Davidson, William Lee, letter from, 24
Davies, William, certificates by, 68, 121, 172, 182; letters from, 20, 69
Davis, Elisha, deserted, 163
Day, Aaron, 29
Dayton, Elias, 28
Dayton, Jonathan, 29
De Lisle, Monsieur de, blackguarding the army, 145
Deane, Silas, 8, 117; letter to, 158
Dearborn, Henry, recommendation for, 17
Dedrick, Rachel, 128
Delaware, governor of captured, 33
Delaware River, enemy ship forced ashore, 21; fortifications on, 33 ships taken on, 81
Deming, Julius, 27
Denny, Samuel, 22
Dickerson, Peter, 29
Dill, Robert, 162
Dillering, Jacob, 16
Dixon, Henry, certificate by, 6
Dockum, William, 23
Dodge, Josiah, 83
Donaher, Daniel, 16
Dotherick, Rachiel, 39
Dougan, Patrick, 89
Driskill, Joseph, 21
Du Buysson des Hays, Charles-Francois, Le Chevalier, aid to de Kalb, 59
Du Coudray, Philippe Charles Tronson, 33
Du Ponceau, Peter Stephen, letter from, 126
Duff, Edward, certificate by, 121
Dunham, Lewis F., 28
Dunlap, Andrew, letters from, 39, 128
Duportail, Louis Lebique, 117; letter from, 109
Dustin, Dudley, 58
Duval, Daniel, 157
Duval, Edward, 125

Dyer, Eliphalet, 123
Easton, Pa., 26
Edwards, Le Roy, certificate for, 68
Elizabeth Town, N.J., forage at, 147
Elliot, Commodore, 180
Ellis, Mr., 73
Ernest, Mathew, 165
Evans, Rowland, complaints by, 185 letter from, 87
Ewing, George, 29, 68
Extracts a Letters, 4, 7, 11, 21, 38, 180
Fairlee, James, 159
Fanning, Mr., 72
Febiger, Christian, letter from, 160
Ferguson, Adam, 180
Fergusson, Henry Hugh, 27, 125; letter to, 10
Fiday, John, 90
Finley, John, 143
Fish, Nicholas, 80; letter from, 161
Fishbourne, Benjamin, signs for Anthony Wayne, 122
Fishkill, N.Y., 40
Fitch, Andrew, 120
Fitch, Mr., 114
Fitzgerald, John, letter from, 43
Fitzpatrick, Richard, 91-103
Fitzrandolph, Mr., 147
Flanagan, Samuel, 29
Fleeman, Thomas, discharge for, 79
Fleming, Charles, 15; certificate by, 171
Flemington, N.J., forage at, 146, 147
Flemister, James, 16
Fleury, Francois-Louis Teissédre de, 58
Food, 9, 13; at the Bakehouse, 65
cattle received, 27, 28, 174
extravagant price of, 36
five days without, 70
for American prisoners, 10, 26;
for POWs, 25-27; official ration set, 63; plenty between camp and Darby, Pa., 4; retained rations, 13, 73-74; shortages for officers, 13, 28-29;

Food, cheese, 9; high prices of, 18-19; shortages in Philadelphia, 3; shortages of, 5, 31, 48, 61, 64, 187 taken from civilians, 68
Forage, 145-48; needed at camp, 31 plenty between camp and Darby, Pa., 4; supply of, 88-89; taken by the army, 187
Ford, Mahlon, 29
Forman, Robert, certificate for, 179
Foster, Wm., 16
Franklin, Benjamin, 176
Franklin, Thomas, 10, 26, 27
Frazer, Mary, 6
Frazer, Nancy, 6
Fredericksburg, Va., 21
French Alliance, celebration of, 158-59, 161-62; joy at, 153, 157
French officers, recommended by Lafayette, 57
French, instruction in, 42
French, Samuel, 119, ordnance report, 103
Furloughs, 7, 73
Furman, Moore, letters to, 145, 165
Galaudet, Edgar, 29
Gartia, John, 22
Gates, Horatio, letters to, 109, 116; opinion of, 115
Germantown, Battle of, 18, 34; militia at, 7; POW negotiations at, 86, 91, 151
Gibbs, Caleb, letter to, 78
Gibson, John, certificate by, 131
Gifford, William, 29
Giles, James, receipt for arms, 176
Gill, Samuel, letter to, 71
Gilman, Nicholas, 113
Gimat, de, 166
Glentworth, James, Oath of Allegiance, 164
Goff, Samuel, payment received, 83
Goodwin, Wm., 9
Gookin, Daniel, 35
Gourley, Thomas, 14
Granberry/Granbery, Thomas certificates for, 3, 6
Grangr, John, 22

Grate/Great, David, discharged from the army, 64
Gray, Samuel, letter to, 123
Grayson, William, 91-103
Green, Burwell, certificate for, 172, 182
Greene, Christopher, 1
Greene, Griffin, certificates by, 15
Greene, Nathanael, 31, 146, 173, 187; at Germantown, 34; letter from, 88; letters to, 110, 126; signs a furlough, 7
Greenleaf, Dr., 119
Hacket, Samuel, 29
Hackettstown, N.J., forage at, 146
Hagan, Robert, 29
Hale, Daniel, 26
Hale, Nathan, 35
Haller, Henry, 26
Hamilton, Alexander, 91-103; letter from, 30
Harper, Mrs., 6
Harrison, Robert Hanson, 24, 91-103, 114; letters from, 75, 86, 153; letters to, 75, 172
Hart, James, 16
Haughy, Robert, 26, 27
Haynes, Aaron, 164
Head of Elk, Md.; enemy landed at, 38; food from, 26; forage at, 88
Health, army in general healthy, 18; army tolerably healthy, 119; fear of smallpox, 127; injuries, 12; shortage of medicine and blankets, 61; smallpox, 108, 122; smallpox inoculation a success, 187-88; very sickly, 70
Heartman, Henry, 173
Henderson, William certificate for, 175
Hennion, Cornelius, 29
Henry, Major, 4
Henry, William, roll of recruits, 89
Hill, Daniel, resignation of, 66
Hill, James, 15
Hill, Thomas, 15, 111
Hite, Matthias, resigns, 160
Hodges, Williamson, 16

Hogg, Thomas, 24
Hollingsworth, Henry, 26, 27
Holmes, Joseph, 26
Hooper, Robert L., 26
Hopkins, James, advertisement for a missing horse, 186
Hopkins, Samuel, 121
Hord, James, certificate for, 77
Horner, Mathew, 89
Horses, descriptions of, 173, 186; taken by the army, 187
Hospital, full of miserable creatures, 61
Howard, Sergeant, 67
Howe, Richard, 54, 55; leaving America, 144
Howe, William, 7, 27, 33, 49, 52, 53, 54, 91, 92, 93, 94, 95, 96, 98, 119, 121; leaving America, 144; not expected to advance, 4
Howell, Richard, letter to, 69
Howett, Charles, 22
Hughes, Daniel, letter to, 178
Hughes, Thomas, certificate by, 77
Hungerford/Hungerfoot, James, discharged from the army, 64
Hunt, Russel, 77
Huntington, Jedediah, 31
Huts, 41; construction of, 2, 12; good comfortable, 39
Indians, 187-188
Irvin, Thany, 39
Irwin, Joseph, 123
Irwin, Mathew, letter to, 31
Jackson, Michael, 128
Jameson, John, 38, 56
Jay, Joseph, deserter notice, 82
Jeffries, Isaac, 16
Jehue, Mr., 57
Johnson, Benja., 16
Johnston, James, letter to, 82
Johnston, William, 21, 22, 23
Johnstone, George, 180
Jones, Joseph, 83
Jones, Peter, certificate by, 182
Jones, Samuel, pay certificate by, 79
Jones, Thomas, 123; food at the Bakehouse, 65

letter to, 27; letters from, 63, 162; ration deficiencies, 28; resignation of, 168
Jouett, Mathew, 16
Kalb, Johann de, going to France, 144; letters from, 7, 8, 19, 59, 168
Kalb, Madame de, letter to, 19
Kelly, Anthony, 22
Kennedy, Joseph, deserted, 163
Kersey, William, 29
King, John, 16
Kinnant, Peter, 147
Kinney, John, 29
Kirby, Ephraim, 11, 12
Knine, Hannah, 41
Knox, Henry, 30, letter from, 181
Knox, Lucy, 181
Knox, William, letter to, 181
Lacey, John, Jr., letters to, 64, 86
Lacey, Josiah, letter from, 108; receipt by, 163
Lafayette, Marie Jean Paul Joseph Roch Yves Gilbert du Motier, Marquis de, 35, 59; appoints John Cropper, 148; knows Washington well, 32; letters by, 57, 116, 166, 176; much liked and on best terms with Washington, 19
Lamb, John, letter to, 171
Lancaster, Pa., 25, 26; clothing from, 40
Landais, Pierre, recommendation for, 131
Langston, George, 16
Laurens, Henry, letters to, 30, 57, 59, 131, 157, 166, 168, 176
Laurens, John, 100; signs resignation, 160
Laursee, Abm., 16
Lawrence, Elisha, 147
Lawrie, Mr., Jr., 153
Lee, Charles, 154; exchanged, 144; transportation for, 110
Lee, Elisha, letters to, 114, 120
Lee, Henry, Jr., actions of, 4 defends a stone house, 36, 38, 39, 56-57

Lee, Richard Henry, letter to, 56
Leonard, Nathaniel, 29
Lewes, Manuel, 22
Lewis, Charles, certificate by, 82
Lewis, Naboth, 11, 12
Lindsay, John, 38, 56
Lindsay, William, 4
Lipscomb, Reubin/Reuben, 16, 111
Lipscomb, Thomas certificate for, 171
Livingston, Henry P., 79
Livingston, Robert, Jr.,letter to, 127
Lock/Locke, Thomas, resignation of, 111
Long, Pierce, 36
Loree, Ephraim, 28
Loring, Joshua, 49, 91, 154
Lowrey, Thos, 148
Lowrey, Wm., 147, 148
Lowry, Thomas, 37
Lunt, Daniel, 2
Luten, James, resignation of, 75
Lutterloh, Henry Emanuel, 25, 75, 126; letter from, 30; letter to, 30
Lytle, Archibald, 24
MacKenzie, Robert, 101
Madison, Ambrose, 108
Mansfield, Samuel, letter from, 171
Marcus Hook, Pa., supplies at, 9
Marriner, Mr., 125
Marsh, De., Mr., 147
Marshall, Thomas, 78, 121
Marshall, Thos., 16
Martiniena, Mr. 58
Maudit Duplessis, Thomas Antoine, Chevalier de, letter from, 30
Maussion de la Bastie, Gaston Marie Léonard, letter from, 32
Maxwell, Bethiah, letters to, 66, 117, 126
Maxwell, Hannah, letter to, 5
Maxwell, Hugh, letters from, 5, 66, 117, 126
Maxwell, John, resignation of, 117
Maxwell, William, 184; at Germantown, 34
McCaskey, Alexander, 77
McClintock, Nathaniel, 36

McClure, David, letter to, 35
McClure, James, letter from, 35
McHenry, James, letter from, 183
McIlhany/McIlhaney, James, certificate for, 182
McIntosh, Lachlan, 113; certificates by, 3, 72, 75, 168; letter from, 157; witnesses Oath of Allegiance, 169
McReynolds, Thomas, account of, 69
Meade, Richard Kidder, letter from, 110; letters to, 143, 181; permission for an officer to resign, 28
Mellen, James, endorsement by, 76
Merion Meeting House, Pa., 9
Mersereau, Joshua, 26
Middagh, Lieutenant, 125
Middletown, Pa., 162
Military Stores, 103-107
Militia, N.J., 21
Militia, Pa., 7; of little use, 62; worthless, 115
Miller, Henry, 89
Miller, James, resignation of, 110
Miller, Leonard, receipt for rations, 164
Miller, Peter, 90
Mills, Samuel, 11
Mitchell, John, payments, 187
Money, Continental, useless in New York, 48; high value of Continental, 127; Money, little in the army, 18, 123; of no value, 62
Monroe, James, 23, 160; pass by, 73
Moon, James, certificate by, 182
Moreau, Charles-Hubert, 7
Morein, John, 83
Moreland, Pa., stable at, 69
Morgan, Daniel, 7, 67
Morgan, Ephraim, 176
Morgan, James, 12
Morgan, Mr., 29
Morrell, Thomas, 1
Morris, Mr., 37
Morris, Robert, 151, 152
Morristown, N.J., forage at, 146, 147
Morse, Joseph, discharge for, 78

Mosby, Wm., 16
Mosely, William, 16
Mott, John, 29
Moulder, John, 9
Moylan, Stephen, feed for horses, 83
Muhlenberg, Peter, letter from, 172; letter to, 109
Names, Benjamin, reenlistment bounty, 120
Nash, Francis, at Germantown, 34
Neely, Lieutn., 143
New Castle, Del., 10, 178
New Jersey, forage department in, 145-48
New York City, American prisoners at, 48-55
Newcomb, Daniel, letter to, 118
Newcomb, Joseph, 16
Newtown Square, Pa., supplies at, 9
Newtown, Pa., POW negotiations at, 93
Nicholas, John, 16, 177
Nichols, Francis, 163
Nick, John, 22
Nixon, John, payment from, 83
Norcross, William, 29
Norristown, Pa., 79
Northampton County, Pa., 173
Northover, Recherd, 23
Norvell, Lipscomb, certificate by, 122
O'Hara, Charles, 91-103
Oakley, Ensign, 125
Oath of Allegiance, 164, 169
Officers, American; discontent of, 121; many may resign, 70 promotion of, 103, 155-56; rank disputes, 175; shabby, 62; resignation of, 1, 3, 6, 8, 15, 17, 28, 39, 66, 69, 72, 75, 76, 77, 79, 87, 90, 108, 110, 111, 114, 117, 121, 167, 168, 171, 172, 173, 174, 175, 177, 179, 181, 182; to become artificers, 31, shabby, 62 weeded out, 18
Officers, French, antagonism between, 19

recommended by LaFayette, 57-58; seeking promotion, 30
Ogden, Matthias, letter to, 37
Olney, Jeremiah, certificate by, 156
Otney, John, 89
Paine, Major, 51, 52
Palmer, John, 187
Parker, David, 83
Parker, Richard, certificate by, 108; letter from, 181
Parramore, Thomas, resignation of, 174
Parrish, John, 129
Paterson, Edward, 29
Paterson, John, 13; discharge by, 78
Paterson, Thomas, 29
Patten, John, 75, 103
Patterson, Phill., 16
Patterson, William, 43
Pay, 14, 37, 82; bounty for reenlisting, 15-16, 83, 120; lack of 58; receipts for, 21-23; received, 56
Peeks Kill, N.Y., 26
Pendleton, Philip, 86
Penhallow, Deacon, 36
Penn, John, 87
Pennsylvania, has most traitors on the Continent, 116
Periam, Joseph, 29
Perkins, Hardin, certificate for, 131
Peters, Thomas, 26
Pettit, Charles, fords on the Schuylkill River, 169; letter from, 165
Peyton, Henry, 4
Philadelphia, Pa., 14, 115, 121, 184; food shortages in, 3; stores at, 33
Physick, Edmund, 185; letter to, 87
Pickering, Timothy, Jr., letter from, 4 report on New Jersey Regiments, 20
Pierce, John, Jr., letter from, 37
Pintard, Lewis, 53
Pittstown, N.J., forage at, 146
Pomeroy, Jno., 147
Pompton, N.J., forage at, 146, 147
Poor, Enoch, letter by, 16

Porterfield, Charles, certificate by, 39
Posey, Thomas, 16, 111
Potts Landing, Pa., supplies at, 9
Potts, Mr., 79
Pottsgrove, Pa., 162; forage at, 77
Powel, Samuel, 180
POWs, American, 10; treatment in New York, 48-55
POWs, care of ordered, 24-27; enemy; supplies for detained, 43; exchange of, 125, 184; meetings to exchange, 86, 90-103; officers to be sent to Pa., 178; to be sent to New York, 181
Prentice, Samuel, 72
Preston, Conn., clothing from, 12, 176
Pride, William, certificate by, 122
Priestly, John, 126
Pritchard, Jonathan, 186
Pulaski, Casimir, 116
Quakers, 18
Rahway, N.J., forage at, 147
Reading, John, 29
Reading, Pa., 25, 26; forage at, 88
Reagan, Daniel, resignation of, 39
Reamstown, Pa., miitary stores at 103-107
Redfield, William, 163
Reed, Joseph, 4, 152
Reed, Thomas, deserted, 163
Reese, Wm., 9
Regnier de Roussi, Pierre rank of, 175
Religion, 6, 108, 118, 122, 124, 126
Rhode Island, enemy at, 145
Rice, George, 39
Richeson, Robert, 16
Riker, Abraham, death of, 159
Rix, James, letter from, 58
Rix, Miriam, letter to, 58
Roads, poor condition of, 57
Robert, to his mother, 13
Roberts, John, 9
Robertson, James, 49, 50, 51, 52, 53, 54, 151, 152
Robertson, John, advertisement for a missing horse, 186

Robinson, James, 27
Roche, Edward, letter by, 178
Rodney, Caesar, 178
Roe, Hugh, allowed to resign, 28
Ross, John, 29
Rowell, William, 35
Rucastle, John, 29
Russell, Andrew, certificate by, 122
Russell, James, 22
Russell, William, discharges a soldier, 67; endorsement by, 68 letter to, 69; signs discharge, 59
Salem County, N.J., militia of, 21
Samson, John, 16
Sandford, William, certificate for, 108
Saunders, Robert Hyde, resignation of, 177
Scammell, Alexander, 17, 144
Schuylkill River, Pa., 33; fords of, 169-70
Scobey, James, 29
Scott, Charles, 85, discharge by, 64; letter from, 71; letter to, 173
Scott, John Morin, 161
Scott, Mathew, 89
Scribner, Asa, 108
Scruggs, Gross, certificates for, 121
Segond, Chevalier de, recommendation for, 116
Shackelford, Leond., 16
Shephard, William, letter from, 66
Sheppard, Abraham, certificate by, 171
Sheppard, Thomas, 22
Sheriff, Cornelius, notice by, 186
Sherrard, John, 147
Shipard, Samuel, 28
Ships, Bellefonte, 153
Shoes, 3, 13, 21, 31, 59, 122, 172
Shute, William, 29, certificate by, 73
Skirmishes between the armies, 4, 11, 36, 38, 39, 41, 56-57
Smallpox, over 4,000 inoculated, 187-88. See Health
Smallwood, William, 33
Smith, Ebenezer certificate by, 90

Smith, Frederic, 15
Smith, John, 9, asks to resign, 173
Smith, Joseph, 28
Smith, Kent, 16
Smith, Robert, 91
Smith, Simon, certificate for, 15
Smith, William Stephens, 43
Soldiers, 79; discharged, 59, 64, 66, 67, 71, 78, 79, 82 recruited, 89-90
Southall, Stephen, appointment of, 103
Spencer, Joseph, 16, 111
Spencer, Oliver, 40, 111; letter from, 117
Spencer, Robert; certification by, 114
Spirits, 9, 19; captured, 21; shortages of, 61
Spotswood, John, 86
Springfield, N.J., forage at, 147
Staats, Jno., 147
Stagg, John, 23
Star, Richard, 89
Stedman, Charles, 180
Steel, Alexander, 68
Stephen, Alexander, guilty of drunkness and discharged, 34
Stephens, Humphrey, 91-103
Steuben, Friedrich Wilhelm Augustus, Baron de, discplining the army, 116 144; equipment for, 126; horses from, 166; letters from, 131, 157
Stevens, Edward, certificate by, 17
Stevens, John, letters to, 151, 153
Stevenson, Stephen. advertisement for deserters, 163
Stewart, Charles, letter from, 123; letter to, 120
Stewart, Walter, 89; discharge by, 79 letter from, 120; letter to, 183
Stirling, Lord, see Alexander, William
Stivers, Edwd., 16
Stokes, John; certificate by, 82
Stratton, Mr., 125
Straw, needed for beds, 40

Street, David, discharged from the army, 67
Strickland, Amos, 91
Strickland, Mr,, 93
Succasanna, N.J., forage at, 147
Suckasunny, N.J., forage at, 146
Sullivan, Ebenezer, 145
Sullivan, John, at Germantown, 34, 35; letter to, 144
Sumner, Jethro, certificate by, 3
Supplies, near Chester, 9
Sutten, Wm., 16
Swede's Ford, Pa., 4; army crossed at, 11
Swift, Heman, 56, 72, 176
Swift, Mr., 121
Syme, John, resignation of, 17
Taliaferro, William, 85
Taylor, Edward, 15
Taylor, Francis, 179
Taylor, Richard, advertisement by, 179
Temple, Seth, 67
Tenny, Samuel, letters from, 70, 128
Ternant, Jean Baptiste, Chevalier de, 183
Thayer, Nathan, certificate for, 90
Thompson, Ben, 67
Thompson, Humphry, letter from, 149
Thompson, Thomas, 171
Thomson, Charles, 168
Tilghman, Tench, 123; letters from, 40, 78, 111; letters to, 110, 117
Till, Hannah, 188
Till, Isaac Worley, baptismal record, 188
Todd, Jonathan, Jr., 56
Tood, Mr., 171
Torten, Andrew, 9
Towles, Oliver, letter to, 85
Transportation, hundreds of horses starved, 119. See wagons
Trenton, N.J.; forage at, 88, 147
Trumbull, Jonathan, 32
Trumbull, Jonathan, Jr. letter to, 37
Tryon, Betsy, 128

Tryon, Fanny, 128
Turner, Isaac, resignation of, 167
Turner, Peter, letters to, 70, 128
Turnley, John, discharged from the army, 66
Turpin, Horatio, pay certificate for, 79
Uwchlan Meeting House, Pa., supplies near, 9
Valfort, de, Captain, 8
Valley Forge, looks like an Indian city, 36; strongly fortified, 121
Van Cortlandt, Philip, 80, 161, letter from, 158
Van Cortlandt, Pierre, letter to, 158
Van Dyke, Abraham C., 51
Van Lear, John, 123
Van Schaick, Goose, 130
Van Swearingen, Capt., 143
Van Vechten, Jacob, 130
Van Waganer, Tunis, letter from, 130
Vandeering's Mills, Pa., 11
Varick, Richard, letters to, 80, 161
Varnum, James Mitchell, letters from, 1, 144, 167
Vaux, James, grain from, 83
Vergennes, Charles Gravier, Comte de, 7
Villefranche, Jean-Louis-Ambroise de Genton, chevalier de, 109
Virginia, recruits from, 144
Virginia soldiers, sent home, 71
Vose, Joseph; letter from, 66
Wagons, 40; captured 7; to be impressed, 64; from Northampton County, 173; shortages of, 30-31
Wain, Benja., 16
Wakely, John, 163
Waldo, Albigence, certificate by, 12 poem by, 132; report on innoculation, 187
Wallace, John, Jr., pass for, 73
Waples, Samuel, furlough for, 7; resignation of, 172
Ward, Joseph, letter from, 80; patriotic appeal for men to enlist, 124-125
Warfield, Josiah, 67

Washingon, George, 14, 43, 50, 54, 75, 78, 93, 94, 96, 98, 125, 155, 156; a Roman general, 36; adored by the army, 145; appoints POW exchange commissioners, 91, 151; approves a resignation, 160; arranging officers, 72; audacious attack at Germantown, 34; Battle of Germantown, 18, 35; calmness under diversity, 32; care of POWS, 48; civilians discontent with, 115-16; directs that river fords be guarded, 4-5; has performed wonders, 34; letters from, 69, 78, 89; letters to, 1, 16, 66, 76, 110, 114, 117, 167, 174; loved by the soldiers, 116; on muster practices, 80; opinion of, 115; orders impressment of wagons, 31; orders of, 11; poem in praise of, 132-142; recruiting instructions, 24; refuses to allow succor for Philadelphians, 3; religion of, 33; reports to, 103; talks to men, 13-14; very busy, 40; wants soldiers dressed alike, 72; wisdom of, 124
Washington, Martha, 14
Watkin, Thomas G., 179
Watkins, Thos., 16
Watson, Titus, 77
Wayne, Anthony, 40, 155, 156, 187 at Battle of Germantown, 34; letters from, 3, 122; surprised at Paoli, 33
Weather, 13, 137; Battle of the Clouds, 33; forced a ship ashore, 21
Webb, John, 16, 111
Weedon, George, letter from, 56 signs discharges, 64, 66
Weiss, Jacob, 165
Weissenfels, Frederick, letter from, 110
Welsh, Hugh, deserted, 82
Wesson, James, 76, certificate by, 110
West Chester, Pa., 79

West, Charles, certificate by, 8
Wharton, Thomas, Jr., letters to, 122, 155
White Horse, Pa., flour at, 77
Whitworth, Lieutenant, 125
Whorley, Math., 15
Wigglesworth, Edward, 90
Wilkins, John, resignation of, 111
Wilkinson, Edmund D., 29
Wilkinson, Nathan, 29
Williams, Captain, 24
Williams, Ezekiel, 26, letter to, 181
Williams, William, letter from, 155
Williamson, M., 147
Willobey, Edlen, 16
Willobey, Wm., 16
Wilson, James, certificate for, 171
Wilson, John, certificate by, 72
Winchester, Va., 26
Winslow, John, letter to, 125
Women, dearth of, 141-142, birth at camp, 188
Woodbridge, N.J., forage at, 147
Woodford, William, letter from, 85
Woodson, John, advertisement for a missing horse, 173
Wrights Ferry, Pa., 88
Wroe, William, discharge for, 59
Yellow Springs, Pa., 33, 186
York, Pa., 26, 179
Young, Charles, letter to, 30
Young, Henry, report on the Seventh Virginia Regiment,, 111
Young, Nathaniel, 83

Heritage Books by Joseph Lee Boyle

*"My Last Shift Betwixt Us & Death": The Ephraim Blaine Letterbook, 1777–1778*

*"Their Distress is Almost Intolerable": The Elias Boudinot Letterbook, 1777–1778*

*From Redcoat to Rebel: The Thomas Sullivan Journal*

*"this grand supply": The Samuel Hodgdon Letterbooks, 1778–1784*
Volume 1: July 19, 1778–March 31, 1781
Volume 2: April 3, 1781–May 24, 1784

*Writings from the Valley Forge Encampment of the Continental Army: December 19, 1777–June 19, 1778*
Volume 1

*Writings from the Valley Forge Encampment of the Continental Army: December 19, 1777–June 19, 1778*
Volume 2, "Winter in this starved Country"

*Writings from the Valley Forge Encampment of the Continental Army: December 19, 1777–June 19, 1778*
Volume 3, "it is a general Calamity"

*Writings from the Valley Forge Encampment of the Continental Army: December 19, 1777–June 19, 1778*
Volume 4, "The Hardships of the Camp"

*Writings from the Valley Forge Encampment of the Continental Army: December 19, 1777–June 19, 1778*
Volume 5, "a very Different Spirit in the Army"

*Writings from the Valley Forge Encampment of the Continental Army: December 19, 1777–June 19, 1778*
Volume 6, "my Constitution got quite shatter'd"

*Writings from the Valley Forge Encampment of the Continental Army: December 19, 1777–June 19, 1778*
Volume 7, "I could not Refrain from tears"

*Writings from the Valley Forge Encampment of the Continental Army: December 19, 1777–June 19, 1778*
Volume 8, "called to the unpleasing task of a Soldier"